M000248331

"At the beginning of the Second World War, the prevailing view was that women didn't have the education, intellect or ability for intelligence work. With a lively mix of personal testimony and scholarly analysis, Sarah-Louise Miller shows how in fact women performed superb work in the WAAF as radar operators, signals analysts, photo interpreters and in many other fields. *The Women Behind the Few* restores the WAAFs to their rightful place in the full narrative of the conflict."

Taylor Downing, author of *Spies in the Sky: The Secret Battle for Aerial Intelligence during World War II*

"The vital contribution of the enterprising and courageous women who helped to win the battle of the air in the Second World War is brought to life in Sarah-Louise Miller's important and absorbing book."

Wendy Moore, author of *Endell Street: The Women Who Ran Britain's Trailblazing Military Hospital*

"A rip-roaring read about a previously hidden aspect of the Second World War. Dr Miller shows how behind every good RAF officer there was a brilliant female intelligence officer."

Professor Michael Goodman, King's College London

"Sarah-Louise Miller presents an animated, in-depth account of the crucial role of the Women's Auxiliary Air Force in the intelligence services during the Second World War. Her book makes an important and welcome addition to scholarship on wartime women."

Professor Penny Summerfield, University of Manchester

"A marvellous account of a hitherto unknown subject of immense importance."

Diane Atkinson, author of *Rise Up, Women! The Remarkable Lives of the Suffragettes*

THE WOMEN BEHIND THE FEW

THE WOMEN BEHIND THE FEW

THE WOMEN'S AUXILIARY AIR FORCE AND
BRITISH INTELLIGENCE DURING
THE SECOND WORLD WAR

SARAH-LOUISE MILLER

Biteback Publishing

First published in Great Britain in 2023 by
Biteback Publishing Ltd, London
Copyright © Sarah-Louise Miller 2023

Sarah-Louise Miller has asserted her right under the Copyright, Designs and Patents Act 1988
to be identified as the author of this work.

All rights reserved. No part of this publication may be reproduced, stored in a retrieval system
or transmitted, in any form or by any means, without the publisher's prior permission in writing.

This book is sold subject to the condition that it shall not, by way of trade or otherwise, be
lent, resold, hired out or otherwise circulated without the publisher's prior consent in any form
of binding or cover other than that in which it is published and without a similar condition,
including this condition, being imposed on the subsequent purchaser.

Every reasonable effort has been made to trace copyright holders of material reproduced in this
book, but if any have been inadvertently overlooked the publisher would be glad to hear from them.

ISBN 978-1-78590-785-2

10 9 8 7 6 5 4 3 2 1

A CIP catalogue record for this book is available from the British Library.

Set in Adobe Caslon Pro

Printed and bound in Great Britain by
CPI Group (UK) Ltd, Croydon CR0 4YY

FSC
www.fsc.org
MIX
Paper | Supporting
responsible forestry
FSC® C171272

For Isaac, who makes it all possible.

CONTENTS

ABBREVIATIONS

AAA	anti-aircraft artillery
ACIU	Allied Central Interpretation Unit. The ACIU was known as the CIU until 1 May 1944, when it was renamed to reflect the increasing involvement of American service personnel in photographic reconnaissance and interpretation in Britain.
ATA	Air Transport Auxiliary
ATS	Auxiliary Territorial Service, the women's branch of the British Army during the Second World War
CH	'Chain Home' radar
CHL	'Chain Home Low' radar
CIU	Central Interpretation Unit
CO	Commanding Officer
FANY	First Aid Nursing Yeomanry
F-Section	The section of the SOE responsible for operations in occupied France
GC&CS	Government Code and Cypher School
GCI	ground-controlled interception (radar)
HDU	home defence unit
HQ	headquarters

IFF	identification friend or foe
JIC	Joint Intelligence Committee
MI5	British domestic counter-intelligence and security agency
MI6	British foreign intelligence service
NCO	non-commissioned officer
PI	photographic intelligence
PIU	Photographic Interpretation Unit
PPI	plan-position indicator (radar display)
PR	photographic reconnaissance
PRU	Photographic Reconnaissance Unit
R/T	radio telephony
RAF	Royal Air Force
RDF	radio-direction finding (radar)
ROC	Royal Observer Corps
SIGINT	intelligence gathering by the interception of signals
SIS	Secret Intelligence Service (also known as MI6), the British foreign intelligence agency
SNCO	senior non-commissioned officer
SOE	Special Operations Executive
SOS	international Morse code distress signal
Station X	Bletchley Park
V-weapons	Vergeltungswaffen – German 'vengeance' weapons
V-1	German remote-controlled flying bomb (also known as the 'doodlebug' in Britain), an early cruise missile
VE Day	Victory in Europe Day, celebrated 8 May 1945, marking the formal acceptance by the Allies of Germany's surrender
W/OP	wireless operator

WAAC   Women's Army Auxiliary Corps (First World War)
WAAF   Women's Auxiliary Air Force
WRAF   Women's Royal Air Force (First World War and
          1949–94)
WRNS   Women's Royal Naval Service
Y Service Organisation tasked with the monitoring and
          interpretation of enemy radio transmissions

PROLOGUE

'Never in the field of human conflict was so much owed by so many to so few.'¹ Winston Churchill's famous words appear on the plaque at Yale College, Wrexham, commemorating one of its most honoured and extraordinary pupils – Air Chief Marshal Sir Frederick Rosier. A Royal Air Force fighter pilot in the Second World War, Rosier destroyed a Messerschmitt 109 and damaged another on 18 May 1940, shortly before being shot down himself. He escaped his burning Hurricane, receiving facial burns and other injuries which he would recover from in hospital. The group of Messerschmitts had appeared in force and without warning, as he, along with his weary and depleted squadron, had taken off from an airfield in northern France. Speaking later of his experience, he blamed the lack of intelligence for what had happened. Had they had any reliable information on how, when and where the enemy would appear, he argued, the RAF pilots might have stood a chance. Instead, they were caught at a major disadvantage and the already battered force sustained further damage and loss.

This lack of intelligence, and the feelings of isolation and help-lessness which it induced in RAF pilots, would not last long. De-velopments in technology would greatly increase the ability of the military services to collect, analyse and disseminate intelligence that was so badly needed if the numerically inferior RAF was to be able to continue, and perhaps even win, its fight against the Luftwaffe.

In his August 1940 speech, Churchill attributed the smaller number of casualties in the second of the twentieth-century world wars in part to the 'Few' – the courageous pilots of the Royal Air Force. He also acknowledged that improved strategy, organisation, technical apparatus, science and mechanics were playing a vital role in keeping the RAF flying. Indeed, the planes and weapons used by the British armed forces, and the ability of the aircrew who so famously and gallantly flew in the Battle of Britain, were critically important to any potential British victory. There were, however, more secret developments in technology, as well as a number of personnel who were highly trained in using new machines and systems as they were developed and commissioned for duty. While the dogfights took place in the skies above Britain, RAF personnel laboured behind closed doors, using this new technology to collect, process, analyse and disseminate the vital intelligence that would keep the RAF functioning and ensure that Britain remained in the war.

Among these personnel were many women – women who, like Aileen Clayton, were members of the Women's Auxiliary Air Force. Air Chief Marshal Rosier worked closely with Aileen, who was the first WAAF member to be commissioned for intelligence duties when she was promoted to officer rank in July 1940. She worked in the Y Service, an organisation tasked with the monitoring and interpretation of enemy radio transmissions. Rosier considered her an extremely important member of the Y Service, acknowledging that she was a 'woman in a man's world'.[2] Aileen and her colleagues passed RAF Fighter Command warnings of impending enemy raids, their targets, their identities and other vital intelligence which made it possible for attacks to be successfully countered. Technical developments, Rosier admits, contributed greatly to British success in both the Battle of Britain and the Second World War. Equally as vital in both, however, was the 'extraordinary resilience and adaptability of women who showed that they were supreme' in using such technology. Rosier suggests that without these remarkable and courageous women, the direction of events in and the ultimate outcome of the Second World War 'might have been very different'.[3]

When intelligence work is done well, it is expected that it will remain hidden from public view. For decades after the conclusion of the Second World War, very little was publicly known about intelligence operations and systems that had functioned for its duration. After the revelation of the Ultra secret – the wartime work of the Government Code and Cypher School at Bletchley Park – in the mid-1970s, the story of British codebreaking and wartime intelligence work began to finally be told. 'Ultra', the name given to wartime signals intelligence obtained by the decryption of enemy radio and teleprinter communications, became the star of the 1940s British intelligence show and has been the subject of much research, as well as many books and screen tellings of the story of how the Enigma codes were broken. It is, however, only a small part of a much larger story and the monitoring of enemy signals traffic was not limited to Bletchley. There were many other men and women involved in producing information, without which the Allied knowledge of the enemy's tactical dispositions and intentions would have either been incomplete or missing entirely. Among these men and women were Aileen Clayton and her WAAF colleagues, who were employed in intelligence work throughout the Second World War.

The very nature of intelligence work creates challenges for historical researchers when it comes to investigating intelligence history. Intelligence and espionage are inherently extremely secretive and for much to be publicly known about the intelligence world somewhat defeats the point of its existence. Historians look to primary sources for their information – sources from the historical time period they are studying. In the realm of intelligence history, these records can be difficult, and sometimes impossible, to find and access. Despite the decades that have passed, some intelligence files from the Second World War remain classified and sealed. The National Archives continues to declassify records and make them accessible, but classification issues, post-war upheaval, archive fires and disasters and a process known as 'weeding' mean that sometimes the files have been locked, lost or destroyed. Historians of the intelligence world can and must use official records, and for this book, the files used are housed in the National Archives, the Imperial War Museum, the Military Intelligence Museum, the International Bomber Command Centre, the Bawdsey Radar Trust, the Association of RAF Fighter Control Officers, the Air Historical Branch, the Medmenham Association and Bletchley Park. The intelligence world can be murky and spectral, however, and to be able to gain as full a picture as possible of its history, it is critically important to remember that it is, and has always been, populated by people. Many of these men and women, sworn to secrecy until they were released from their oaths, have left behind their personal memories, in the forms of diaries, oral histories, letters, written accounts and interviews. These sources are invaluable and help to fill the inevitable gaps in the official records. They are especially precious when it comes to studying women in intelligence history. Intelligence historians Christopher Andrew and David Dilks call intelligence the 'missing dimension' from 'most political and much military history'.[4] Within this dimension, they say, there is another missing dimension – that of women. Historical records tend to be recorded by men about men and it is common for them to omit or mis-record women and their work. This is even more true in the world of intelligence, where it is commonly assumed that women were typists and secretaries and not much else. Sometimes misleading and inaccurate nomenclature was intentionally used to hide what women were truly doing, on the grounds of intense secrecy. In other instances, their work may have genuinely been misunderstood. Personal records – from men and women – are therefore critical in helping us to understand not only *what* women did but what it meant and how they felt about it. In this book, both official primary source records and the personal words and memories of those involved have been used to tell the story of wartime WAAFs working in British air intelligence.

In the extensive coverage of the Battle of Britain by authors and researchers, it is almost always the brave young pilots of Fighter Command who are the focus. In recent years, the parts played by Bomber and Coastal Commands have rightfully begun to be recognised and celebrated too. The gallant and sacrificial work of these commands must never be forgotten, and the men who served within them are deserving of the glory bestowed upon them in British history and national memory. Consisting of around 3,000 aircrew from fourteen different nations, the international force known as the 'Few' are as precious to the British public today as they were during the summer of 1940, as a symbol of courage and determination towards victory in the face of the grim situation the country faced. During the battle, the daily news reports and visible dogfights overhead gave the people of Britain proof that all was not lost. They were needed, as a tangible sign of hope. Their story, though, is part of a much wider narrative of the Battle of Britain.

Unseen and yet vital to the success of Fighter, Bomber and Coastal Commands, there were thousands of men and women assisting in the battle in various capacities. Though the balance of history has, in some respects, been redressed in the study of Bomber and Coastal Commands, there remains another hidden few. Responsible at least in part for Britain's victory in the summer of 1940, and in other major aerial victories, but generally not included in the popular telling of their stories, were thousands of members of the Women's Auxiliary Air Force, working to collect and disseminate intelligence that would greatly assist the Royal Air Force in its fight against the Luftwaffe. This book, while not wishing to diminish the marvellous achievements of the Few, focuses on these women, who have hitherto been neglected or have gone unnoticed, despite their vital intelligence contributions. Unlike Churchill's Few, for the WAAF intelligence personnel there was no publicity and no glamour – in fact, there was barely any recognition at all. Behind the Few, they worked day in, day out, supplying the RAF with life-saving, resource-preserving, force-multiplying information, playing a significant role in the saving of lives, the winning of battles and, ultimately, the Allied victory in 1945. Here is the story of this other missing few, and with it, a true redressing of the balance of the history of British aerial warfare in the Second World War.

1

THE WAR, THE WAAF AND WOMEN IN INTELLIGENCE

WOMEN IN ANOTHER WORLD WAR

We got on with it, it was what we had to do. After the bombing stopped, we'd have a cup of tea – that calmed the nerves. Once, when a raid during the Blitz knocked out all of our windows, the chair back covers from our neighbours' armchairs floated into our front room and we had to sort out whose were whose and return them.[1]

For Mary Knight and her family, dealing with bombing raids in their home city of London became a part of life in the early years of the Second World War. Absconding chair back covers the least of their worries, British people learned to cope with danger and difficulty on a daily basis, problem-solving and experimenting in different ways to greet and overcome the many new challenges they faced. They made things, mended others and made do with what they had, and rationing of food, fuel and other materials altered life considerably. These weren't just social responsibilities – they were necessary activities, as the German war machine ravaged Europe and cut off vital supply lines. The conditions of this total war blurred the boundaries of social spheres and plunged Britain into a fight for survival, in which every person was required to play a part. The bombing offensives, made possible by advances in air power and weapons technology, brought the war to villages, towns, cities and everyday lives, inevitably involving men, women and children in the fight. The way in which people fought differed, ranging from creating new recipes to cope with rationing to flying fighter planes to defend the country in battle. Men were needed in the military services in great numbers and as they were recruited and conscripted, a vacuum appeared in the workforce. Just as they had in the First World War, women stepped into this void, filling roles that had long been strictly the domain of men, as well as those that resembled their peacetime work.

They worked with the Women's Land Army, producing food and keeping British agriculture going. These women, numbering around 80,000 at their peak, made a significant and valuable contribution to Britain's food production during the Second World War as a rural workforce. They also staffed factories and shipyards, building ships and aircraft and manufacturing munitions. They served as drivers in buses, fire engines and ambulances, worked as engineers and mechanics and kept the railway network functioning. They saw Britain through bombing raids as air raid wardens, evacuation officers and fire officers and administered first aid and medical care as nurses and volunteers. Women kept Britain fed and fighting in many civilian capacities, working hard to ensure that the jobs traditionally carried out by men continued to be done.

There was, however, another arena in which they were badly needed, as another manpower vacuum appeared – in the military services. War, the great destabiliser of the twentieth century, necessitated military experimentation, and as more and more men were needed in combat and overseas positions, the British government appealed to women to step into military roles previously unavailable to them. The integration of women into the British armed forces was, in some ways, an experiment, necessitated by the incessant demands of war. Fighting and warfare had long been considered a strictly male sphere, but such a move was not without precedent.

SETTING THE PRECEDENT: WOMEN IN THE FIRST WORLD WAR

'She has taught the bravest man among us a supreme lesson of courage; yes, and in this United Kingdom … there are thousands of such women, but a year ago we did not know it.'[2] Addressing the House of Commons, British Prime Minister Lord Asquith was speaking about Edith Cavell, the British nurse famous for her indiscriminate saving of soldiers' lives on both sides and for her part in aiding the escape of over 200 Allied soldiers from German-occupied Belgium during the First World War. For her now celebrated acts of courage, Edith was arrested by the Germans and accused of treason, resulting in her death by firing squad on 12 October 1915. Following her execution, she became a public symbol of the Allied cause, appearing in recruitment posters and messages around the world. Her story was, as Asquith pointed out, a revelation to the world of the kind of courage in the face of danger that a woman could possess, and it proved that women could carry out roles unexpected of them during wartime. The prevailing attitude towards women in military service during the First World War was, unsurprisingly given the historical context in which British women had no right to vote and no independent legal status, that if they absolutely had to serve it should be in a non-combatant, non-dangerous support capacity only. Society's praise and admiration went to those women who did what was

3

expected of them by remaining at home as sources of unwavering support, fortifying their menfolk to go to war while they took care of the family. In 1914, the 'separate spheres' ideology, which dictated that a woman's place was in the domestic realm of her home, was firmly ingrained in British society. Women were expected to care for their children and keep their homes in order, providing support for the men of the military from the comfort and safety of their kitchens and living rooms. Necessity for their involvement with the armed services was dictated by the ongoing, bloody war and the increasing shortage of able-bodied men to fight it.

The First World War witnessed the creation of various military auxiliaries and capacities in which women could serve in aid of the war effort, and they did so in vast numbers. The Women's Army Auxiliary Corps (WAAC), the Women's Royal Naval Service (WRNS) and the Women's Royal Air Force (WRAF) recruited women who would march and carry out drills, wearing uniforms just as their male counterparts did. There was, however, at no point any question that these all-female auxiliaries were anything more than support units. Established in December 1916, the WAAC's members served as cooks, clerks and office workers or secretaries, messengers, waitresses, driver-mechanics and domestic workers of various sorts. The War Office had identified that these non-combat jobs were being carried out by men who were needed in battle, and so male soldiers were replaced by women from the auxiliaries in canteens, offices, transport, stores and army bases. Over 57,000 women served with the WAAC, in Britain and overseas, before it was disbanded in September 1921. Formed in November 1917, the WRNS carried out similar tasks, but members did not serve aboard active-duty warships. It was in the final year of the First World War that air power really came of age. Initially, the Royal

Flying Corps and the Royal Naval Air Service bore the brunt of the responsibility of air defence, but on 1 April 1918 the two combined to form the newly established Royal Air Force – the first separate, entirely independent air force in any country. The RAF was given its own ministry, the 'Air Ministry', with a secretary of state for air, and over 290,000 personnel lined its ranks.[3] Before the creation of the RAF, members of the WAAC and the WRNS worked with the Royal Flying Corps and the Royal Naval Air Service. When the RAF was established, its leaders were so concerned about the loss of their specially trained women that it was decided to simultaneously create a women's air service, which could continue to train women to work on air stations. On 1 April 1918, the Women's Royal Air Force was established and over 2,000 of its recruits had previously served with the WRNS, in the Royal Naval Air Service. Like its naval and army counterparts, the WRAF served mostly as a support unit and in very similar capacities. In 1918, women could choose from four basic trades: clerks and store-women; household; technical; and non-technical. By 1920, the number of available trades had increased to fifty and included tailoring, catering, driving, pigeon-keeping and photography. WRAF members were either 'immobiles', meaning that they lived at home and served at their local station, or 'mobiles', who could be transferred to other stations if necessary. Some members – namely domestic personnel, medical and clerical staff and drivers – were sent on overseas service after 1918, in France and Germany. In 1919, the order was given to close down the WRAF contingent on the Rhine, and the RAF sections there were so unwilling to lose their airwomen that they delayed the disbandment as long as they possibly could. By April 1920, the WRAF had employed 32,000 women and they had shown themselves to be an extremely valuable asset to the RAF.

This experimental service, formed out of nothing but sheer necessity, had had irrefutably successful results.

All three women's military auxiliaries were formed towards the end of the First World War and only after heavy manpower losses and casualties were military jobs officially handed to women. The British government and military leaders had resisted for as long as possible, their traditional patriarchal views and attitudes unwavering, but eventually they had little choice but to allow the recruitment of women. Though the women of the auxiliaries proved themselves to be capable and courageous, their service did not change the situation or status of women in the short term. Women were doing things that they had not previously been allowed to do, but the War Office and the British government made it very clear that these special concessions had only been made under the emergency conditions of war. Though these women wore uniforms, in many cases they had to buy their own, and they were not given traditional ranks or badges. They were not referred to as soldiers but as 'workers' or 'amazons', or by the War Office as 'camp followers'. They were considered members of the women's services rather than the British military, and because they were legally civilians, they were not integrated into the armed forces. By 1921, all three of the women's military auxiliaries had been disbanded. The Great War placed immense pressure on the British economy, which did not witness a swift return to its pre-war state. By 1921, unemployment was at a record high in Britain and working women were forced to give up their jobs to men who had returned from battle. The economic cuts and concessions by women extended to the military auxiliaries, which were deemed unnecessary and were axed. No peacetime women's auxiliaries existed. Ultimately, it seemed as if the British government and military were keen to return to a world where women were not involved in the armed forces, their argument being that women had only ever been put in uniforms to replace absent men who were needed on the front. Now that the men had returned and were not required in mass numbers to fight a war overseas, women in uniform became an unwelcome sight and a redundant concept. The only military capacity in which the British authorities were willing to permanently allow women to serve was that of nursing, which was recognised as a necessary part of the services. The Nurses Registration Act was passed in 1919, formally recognising nursing as a profession and integrating nurses into the military. Apart from this, there had been very little lasting change for women in the British military services as a result of their work in the First World War auxiliaries. Nevertheless, the experiment had proven a point. Asquith recognised that the war had revealed women of conspicuous courage, like Edith Cavell, through providing them with opportunities to demonstrate their bravery and abilities – abilities that, prior to the war, the government and the military were sure they could not possess. Such bravery was not easily forgotten, and in 1939, as the world went to war again, women once more found themselves working in environments and roles unfamiliar to them.

WOMEN IN FIRST WORLD WAR INTELLIGENCE

In 1909, the British Secret Service Bureau was established with separate sections for foreign intelligence (later the SIS or MI6) and domestic intelligence (MI5). From then to 1919, over 6,000 women served in the bureau, which would not have been able to function efficiently without them. Though for a large portion of this period they could not vote, let alone hold political office or work in permanent civil service roles, they were recruited to work for the bureau in their thousands. Their work was mostly clerical in nature and they laboured behind the scenes to record messages, organise files and provide refreshments for the (all-male) senior staff. Due to the increasing unavailability of men as they were sent to the front to fight, women became a vital, if unseen, element of First World War intelligence organisations. Their work included the organisation and analysis of surveillance information and the dissemination of this information to the appropriate civil and military authorities, but this contribution was very much peripheral. When classified documents on British intelligence were opened for the first time in 1998, they made little to no mention of women or their contribution to intelligence work in the First World War. This is hardly surprising, given that clerical workers in any setting remain almost always in the background, and is especially understandable in the intelligence world, where due to the fascination with spies in popular culture, secretaries would inevitably remain in the shadow of the glamorised secret agents.

Whether or not they were noticed, or whether anyone thought to record their presence or the significance of their work, they were certainly there, working to ensure that British clandestine activity continued effectively and efficiently. The Registry at the Secret Service Bureau was expanded during the First World War and by November 1914 it was staffed solely by women, with Lily Steuart at its head. Women played a 'more important role in the Security Service than in any other wartime government department'.[4] Though restricted to administrative work, the women involved in secret work proved to be vital to the smooth running of the service. Despite their clear ability to carry out hard work under pressure, the women were expected by most of their male colleagues to be 'good ladies serving tea and finding files'.[5] A post-war 'Report on Women's Work' stated that the service had been looking for women who possessed 'intelligence, diligence and above all, reticence'.[6] Though they were looking for clever women who could be restrained enough to keep secrets, the British intelligence authorities believed that behaving in such a way was difficult for women. In 1915, it was decided that the service would not recruit women over the age of forty, and in 1916 the maximum age was lowered to thirty, 'on account of the very considerable strain that was thrown on the brains of the workers'.[7] Women, it seems, were not considered wholly capable of intelligence work, even as clerks and secretaries. It was believed that the only women who might possess the desirable qualities to be able to work in intelligence were those who were educated and who naturally had inherited a 'code of honour' – 'gentlewomen who had enjoyed a good school, and in some cases a university education'.[8] Despite the class and age restrictions and the limited opportunities within British intelligence, women did prove themselves to be capable and essential during the First World War.

By 1929, MI5, now distinct from the SIS as Britain's domestic intelligence agency, had two branches. 'A Branch' was responsible for administration, personnel, records and protective security (then called 'precautionary measures'), and 'B Branch' was responsible for conducting investigations and inquiries. Within A Branch, the Registry continued to be staffed and run by women and of the branch's four section heads two were women, though neither of them was allowed to hold officer rank. Mary Dicker ran the Registry and was controller of female staff, and A. W. Masterton had become the first female controller of finance in any government department.[9]

By the end of the First World War and into the 1920s and 1930s, women had proven themselves to be reliable and capable within the British intelligence network.

ANGELIC NURSES AND FEMMES FATALES

Where women in Britain were restricted to clerical work within First World War intelligence services, elsewhere in Europe women did labour as field agents and spies. 'La Dame Blanche' was a network of spies in German-occupied Belgium which provided intelligence on German troop movements to the Allies. By the end of the war, La Dame Blanche consisted of almost 800 members, many of whom were women.[10] Among them were nuns, nurses and midwives, all of whom could move around unrestricted, carrying intelligence reports in their whalebone corsets or disguised in soap or chocolate.

When British nurse Edith Cavell was arrested for helping Allied soldiers escape occupied Belgium, the Germans claimed that her network was also smuggling intelligence back to the Allies. Edith was sentenced to execution for espionage and chose not to appeal her sentence. Even those British intelligence officers aware that she was feeding them intelligence found it inappropriate to execute a woman, and an image was circulated in British propaganda which ignored the allegations against Edith and instead stressed her role as a nurse to patients from all over the world. Surely, they declared, this angelic, caregiving woman could not be suspected of being an agent. Edith became a public martyr and the British government seized the opportunity to capitalise heavily on her execution. News reports, postcards and posters cited Edith's 'murder' as a recruitment technique. It worked – after her execution, British Army recruitment did noticeably increase. The extent to which Edith was actually involved in British intelligence remained unclear, but the British reaction to the accusation against her reveals much regarding attitudes towards the involvement of British women in espionage during the First World War.

When women in the La Dame Blanche network were caught, some were treated equally to Edith Cavell. Gabrielle Petit, a Belgian woman who passed intelligence to the British Secret Service, was executed by firing squad in 1916. She had been offered amnesty in exchange for information on her colleagues, but she heroically turned the offer down and remained silent. The British intelligence community were willing to work with foreign female spies and accept intelligence from them, well aware of the risk they were taking in obtaining and disseminating it. This willingness, however, apparently did not extend to risking the lives of British women – at least not publicly. The outrage in Britain over Edith Cavell's death was twofold. Britain was rocked not only because the Germans had dared to kill a woman essentially in cold blood but also because they had dared to kill a British subject. The combination of imperialist superiority and traditionalist patriarchy evidenced in the reaction to Edith's death, both by the British leaders who circulated the propaganda and by the public who reacted to it, explains why women were not wanted in First World War British intelligence in any other capacity than serving tea and finding files.

In stark contrast to Edith Cavell but also illustrating why women were not welcome in British intelligence is the example of Mata Hari. The First World War reaffirmed the enduring image of female spies as charming seductresses who used their sexuality to ensnare powerful men and prise information from them. This image was firmly lodged in the minds of important men through the case of

Mata Hari. A Dutch exotic dancer and courtesan, Mata was famous throughout Europe for her shows, which usually involved exotic dancing and the removal of most of her clothing. Eventually, she supplemented her income by seducing government and military officials, including Germans, honey-trapping them into giving up intelligence. As the First World War continued, such liaisons brought her to the attention of the British and French intelligence services. She claimed she was trying to help France with her plan to embed herself within the German High Command but was named as a spy by a German attaché in some papers he sent to Berlin, which were intercepted by the French. She was convicted of being a spy for Germany and was executed by firing squad, just as Edith Cavell had been. Such an example contributed to the already existent archetypal idea of the 'femme fatale', a female character who relied on charm and seduction to manipulate men into giving up national secrets. Men, it seemed, could make honourable, trustworthy spies, like Richard Hannay in John Buchan's *The Thirty-Nine Steps*, or Ian Fleming's James Bond. Women, on the other hand, were not trustworthy and had proven traitorous and deceitful as spies in the past. The ingrained fear of women like Mata Hari was evident in depictions of such female characters in popular culture, both before and after Mata had been identified as a spy. This popular and enduring image of the seductress spy is an ancient idea stemming from biblical examples such as Eve and Delilah. Sir Arthur Conan Doyle's depiction of such a woman in the form of Irene Adler appeared in 1891 in 'A Scandal in Bohemia'. Mata Hari, it seemed, merely confirmed that men should be worried about and fearful of female spies. This image was indeed enduring, and by 1939 the British intelligence services remained in no hurry to recruit women. Despite providing abundant evidence of how effectively they actually could work in intelligence and how vital their contributions were, women were remembered more for their ability to use sex as a weapon to bring down men, kings and countries than they were for their successes and trustworthiness.

THE SECOND WORLD WAR WOMEN'S AUXILIARIES

As the coming of another war looked increasingly likely in the late 1930s, all three of the women's military auxiliaries were reformed in preparation for its outbreak. The Women's Royal Naval Service retained its original name, but the WAAC was renamed the Auxiliary Territorial Service (ATS) and the WRAF became the Women's Auxiliary Air Force (WAAF). The Munich crisis in September 1938 brought about the hasty formation of the ATS and every British county was tasked with raising several companies within the ATS which would be affiliated to a local male army territorial unit. One of these companies was to be a Royal Air Force ATS company, which would be affiliated to an auxiliary RAF unit. On 28 June 1939, just two months before the outbreak of the Second World War, the RAF ATS companies separated from the ATS altogether and by royal warrant the WAAF was established. The WAAF was not to be an independent organisation, but it was not completely integrated with the RAF either. The Air Ministry recognised the need to economise manpower if Britain stood a chance at winning the war, and they also recognised the need for trained 'womanpower' in being able to provide enough men to fight. It was proposed to 'employ women on certain operational duties' in the place of men, with a view to keeping the RAF flying.[11] In December 1941, the British government passed the National Service Act (No. 2), which made provision for the conscription of women. Women could choose to enter the armed forces, to join the civilian Women's Land Army or to work in industrial production of war commodities, such as munitions, tanks and planes. To begin with, the Act made all single women between the ages of twenty and thirty liable for conscription, and the WAAF received a flood of applications. Following this, a royal proclamation on 10 January 1942 activated the National Service Act, calling up all those born in 1920 and 1921, which was later extended to include all those born between 1918 and 1923. As a result, the WAAF continued to grow, and by July 1943, it was at its peak strength, containing 181,000 women. These women comprised 15.7 per cent of the total strength of the RAF.[12]

The three services trained their members to provide vital support towards the war effort, and by 1944, some 494,000 women had served within their ranks. Many of them provided clerical and domestic assistance to the British government and armed forces, just as they had in the First World War. Though in some respects their position in the military had not changed, in other respects, it had to. Again, necessitation born out of the lack of available men, combined to some degree with increasing and developing availability of opportunities for women in a world where they were now able to vote, resulted in a different women's military to that which had existed in the First World War. Along with the important and valuable clerical and domestic roles they filled, women were invited to work with anti-aircraft artillery and on radar stations, learned to encode and decode vitally important secret messages and were even parachute dropped into Nazi-occupied countries as clandestine agents with the Special Operations Executive. That being said, the eventually wide array of opportunities available within the women's military services was not immediately on offer when the WAAF was formed in 1939. Initially, the WAAF endured social ostracism, harsh conditions and occasional governmental disapproval, but WAAFs worked hard towards the British war effort, nonetheless. They served in a domestic capacity as drivers, orderlies, batwomen, catering personnel in hospitals and messes, and in a medical capacity as nurses, medical and air ambulance orderlies and dental surgery attendants. They also served as barrage balloon handlers, despite initial concerns in the Air Ministry that they might not be physically strong enough to handle the huge airborne bags of gas in high winds. They served as equippers, parachute packers, meteorologists, assistant armourers and many other clerical and support roles. WAAF members did not fly unless it was by sheer necessity or to carry out air checks. Some did receive special permission to accompany aircrews on training flights, but these were usually within the UK or were after the tide of war had turned, in territories controlled by the Allies. The only instance where they flew themselves with official permission was when the RAF begrudgingly allowed thirty (out of almost 1,500 volunteers) female service pilots to serve with the Air Transport Auxiliary, ferrying planes between airfields and factories.

A common misconception about women's military service in the twentieth century is that their involvement in the First World War led to immediately wider opportunities in the Second. To begin with, entirely the opposite was true. Rather surprisingly considering the advances women had made, which included obtaining the vote, the classes of employment of the WRAF in 1918 were 'very much more numerous' than those proposed for the WAAF in 1939.[13] In 1918, women in the WRAF could be involved in administrative work, household work (cooks, mess orderlies and waitresses, laundresses, general duties, pantry maids and vegetable women), non-technical work (shoemakers, tailors, fabric workers, motorcyclists, washers and telephonists) or technical work (acetylene workers, armourers, camera repairers, coppersmiths, electricians, aero-engine fitters, instrument repairers, machinists, magneto repairers, tinsmiths and sheet workers, turners, vulcanisers, wireless mechanics, drivers, draughtswomen, upholsterers, painters, carpenters, dopers, sign writers, photographers and store-women). In 1939, their somewhat underwhelming choices were those of cooks, light car drivers, equipment assistants, clerks (including General Duties) and fabric workers. The whole question of a women's reserve had been raised in 1936 but was considered at that time 'not desirable'.[14] Such an attitude is evident in the lack of options for women's work in the WAAF at its formation, despite how useful and effective women had proven to be in the WRAF in the First World War. Their work had not resulted in changed attitudes and views towards women and war work. Though some women had broken out of their traditional roles into fields that were usually reserved for men, this had not had a lasting effect as is sometimes claimed. Very early on in the Second World War it became clear that the manpower situation for the future was serious and that in order to solve the problem, women would have to be trained to do jobs within the RAF to release more men for duty. Just a month into the war, RAF stations were desperately asking for airwomen, voicing a need in particular for personnel to operate teleprinters, telephones and radar equipment. It was soon evident that many of the roles keeping men at home when they could be sent into action elsewhere were those relating to intelligence and communications. Just as war had forced the British government to stray into uncharted territory by creating first the WRAF and then the WAAF, the RAF would stray even further in the Second World War, by employing women in highly secret work gathering and disseminating information. The

Air Ministry searched for intelligent women in the WAAF who could be trusted to work behind the scenes, in secret intelligence branches and organisations, as very few women had before.

BRITISH INTELLIGENCE IN THE SECOND WORLD WAR

Historically, intelligence in Britain was gathered by the individual branches of the military. In 1909, however, the Secret Service Bureau was founded, containing various departments with different purposes and roles. MI5 was the domestic arm of the service and the Secret Intelligence Service (SIS, also known as MI6) was the foreign section, responsible for gathering intelligence overseas. In addition, the Government Code and Cypher School was founded in 1919 and was responsible for providing signals intelligence to the government. In 1936, the Joint Intelligence Committee was established and became the senior government intelligence body in Britain, encompassing MI5, MI6 and the GC&CS. Working alongside and yet independently of the JIC were the military intelligence branches. The British Army delegated intelligence duties to the Directorate of Military Operations and the Directorate of Military Intelligence, and the Royal Navy contained the Naval Intelligence Department. The Royal Air Force utilised its Air Intelligence Branch. In 1939, therefore, British intelligence was not the responsibility of one single organisation. Rather, these several bodies within the British government and armed forces shared the responsibility, all with different individual duties and methods. The outbreak of the Second World War acted as a catalyst for a mass reorganisation of British intelligence apparatus. While centralisation of intelligence was not always practical, it was, to some extent, desirable, as it would prevent the wastage and duplication of resources and would aid timeliness in the provision of accurate and useful intelligence. The need to better coordinate intelligence collection had, to some extent, been realised after 1918, but it did not result in action until 1939. By 1940, the individual organisations were finally beginning to successfully coordinate and collaborate, sufficiently enough that they managed to produce a much more efficient, if still not perfect, system.

British intelligence was split into two different types: 'special' intelligence was civilian in nature, encompassing MI5, MI6 and the GC&CS, and was not primarily concerned with military matters. Rather, it reported on political issues and handled overseas human intelligence operations. Under Foreign Office supervision, the Government Code and Cypher School at Bletchley Park came under this category. 'Service' intelligence, on the other hand, was military in nature. The Admiralty, the War Office and the Air Ministry produced, through their various individual intelligence sections, material which was concerned with facts about the enemy's military position. The relationship between military and civilian intelligence organisations was often uneasy. Military leaders preferred impressive field command and military tactics to spying, which they deemed dirty work. It was obvious, though, that cooperation and collaboration between the two different types of organisations was essential if the Allies were going to win the war. The RAF needed to know certain things about its German counterpart, the Luftwaffe. It helped to know, for instance, what kind of aircraft it possessed, in what numbers, where they were located and what they were capable of. It was useful to know where they might take off from and where they were stored when they were not flying. Knowledge of the basic tactics the Luftwaffe used, and any changes in these tactics, was valuable. This information could be obtained in various different ways and would provide the RAF with a major advantage in the coming war.

WOMEN IN BRITISH INTELLIGENCE DURING THE SECOND WORLD WAR

In the historical context of the First World War, entrenched traditionalism, separate spheres ideology, patriarchy and to some extent imperialism all contributed to the argument against using women in wartime British intelligence. By 1939, with another world war looming, the argument was growing weaker with the increasing mobilisation of women. However much they did not want to, the British intelligence services had no choice but to turn to women to fill positions that were at risk of being left empty if kept only for men. By 1939, the Registry at MI5 was an exclusively female preserve. Women were working at MI5 and the SIS as clerks and secretaries, also involved in propaganda, censorship and misinformation. There were, however, no female intelligence officers in either service. Over the course of the Second World War, the number of women employed in both MI5 and MI6 increased heavily, most of them in clerical and office roles, subordinate to the male intelligence officers who begrudgingly accepted them.

In addition to the fear of Mata Hari-type women and ideas about the general lack of capabilities women possessed, there were those men who did not consider it safe for women to be employed in intelligence roles, due to their inevitable proximity to areas susceptible to enemy bombing raids. The reality was that German bombing was often indiscriminate, rendering most of Britain unsafe, not just government and military installations. The weakness of this argument is also obvious in a proposal for the formation of the WAAF from April 1938, in which it was pointed out that 'a woman working at an RAF operational station is probably much safer than a woman working in an aircraft factory'.[15] Writing in 1943, Leonard Taylor, the editor of the *Air Training Corps Gazette*, questioned whether war work was 'suitable' for women, or if it was 'unfeminine' and might 'lessen a woman's charm'.[16] Agreeing with the author of the proposal document, he concluded that if war work was suitable for housemaids and factory workers, then it was suitable for women to work towards the war in a military capacity. The work being carried out in factories and by housemaids was hard, dirty and underpaid and yet was socially accepted and even encouraged. Women joining the military, on the other hand, were treated with suspicion and even disdain by men and by some of their female peers. The work they would be doing, being initially domestic and clerical in nature, was often much more contemporarily suited to women than factory work would have been, and yet they encountered such attitudes. In truth, it was not the work that was the issue – it was the fact that women would be doing it while wearing military uniforms, posing a great threat to conventional understandings of gender and therefore to social order in general. The potential for such upheaval and change naturally worried men, and some women, throughout the country. RAF officers charged with training incoming WAAF recruits were dubious – a Wing Commander Carnegie at RAF Wittering took WAAFs on his station 'only because the CO at a nearby bomber station refused to take them'.[17] Such entrenched refusal to accept women as part of the military or intelligence world was as common in the Second World War to begin with as it had been in the First, as changes in attitudes failed to keep up with the changes taking place in British society, despite the increased pace under conditions of war.

In addition to questioning whether or not women should be doing military work were those asking whether or not they were actually capable of it. As there had been in the First World War, there was in the Second an attitude that men were intellectually superior to women, and one of the primary concerns of RAF intelligence sections was that women did not have the intellect or education to be able to understand the work that they were doing well enough to do it accurately. Women often proved this assumption wrong during training. WAAF recruit Molly Sasson went straight from her initial training into specialist courses, focusing on languages and intelligence matters. She was the youngest and most junior of the twenty-three officers on her advanced intelligence course, as well as being the only woman. 'It was tough', she says, 'as I had made up my mind to study hard and do the best that I could. Most evenings I studied, while the others enjoyed a drink or two in the mess hall and local pub. This course lasted six weeks. The final exam had most of us panicking.'[18] Molly's hard work was rewarded, and her clear ability evident, when her results revealed that she had come second. She points out, though, that the RAF Squadron Leader who came first had been cheating and had concealed a number of pieces of paper up his sleeve. Molly's first posting after passing these specialist courses was to the RAF's Special Investigation Branch Headquarters in London, where she lived and worked in a large block of flats that had been requisitioned by the RAF. Here she undertook further German and Dutch studies in preparation, before taking a specialist civil service commissioners' examination in both languages, and spent time reading thousands of German letters that were subjected to censorship. 'Any letters of security interest would be translated and forwarded with comment,' she says.[19] Molly dealt with many other German and Dutch documents and was eventually assigned duties that took her to other parts of the country to interview German prisoners of war and civilians who were of security risk or interest. 'There were cases of dubious characters', she recalls, 'whose data was passed on to other authorities such as immigration, police of the Security Service, MI5.'[20] Molly proved that WAAFs were definitely capable of intelligence work – but more than that, she proved that they could be very good at it. However, it is clear in how some women were treated that their male colleagues often had a difficult time believing in their ability. Women did not receive the same education in mathematics and the sciences that men received, so how could they be expected to be allowed to do jobs where they would need to calculate things and carry out mechanical procedures? Technical signals officer Dorothy Henderson describes an encounter early on in her career:

> I recall the first time after I was posted as a Technical Signals Officer, picking up my phone to answer, 'Signals Officer here', and hearing the amused comment in the background the other end, 'There's a little WAAF here calling herself a Signals Officer!' Then to me, 'You mean a Code and Cypher Officer, don't you dear?' I said, 'No, I meant Signals Officer.' 'Oh God,' said my caller. 'Women Signals Officers.' I later had splendid support and loyalty from male SNCOs. It was they who had found the idea hardest to accept at the beginning.[21]

It was commonly claimed that women in uniform would undermine the morale of male soldiers and fail in the work that was required of them, due to physical and emotional weakness. Women, it was thought, should not be involved in military intelligence work, were not entirely capable of it and could not be trusted with secrets because they had not historically proven to be trustworthy or capable of discretion. Not all women met with constant opposition – Aileen Clayton found the men she worked with to be 'kind and tolerant in their attitude towards the motley assembly of young women which had been inflicted on their erstwhile all-male existence'.[22] Many WAAFs, however, were not so lucky. A BBC broadcast by an RAF officer, who believed that 'war was a job for men, that in war women could tackle the more quiet and comfortable civilian jobs and leave it to fathers, brothers and cousins to fill the fighting services', was more indicative of the common attitude towards women in military roles of any sort. The same officer heard that women were to be employed in intelligence capacities, in operations rooms, manning signals and teleprinters, and was 'inwardly rather resentful, slightly amused, believing that it could not last; that it might be pretty-pretty during the quiet days, but when the going got tough the folly of it would be seen'. After the war, the RAF officer in question went on air with the BBC to declare himself a 'converted man'. The first few WAAFs who were added to the RAF were, in his later opinion, a 'sign of strength, not weakness'. He noticed through the war that efficiency was maintained and often increased because of the WAAFs and was proud enough of them to publicly proclaim how 'darned well' they had worked, especially in helping to win the Battle of Britain.[23] WAAFs were employed in many roles and capacities throughout the vast and intricate network that made up British military intelligence, and they performed this work with skill, effectiveness and discretion not initially expected of them.

The combination of necessary change, differing opinions and clashing personalities within the British government, military and intelligence organisations and the special circumstances of war culminated in a British intelligence network that was complex and often confusing. An accurate and reliable picture of enemy intentions and capabilities could only be supplied by a jigsaw puzzle consisting of many pieces, each one of which was needed to obtain a complete picture. Across this puzzle, in many of the pieces – some of them the most vital – were members of the Women's Auxiliary Air Force. No single organisation or department was responsible for the collection and dissemination of intelligence that was crucial to informing some of the most important decisions taken by the Allies in the war. The whole system was needed for this, and hidden in many of the individual sections were members of the WAAF.

Intelligence consists of three main functions: the acquisition of information; the analysis and interpretation of that information; and the dissemination of the results to those who can make operational decisions based upon the intelligence provided.[24] Members of the WAAF performed all of these functions in their work within the complicated web of intelligence in Britain throughout the Second World War. They were involved in both special and service intelligence, and their contribution was vitally important to the British war effort and the Allied victory in 1945. They worked to gather intelligence on enemy aircraft, airfields and bombing targets and generated reports on the effectiveness of Allied bombing raids and on enemy and Allied air activity in general. WAAFs were heavily involved in this work in various RAF sections and departments, including in the photographic reconnaissance and interpretation unit at RAF Medmenham. The Y Service monitored enemy signals and generated the raw intelligence material that was sent to Bletchley Park. The Dowding System used radar to monitor where enemy aircraft were and to help the RAF intercept them and aid in timely air raid warnings being given. These organisations were used in defence of Britain in the early stages of the Second World War and aided Bomber Command's offensive and the D-Day landings as the war progressed. In all of them, WAAFs were present and instrumental in the collection and dissemination of intelligence. Their contribution, though hidden, was vital.

2

CARELESS TALK AND KEEPING MUM

Women were accepted into intelligence roles within the British armed forces in the Second World War predominantly out of necessity. As men were funnelled into combat positions, women filled the roles they left empty in Britain. This war is remembered as the 'People's War' in that the British war effort involved members of every class and gender across the nation. In many ways, the war effort transcended gender boundaries, as women filled jobs across industry, agriculture and in the armed forces that had previously been the exclusive domain of men. There was also, however, a curious contradiction to this new trend and, in some ways, gender divisions were also reinforced. Though women were working in military intelligence roles that they had previously been excluded from, their work generally fit comfortably within the definition of what was deemed appropriate 'women's work' in the 1940s. By remaining in Britain and working in what were essentially offices, albeit on RAF stations which were subject to Luftwaffe bombing raids, WAAF intelligence personnel were seen to be supporting the fighting men who were off winning the war at the battlefront, on land, at sea and in the air. Perhaps thinking of it this way made it easier for the RAF to afford WAAFs new opportunities, though they were often afforded begrudgingly, as various ingrained ideas and fears fed into the doubt that women would be able to successfully fill intelligence roles.

WOMEN AND SECRETS

In his mission to transform Britain into a total war economy, Minister of Labour Ernest Bevin made the controversial decision to conscript women for war work, despite the general reluctance of men and trade unions to accept women into skilled professions. This reluctance was felt to an even greater degree by the majority of men in the military and intelligence services, for a variety of reasons. There was the argument that women were inherently unsuited to combat, and to military work in general, due to supposedly being the more emotionally and physically frail of the sexes. Where secret work is concerned, however, the overriding reason for the reluctance of the male-dominated intelligence services and sections to accept female staff was the belief that women were incapable of keeping secrets. In a war where brute force simply was not an option, the British authorities were well aware of the grave importance of intelligence and secrecy. In 1940, the invasion of the Low Countries, the evacuation of the British Expeditionary Force from Dunkirk and the fall of France left Britain isolated, its people anxious as the threat of invasion loomed constantly. This situation, coupled with the Ministry of Information's attempt to encourage secrecy and discourage gossip through a new propaganda campaign, resulted in the creation of an atmosphere of paranoia and 'spy mania'. England, as WAAF operator Aileen Clayton points out, became 'pathologically spy scared', both evidenced and perhaps in some ways encouraged by the now-famous Fougasse 'Careless Talk' cartoon posters in public places, warning everyone that German spies, or even Hitler himself, might be listening.[1] In this atmosphere, common fear of the 'fifth column', coupled with memories and perceptions of traitorous women like Mata Hari, reinforced the existing idea that women could not be trusted and were inherently incapable of keeping secrets. Such an attitude was prevalent in the military and intelligence services, as is clear in the experiences of many WAAFs involved in intelligence work.

The initial distrust of women by the British military and intelligence services was twofold. On one hand, it was feared that women could, like Mata Hari, be employed by the enemy as covert spies, acquiring secret knowledge through flirtation and seduction. On the other hand, it was assumed that they would give away national secrets by accident, due to their perceived general inclination to gossip and 'chatter'. The RAF could do its best to ensure that female spies were kept out of the WAAF and well away from secret work by carrying out extensive background checks, but they 'suspected women would surely chatter about top secret information' should they be employed in intelligence work at all.[2] When WAAF recruit Petrea Winterbotham was interviewed prior to her posting to Bentley Priory operations room, she was asked if she could keep a secret and was told that she'd never be allowed to reveal details of her work to anyone. Assuring her interviewer that she could indeed be discreet, she was admitted to the first batch of women to go on watch at the headquarters of Fighter Command. Her warrant officer told her that 'women always chattered and wouldn't keep things secret'.[3] Petrea was determined to prove him wrong. She had a tough job on her hands, though, as it was popularly believed that women could not help but gossip. This view was certainly held by the male-dominated British domestic security service, MI5. Maxwell Knight, an MI5 officer, stated the common view of the service on female agents: 'It is frequently alleged that women are less discreet than men: that they are ruled by their emotions, and not by their brains: that they rely on intuition rather than on reason; and that Sex will play an unsettling and dangerous role in their work.'[4] Despite these prevailing fears and views, the British government, military and intelligence services had little choice under the special conditions of war but to admit women into secret work. This they did reluctantly, taking every possible opportunity to remind the women of the importance and necessity of secrecy, initially convinced that they would be unable to comply.

A personal security form for all employees of the Government Code and Cypher School at Bletchley Park warned against careless talk in May 1942:

> This may seem a simple matter. It should be. But repeated experience has proved that it is not, even for the cleverest of us; even for the least important. Month after month instances have occurred where workers at BP have been heard casually saying outside BP things that are dangerous. It is not enough to know that you must not hint at these things outside. It must be uppermost in your mind every hour that you talk to outsiders. Even the most trivial-seeming things matter. The enemy does not get his intelligence by great scoops, but from a whisper here, a tiny detail there.[5]

The form went on to warn staff not to talk at meals, in transport vehicles, while travelling, in their billets and huts and even by their own firesides. The fear was that spies could pose as waitresses, drivers, travellers, billet hosts, cleaners and maintenance staff and that the slightest indiscretion could give the enemy an unwelcome advantage. This national fear, at times bordering on paranoia, is clear in much of the propaganda of the Second World War, which often used guilt tactics and fear-mongering to try to keep those with access to secret information from leaking it, either intentionally or by accident. The GC&CS form ominously warned:

> If you are indiscreet and tell your own folks, they may see no reason why they should not do likewise. They are not in a position to know the consequences and have received no guidance. Moreover, if one day invasion came, as it perfectly well may, Nazi brutality might stop at nothing to wring from those that you care for, secrets that you would give anything, then, to have saved them from knowing. Their only safety will lie in utter ignorance of your work. There is nothing to be gained by chatter but the satisfaction of idle vanity, or idle curiosity: there is everything to be lost – the very existence of our work here, the lives of others, even the War itself. People will always be curious. They can always learn something from your answers, if you answer, even though you only answer 'yes' or 'no'. Do not suggest, as it is so easy and so flattering to human vanity, that you are doing something very important and very 'hush-hush'. Far too many people in England know about BP already. If ever the Germans come to know it, we may find ourselves a German 'Target for Tonight'.[6]

In a similar attempt to impress upon security and intelligence personnel the importance of secrecy and the possible effects of breaching it, the Ministry of Information released what came to be known as the 'Careless Talk' propaganda campaign.

WOMEN AND PROPAGANDA

Formed on 4 September 1939, the day after Britain declared war on Germany, the Ministry of Information was the central government department responsible for publicity and propaganda during the Second World War. Some of the phrases from its propaganda posters have entered the British common lexicon and remain enduringly famous. One such catchphrase comes from the poster collection which gave the 'Careless Talk' campaign its name: 'Careless Talk Costs Lives'.[7] On one poster sporting the phrase, cartoon versions of Hitler and Göring are depicted eavesdropping on two female shoppers who are supposedly gossiping together. The Careless Talk campaign reinforced the general idea that women were loose-lipped liabilities, responsible for starting and spreading rumours and letting information slip that could help the enemy. The campaign perpetuated a culture of distrust and women talking together in public suddenly seemed dangerous and threatening. The War Cabinet established a Committee on the Issue of Warnings against Discussion of Confidential Matters in Public Places, which met for the first time on 13 October 1939 to consider security in the services and the possibility of a domestic propaganda campaign to discourage gossip and attempt to encourage greater effort towards secrecy.[8] By 14 November 1939, 621,250 posters had been distributed for display in hotels, public houses, Post Office branches, local authorities, labour exchanges and docks. In early 1940, a new campaign was launched and over 2 million display sites were secured for posters, including those by Fougasse. Of the 2,250,100 posters distributed, 734,200 of them were from the Fougasse series, with a further 248,000 printed in March 1940. This propaganda push – particularly the Fougasse prints which focused on public gossip and often pictured chattering women – went some way towards reinforcing the idea that women were natural gossips and could not keep secrets.[9] In addition, Churchill's encouragement of Britons to 'join the Silent Column', combined with the popularity of spy literature and films and with the general war situation in 1940, 'fuelled fertile imaginations' and transformed Britons into a 'nation of spies'.[10]

THE LETHAL WOMAN

The Mata Hari-style 'femme fatale' was not an image that had disappeared with the end of the First World War. The stereotype of the lethal beautiful woman persisted, appearing in various propaganda films in the Second World War. A United Artists film entitled *The Next of Kin* reminded viewers that in relation to espionage, 'popular imagination usually conjures up a vision of a glamorous, exotic female' spy, much like Mata Hari. Though the film pointed out that spies could just as well be very ordinary people and that the 'glamorous, exotic female' spy was perhaps an illusion, the stereotype had existed for many years in the British psyche and could not easily be removed.[11] The combination of alcohol and feminine allure was seen as a particular threat, as shown in the 1942 poster from the Careless Talk collection bearing the phrase 'Keep mum, she's not so dumb!'[12] The poster depicts a blonde-haired woman reclining as officers from all three branches of the armed forces surround her, one holding an alcoholic drink, all seemingly ready to disclose information about their classified work because of her sex appeal. In May 1942, *Advertiser's Weekly* reminded servicemen that 'when in the company of a beautiful woman', they should 'remember that beauty may conceal brains' – the implication being that military personnel needed to be careful around women, who would surely try to wile secrets from them.[13]

In addition to being presented as intentionally subversive or inherently loose-lipped, in some British propaganda relating to secrecy women are presented as being subversive even when they have not actively done anything wrong. The 1943 army short film *Missed Date* shows two servicemen who make a date with two women in a country pub. Receiving no visible or audible encouragement from the women to do so, the men brag to them that 'there's a big do on' and that though they know what it is all about, they 'mustn't say'.[14] On Saturday, the women wait for their dates, eventually wondering why the men do not appear. It is revealed that a man in the pub – a German spy – overheard the conversation and that the servicemen have not appeared because they have died in a German raid on the nearby aerodrome, which was launched based on the information they gave away. Though the two women do nothing in the film to elicit information from the servicemen, their presence is considered to have made the pub a dangerous den of enemy infiltration. A similar situation is presented in the 1943 propaganda film *Hush! Not a Word!* Intended for circulation within the RAF, the film shows details of British secrets being divulged by a soldier writing to his girlfriend, resulting in the bombing of an airfield.[15] Again, the woman involved has done nothing to illicit the revelation from the airman, and yet indirectly in both films women are seen as a security risk purely by being present.

Government advertisements also described stereotyped female characters, like 'Miss Leaky Mouth': 'She simply can't stop talking and since the weather went out as conversation she goes on like a leaky tap about the war. She doesn't know anything, but her chatter can do harm. Tell her to talk about the neighbours.'[16] 'Miss Teacup

Whisper' was also said to be dangerous: 'Everything she knows is so important that it must be spoken in whispers and she whispers all over the town. She's one of Hitler's allies (she does not know that).' The audience of the advertisement was urged to 'tell these people to join Britain's Silent Column', a new campaign deployed to prevent the spilling of secrets.[17] In a context of mass anxiety and threat of invasion in the summer of 1940, the Ministry of Information was looking for ways to curb talk that might further damage the morale of the British public. In June, it was confirmed that rumours had had 'disastrous effects' on morale during the evacuation of Dunkirk and the government was keen to avoid the same thing happening again.[18] Government propaganda urged the British people to join the Silent Column in a new initiative aimed at strengthening security and preventing damaging rumours and careless talk, both of which would, the people were told, aid the enemy. Britons were told to remain silent – to keep information to themselves and to make sure others did the same. The Silent Column campaign, however, was widely criticised by the British public, who felt that their right to freedom of thought and speech was being violated, some even comparing the government who had issued it to the Gestapo.[19] The campaign was also criticised for the debates it elicited over class, citizenship and identity. It appeared to contradict notions of togetherness and unity, encouraging suspicion and accusations of unpatriotic behaviour among the British people. It perpetuated stereotypes of nationality, race and class and inadvertently encouraged fear and suspicion of 'the other'. For example, the lower echelons of the class system – those with less formal education – might be assumed more likely to gossip, where those at the top were assumed more likely to be able to keep secrets. Immigrant workers might be viewed with much greater suspicion than British nationals. Curiously, while the Silent

Column and Careless Talk campaigns elicited criticism over issues of class, ethnicity and citizenship, they did not draw much pushback over gender. There was little criticism of the campaigns' implication that women were the most likely candidates for giving away national secrets through gossip.

WAAF SECRET-KEEPERS

Despite their fears about women being spies, gossips or a subversive presence, the British authorities and the Air Ministry need never have worried about the ability of the WAAFs to keep secrets. Where it was assumed that they lacked the ability to keep from accidentally chattering about their work, WAAF intelligence personnel actually conducted themselves with an impressive level of discretion and secrecy. Petrea Winterbotham was one of the first women to be involved in secret work in the Battle of Britain and did so without ever illegally chattering about it. Her warrant officer adamantly believed that women could not keep secrets, but he had to admit it when Petrea proved him wrong. 'I think I could have become a feminist at that point,' she says.[20] Secrecy was so well adhered to by WAAFs that most of them had no idea what their colleagues were doing. Compartmentalisation was used heavily to decrease the likelihood of important information reaching the enemy, and in one case, a WAAF cook asked to be transferred to a station where she knew young women were engaged in 'terribly hush-hush' work, only to find that she had in fact been working at the station in question for eighteen months.[21] The same was true at Medmenham, where many WAAFs working in adjacent rooms had no idea what went on outside of their own. The head of Medmenham's Model Making Section circulated a letter in 1945 to his staff which read:

Your loyalty and devotion to duty has been outstanding. Your sense of responsibility and security has been unsurpassed. The latter has brought forth many expressions of admiration from other members of the Station who have only recently learnt of the true nature of the work upon which you have been engaged for so long. The making of models for the briefing of vital operations on land, sea and in the air has put you very much 'in the know' as to the spot where and, to a certain extent, when the next blow at the enemy was to be made. Not once did you break the trust that has been placed upon you.[22]

Measures were taken, often on the initiative of the WAAFs themselves, to try to ensure that security was never breached. Some WAAFs, like radar operator Olivia Davies, were segregated from their colleagues at night in case they talked in their sleep.[23] Others refused anaesthetic when undergoing dental procedures in case they leaked information under its effect, and some refused operations completely, not wanting to take the risk.[24] WAAFs did not speak to their friends, romantic partners or parents about their work, however badly they wanted to. Gwen Reading was well accustomed to the intense security on her radar station and her parents had no idea what her wartime service really entailed.[25] On 8 August 1945, the Air Ministry sent a photographer to Bawdsey radar station, where Gwen was working, and a crew photograph was taken for release in the national press. The official blurb to the photograph read:

Working under the closest secrecy since 1939, over 4,000 WAAF personnel have played an important part in the air victories achieved by radiolocation. They tracked hostile and friendly aircraft, flying bombs and rockets, German E Boats and Allied Merchant vessels, and have guided British and Allied fighter pilots on to enemy aircraft. Trained to use and service some of the most delicate and complicated instruments ever invented, they have carried out their duties with enthusiasm, often under uncomfortable conditions and sometimes under enemy fire.[26]

The revelation of what Gwen and her colleagues had been doing in the Dowding System came at the end of the war, and it was not told by the WAAFs themselves but by their government, which was proud of their achievements. Other WAAFs would continue to stay silent regarding their work long after the war had finished and many of their stories remained secret for decades. Many service-women did not speak publicly about their wartime intelligence work until after 1974, when F. W. Winterbotham's book *The Ultra Secret* revealed the true nature of the work carried out at Bletchley Park. From the late 1970s, women's memoirs and personal accounts of the war began to appear, but many focused on the social aspects of their wartime service and were light on detail concerning the in-telligence work.[27] Inevitably, such restraint contributed to the story of WAAFs in air intelligence remaining untold and is testament of the ability of the women to defy expectations and keep secrets.

In some cases, WAAFs were even employed in roles to ensure that secrecy was upheld. The famous leader of the 617 Squadron Dambusters, Guy Gibson, was 'almost fanatical about security' and was 'unsparing in his anger' towards anyone caught giving away even the slightest operational detail.[28] Gibson was deeply alarmed when his WAAF intelligence officer informed him that details of the impending operation were 'common knowledge' at the Air Ministry, listing the specifics of what was known and to whom. In this instance, secret information had been leaked by male staff, and a WAAF operator had been the one to recognise the possible resulting danger and to correct the situation. Other WAAFs were intentionally employed to look out for lapses in secrecy. Ruth Ive was sent around the country to military camps and RAF stations where special exercises or operations were taking place and was heavily involved in efforts to clamp down security prior to them doing so. Ruth knew how to 'bug' a telephone exchange and one of her tasks was to plug into a camp or station's exchange to listen for unauthorised phone calls. The night of the Dambusters raid, she was driven to the Dambusters' airfield and spent the night waiting to intercept telephone calls. She recalls:

On this particular raid they weren't allowed to make telephone calls at all. So we knew if our lines were being used by a little light or flickering ball. Anyone making a call would be going against the rules because there was a 24-hour clamp down on security and all telephone calls. They put a fix on the officers' mess and various other places, and I had to listen to the telephone calls and make a note of any indiscretions and disconnect the call at the same time.[29]

Maxwell Knight, the MI5 officer who had stated the risks of using female agents, ate his words after working with women in intelligence. He later wrote that his own experience of working with them had been 'very much to the contrary' of what he had expected. Having worked with Olga Gray, a female agent who had managed to penetrate the pro-Nazi Right Club, he wrote:

During the present war, M.S. [his department] has investigated probably hundreds of cases of 'loose-talk': in by far the greater proportion of these cases the offenders were men. In my submission this is due to one principal factor: it is that indiscretions are committed from conceit. Taking him generally, Man is a conceited creature, while Woman is a vain creature: conceit and vanity are not the same. A man's conceit will often lead him to indiscretion, in an endeavour to build himself up among his fellow men, or even to impress a woman; women, being vain rather than conceited, find their outlet for this form of self-expression in their personal experience, dress etc.[30]

Indeed, where it was feared that women would reveal secrets through absent-minded gossip, it was actually much more common that men revealed sensitive information through arrogance or conceit, as suggested by Knight. A letter from Bletchley Park to its Gawcott outstation detailed one such situation:

Sergeant S is in the habit of talking foolishly and perhaps dangerously about his work and implying a knowledge of our work at BP in front of his billeters and others. He appears to be one of those who want to shine before men (and no doubt women). He has bragged about how busy the Middle East battles have made him: 'Of course, you know all about that at Bletchley etc.' Sheer stupidity no doubt but undesirable. If I might suggest it a talking to would do him no harm even if there is not very much in it.[31]

In these situations, like the one depicted in the propaganda film *Missed Date*, it was easy and perhaps desirable to the British authorities to blame the women that the men were bragging to. It was also highly unfair and unwarranted, certainly in the case of the WAAFs, who did not live up to the popular stereotyping of them as gossips and wily subversives. On the contrary, they performed their work capably and efficiently and with the utmost discretion and secrecy, defying the stereotypes and expectations placed upon them by their government, the military and the British public. The fact that much of their work remained secret until decades after the war had ended is testament to the fact that they kept their secrets extremely well, in some cases for much longer than was officially required. Sadly, such success led to the omission of their contribution from historical memory and the story of Allied air operations during the war.

POST-WAR REVELATIONS OF SECRECY

When she was posted to Bletchley Park, WAAF operator Kathleen Godfrey quickly realised that secrecy was 'of the utmost importance'. Kathleen did not reveal what she had done during the war until twenty-five years after it had finished, keeping even her father in the dark, despite the fact that he was Admiral John Godfrey, the Director of Naval Intelligence.[32] Y Service WAAF operator Vera Ines Morley Elkan took her signing of the Official Secrets Act so seriously that she did not speak about her war work until very recently, when she met her German opposite in Hamburg.[33] Similarly, when Petrea Winterbotham married her husband, Frederick Winterbotham, they did not discuss what they had respectively done during the war until 1974. She had no idea until that year, when her husband published *The Ultra Secret*, that he had supervised the distribution of Ultra intelligence. As he had first met her in the Bentley Priory operations room, Frederick was aware of what his wife had been doing, but still they never discussed it until after *The Ultra Secret* was out.[34]

A VE Day Special Order to staff from Commander Edward Travis, the operational head of Bletchley Park, acknowledged that 'the temptation now to "own up" to our friends and family as to what our work has been is a very real and natural one'. It also stated that this temptation 'must be resisted absolutely'.[35] Though the Second World War had ended, the threat of the Cold War loomed and the intelligence and military staffs were aware of the continued need for secrecy. Keeping secrets and stifling openness became an 'automatic reaction' for many WAAFs, many of whom lost the chance to share their stories with loved ones for ever. Bletchley Park remained a particularly well-kept secret and when former staff visited it in the 1970s, some were astonished to find that 'nothing had been left' and 'nobody knew of them'.[36] The women truly understood the gravity of their work and the importance of it being kept secret and were more capable and willing than the authorities ever thought possible in refraining from talking about it. Working at Old Sarum, Gwendoline Saunders received the teleprinter signal from 617 Squadron that reported the breaching of the Möhne and Eder Dams by the Dambusters. She was aware that the raid was important and despite the excited staff crowding around her desk, she knew that 'nothing was to be repeated outside of the office'. For Gwendoline, secrecy became 'automatic' and after the war she said simply, 'You just didn't discuss it.'[37] Jean Hilda Mills worked as a plotter and was 'quite proud' to be involved in secret work, aware of the fact that lives depended on her ability to keep information about radar out of German hands.[38] When she was recruited for Special Duties work, Muriel Gane Pushman was told by an RAF officer:

I cannot stress too strongly the secretive nature of this work. You will be asked to swear an oath that you will never mention what you are doing to another human being – parent, husband, brother, sister, boyfriend, the man in the street, or the barmaid in the pub. Should you ever break this oath, either deliberately or through indiscretion, you will be dishonourably discharged.[39]

Following the war, Muriel said, 'Torture would not have induced me to say what I had eaten for breakfast, let alone divulge the nation's secrets.'[40] Her WAAF colleague in radar Anne Stobbs took a similar oath and kept it 'absolutely faithfully throughout the war'. Anne says, 'They say that women can't keep a secret, but it really isn't true.'[41] In the case of the WAAFs, the evidence suggests that she was right.

3

THE GREAT AIR BATTLE

OPERATION SEALION

In his address in the House of Commons on 20 August 1940, Winston Churchill referred to the aerial conflict that had been raging in Britain's skies since July as the 'Great Air Battle'. The importance of this battle was not lost on the Prime Minister, and he had anticipated it months before. 'The Battle of France is over. I expect that the Battle of Britain is about to begin,' he had said to the House of Commons on 18 June.[1] The Great Air Battle was part of Germany's ultimate plan to invade and take control of Britain, which it needed to do to ensure victory in Europe. As long as Britain remained free from German control, a base existed from which the war against the Axis could be fought.

Following the fall of France, on 16 July Hitler issued Directive No. 16, containing the formal approval of the invasion of Britain. 'Operation Seelöwe', or 'Operation Sealion', was the codename for the Nazi plan to carry out a landing operation in Britain, the aim of which was to 'eliminate the English motherland as a base from which the war against Germany can be continued, and, if necessary, to occupy it completely'.[2] Joseph 'Beppo' Schmid, commander of the

Luftwaffe's Military Intelligence Branch, recognised in November 1939 that from Germany's point of view, Britain was 'the most dangerous of all possible enemies'. The war, he said, could not be ended in a manner favourable to Germany as long as Britain had not been mastered. Germany's war aim 'must therefore be to strike at Britain with all available weapons, particularly those of the navy and the air force'.[3] The success of Operation Sealion rested on this strike.

RAF reconnaissance confirmed the assembly of a German Army and invasion force along the coasts of occupied Europe, and decrypted German signals indicated that invasion was imminent. Though Hitler considered the British military situation in July 1940 to be hopeless, he knew that in order to successfully execute Sealion he would need to remove Britain's ability to protect itself. As an island, Britain's gravest threats had traditionally come from the sea and the country had always relied on its navy for protection. The German Navy, the Kriegsmarine, had suffered significant losses in the Norwegian campaign, which had severely weakened it. In order to land an invasion fleet on British shores, Hitler needed air superiority. With his ships outnumbered, it was critical to have control of British airspace so that the landing force could be protected from above. The most dangerous threat Britain faced in June 1940 was therefore not from the sea but from the air, in the form of the German air force, the Luftwaffe. If the RAF was left undefeated, Sealion's objectives would likely not be achieved. Nicknamed the 'junior service' due to its being the youngest of the three British military services, the RAF would be at the forefront of the forthcoming fight for Britain's survival. Aware that he could not successfully invade Britain without the removal of the RAF as a threat, Hitler ordered the head of the Luftwaffe, Reichsmarschall Hermann Göring, to defeat this 'junior service' so that Sealion could proceed.

In his famous speech on 'the Few' in August 1940, Churchill acknowledged that while the Second World War was, in his opinion, a continuation of the First World War, there were 'very great differences in its character'. He proclaimed his thankfulness that due to evolving strategy, organisation, technical apparatus, science and mechanics, the 'prodigious slaughter' in the Great War was replaced by a different means of fighting which resulted in a much lower casualty rate.[4] One of the results of such evolution was the maturation of British air power. In the First World War, the aeroplane had been in its infancy and remained a secondary support for land and sea operations. By 1939, it would be a critically important primary weapon, playing the dominant role in the war that lay ahead. In a memorandum to the Cabinet on 3 September 1940, Churchill cited the RAF as 'the means of victory', voicing his belief that while the navy could lose the war for the Allies, 'only the Air Force can win it'.[5] In 1939, Luftwaffe aircraft numbers far exceeded the number of British planes available for frontline service. At the height of the battle, the RAF had 749 fighter aircraft available, compared to the Luftwaffe's 2,550.[6] Brute force was not an option for the RAF and its inferior material strength meant that it would need to look for a different kind of advantage. That advantage would be found in the form of a state-of-the-art integrated air defence system, which would collect intelligence using newly developed technology and disseminate it to fighter pilots using a vast and efficient communications network. The technology was radio direction finding – better known today as radar – and the network was known as the 'Dowding System'. In every instance where British fighter pilots successfully contributed to victory, behind them were teams of intelligence personnel guiding and supporting them to ensure the best use of resources against a superior enemy. In this war where air power was of vital importance to victory, so too was the intelligence behind the deployment of planes and pilots, and the combination of the two proved more than a match for the Luftwaffe. The resources of the Luftwaffe were 'superior in numbers and of a high quality', and though there had been aerial battles in the First World War, this was the first large-scale aerial battle for air dominance that could potentially determine the outcome of a war. From 26 June 1940, the Luftwaffe carried out scattered day and night attacks over Britain, concentrating on ports, shipping targets and locations where aircraft were being manufactured. By 6 September, the attacks had increased and were larger and were targeting more RAF facilities and aircraft industry with a view to weakening and ultimately removing the ability of the RAF to defend Britain. The ground personnel of the RAF, including thousands of WAAFs, were directly involved in the fight, facing the change in Luftwaffe tactics head-on.

On 6 September 1939, a coastal searchlight battery on Mersea Island in the Thames Estuary reported the sound of an aircraft above them. It was a foggy morning, so they could not see the aircraft clearly enough to be able to positively identify it. The battery reported the aircraft to RAF 11 Group Headquarters and as it remained unidentified, the North Weald Sector commander was ordered to scramble fighters to investigate it. RAF 56 Squadron launched Hawker Hurricanes to intercept and report on the aircraft. As they gained altitude, the Hurricanes were picked up by radar equipment at a radar station in Essex. Unfortunately, there was no way to distinguish between friendly and enemy aircraft when they both appeared as the same 'blip' on a screen, and the Hurricanes were mistaken for German aircraft. Believing that the Luftwaffe was on the doorstep about to burst in, the RAF launched Spitfires from Hornchurch and South Weald, instructing them to intercept the supposed enemy raiders. The interception resulted in the downing of two Hurricanes by friendly fire and the first RAF fighter pilot casualty of the war, as pilot officer Montague Hulton-Harrop was killed. The incident, which came to be known as 'the Battle of Barking Creek', revealed the cracks and problems in Britain's existing early warning system. Operators needed to be better able to distinguish enemy raiders from friendly aircraft. Eventually, identification friend or foe (IFF) technology would take care of this problem. There needed to be better visual identification of aircraft – if visibility issues caused by bad weather conditions made this difficult, then pilots needed to be adequately trained to be able to make positive identifications before opening fire. Critically, though, there needed to be better communication between airfields and stations about the deployment of aircraft. If the Essex radar station had known about the Hurricanes, the Spitfires likely would not have been scrambled to intercept. Though tragic, the Battle of Barking Creek taught RAF Fighter Command a valuable lesson. It showed what needed to be fixed to ensure that an efficient air defence system was in place in case of enemy operation. Thanks to this incident, the problems had been solved by the start of the Battle of Britain.

THE DEVELOPMENT OF RADAR TECHNOLOGY

Prior to 1914, British military home defence focused predominantly on the coastline, with any expected attack coming from the sea. During the First World War, however, Britain came under attack from the air and was ill-prepared to deal with assaults from German airships and aircraft. The damage caused by Zeppelins and Gotha bomber planes brought the front line home and placed the British people in direct danger – a taste of what was to come in the Second World War. The country had no choice but to adapt and began the first blackouts, mobilising military aviators in an attempt to assist anti-aircraft guns against the airborne enemy. By June 1917, mighty German bomber aircraft were carrying out raids over Britain and it became clear that in order to counter these attacks, British air defence would have to alter and improve tactically. The timely scrambling of British fighter-defenders relied upon a system of observation and reporting of enemy positions, as well as the use of wireless communication, and in this new fight for survival, scientific innovation and engineering would begin to play an integral role. Following the Great War, it was clear that the aerial threat to Great Britain posed a major challenge which needed to be met with a suitable and effective method of defence. It took over ten years for an air defence exercise to be carried out, and when in 1934 it was, more than half of the bombers involved were able to get past the defences, even with their routes known. Such an outcome was a great worry to the Air Ministry, which turned to science for an answer.

The same year, the Committee for the Scientific Survey of Air Defence was established, chaired by Henry Tizard. The committee was a scientific mission tasked with studying the needs of anti-aircraft warfare in Britain. Initially, it was suggested that scientists develop a 'death ray', which would perhaps be able to disable enemy aircraft, eliminating them as a threat. Physicist Robert Watson-Watt, supervisor of a national radio research laboratory, was contacted and asked to contribute his views on the matter. Watson-Watt dismissed the idea of a death ray, suggesting instead that the focus be the early detection of enemy aircraft. In the 1930s, it was possible to detect aircraft with sound locators, but these only offered a few minutes' warning, which was inadequate time in which to scramble fighters to intercept. Watson-Watt, however, proposed that aircraft could be detected using radio beams. His assistant, Arnold Wilkins, drew up the calculations and the idea was presented. Watson-Watt and Wilkins made a convincing case, which was met enthusiastically by the Air Ministry, and on 26 February 1935, they successfully demonstrated the system using a BBC transmitter, picking up a bomber that was being used as a test target. Funds were then secured from the Treasury to continue the development of this new technology. In May 1935, Watson-Watt, Wilkins and a small team of scientists conducted a series of experiments over the sea at Orford Ness, and by February 1936, they had moved to Bawdsey Manor Estate, converting most of its buildings to workshops. On 24 September 1937, RAF Bawdsey became the first fully operational radar station in the world. A system of around twenty similar stations to be spaced out around the coast of Britain was planned and was dubbed the 'Chain Home' system. In 1937, Bawdsey, with its 240-foot wooden receiver towers and 360-foot steel transmitter towers, was performing well in air exercises. By the outbreak of war in 1939, the Chain Home system had been set up and was in operation around the coast of Britain.

RAF Bawdsey was unique in that it had three different types of radar equipment together on one site – Coastal Defence (CD), Chain Home (CH) and Chain Home Low (CHL). With its location on the east coast making it vulnerable to enemy attack, the scientific development team was relocated from Bawdsey to Dundee in September 1939, and Bawdsey became an operational radar station.

Map showing radar coverage around the British coast
from September 1939 to September 1940

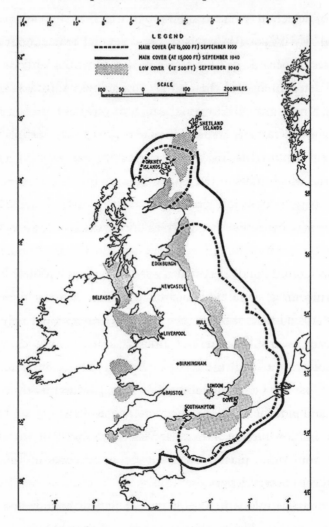

Multiple radar systems were developed during the Second World
War. Chain Home (designated Type 1 by the RAF) was able to
detect aircraft flying in at 15,000 feet to 20,000 feet and provided
what was essentially long-range surveillance over the sea approaches
to Britain, with stations spaced out at roughly thirty-mile intervals

around the coast. CH transmitted a broad beam of radio pulses, from towers at stations located on cliffs or high ground to increase the range of detection (which was up to 200 miles). CH units were designated 'AMES', or Air Ministry Experimental Station, for secrecy purposes. It became quickly apparent that incoming aircraft could escape detection by CH radar if they flew at lower altitudes. For this reason, a new, ground-based radar system was developed to detect low-flying aircraft and ships. Designated Type 2, Chain Home Low radar was deployed at AMES bases around the coast, using a rotating aerial which transmitted a narrow beam. It could detect aircraft flying at 152 metres (500 feet) at ranges up to 110 miles. CHL stations were either set on cliff tops or in low-lying coastal areas, where the aerial was mounted onto a high tower, usually 200-feet tall. One drawback of CH and CHL radar was that both systems could only detect incoming aircraft approaching from the sea. Once the enemy planes crossed the coastline, they would no longer show up on the radar screens, as CH faced out to the sea and CHL was affected by returns from the land surface. This placed great importance on the Royal Observer Corps members, who watched the skies to visually locate and plot the positions of aircraft as they flew over land.

Information provided by radar was not always completely accurate, sometimes placing British fighters in jeopardy. The radar system was, however, very useful in that it eliminated the need for constant air patrols, which helped to economise aircrews and allow them to rest, thus likely increasing their effectiveness.

Radar developed into a vital instrument of modern warfare, which would alter the balance of air power. The various versions of this new technology were able to provide different pieces of information on enemy aircraft. By transmitting a radio signal, which would hit the plane and be reflected back to the receiver like an echo, it could provide the aircraft's range, bearing and altitude. Range was determined by calculating the time taken for the signal to travel from the transmitter to the aircraft and back to the receiver – the signal was displayed on a calibrated cathode-ray tube. The returning signal was received by two aerials set at right angles to each other, and by comparing the way in which the signal was received by each, direction could be determined.

CH receivers used a calibrated dial, which was turned until the 'blip' in the trace on the screen disappeared – the bearing could then be read off the scale. The aircraft's altitude was determined by connecting the dial to two aerials set at different heights and feeding the reading into an electrical calculator, together with the range and bearing data. The aircraft's position and height then appeared on a display panel, with a grid reference.

Direction finding equipment was invaluable in a signals intelligence process known as 'traffic analysis', which provided a good deal of intelligence even when the enciphered messages could not be read. Each radio network was carefully analysed to identify the units involved and how they interacted on air. The three- or four-letter or figure call signs used to identify each of the stations, which were changed on a daily basis, were tracked and identified, with direction finding providing their locations, and techniques like radio fingerprinting, which identified the transmitters in use by each station, helping to keep track of what the enemy was doing, while operator chatter frequently gave away what each unit was doing on the ground at any one time and what it would do next.

The pace of development on this technology was extraordinary and demonstrated the importance of the integration of science, engineering and military tactics and intelligence. Engineers and intelligence analysts were working together to be able to provide a clear, real-time picture of the aerial warfare situation, using a science-based defence system.

Now that the technology existed that could yield vital intelligence on the air battle situation, a system had to be developed in order for such intelligence to be operationally useful. The task of building and perfecting the world's first operational air defence system fell to Air Chief Marshal Hugh Dowding – a man who well understood the stakes and could see the solution in the system which would take his name.

Where German intelligence had informed the Luftwaffe of the existence of radar technology in Britain, the Dowding System into which it was integrated was a very well-kept secret. Radar and the Royal Observer Corps provided initial raw information, which was then fed into the Dowding System, where it was analysed, assessed and disseminated to reach the fighter squadrons who could put it to operational use in good enough time for them to do so. The development of this technology and the training of RAF and WAAF personnel to use it made it extremely difficult for the Luftwaffe to approach Britain by air undetected.

THE DOWDING SYSTEM

In their Blitzkrieg conquering of Europe, the Germans had demonstrated an impressive ability to prepare for and execute large overseas operations with great speed and efficiency. Fortunately for the Allies, Britain had its own impressive ability, in the form of the collection and utilisation of intelligence. Messages sent in the German Enigma cypher were intercepted by British listening stations and passed to Bletchley Park, where they were deciphered and decoded to reveal their contents. Such intelligence had yielded an early warning of the impending intended invasion and of the subsequent approach of the Battle of Britain. The codebreakers at Bletchley Park could provide information on the Luftwaffe's organisation, order of battle and equipment, which was all of obvious strategic value to the RAF, especially considering its inferior size when compared to the Luftwaffe. As valuable as Enigma's contribution was in some ways, in others it was of little use, as it could not foretell how the RAF would stand up to its German counterpart in the everyday battle arena. Highlighting the difference between special and service intelligence, and demonstrating the importance of having access to both, Enigma offered intelligence that was of no use in forecasting shifts and changes which might occur during a battle and no information on the possible strategic decisions that the German High Command might make as a result.

As Commander-in-Chief of Fighter Command, Air Chief Marshal Hugh Dowding would have to base his strategic defence of Britain and its skies on information other than that which Enigma and its associated signals interception could provide. Fighter Command was an operational unit and in order to operate effectively, it needed up-to-date, accurate information – that is, intelligence. Intelligence on an enemy's intentions and capabilities can be the difference between victory and defeat in war. There are many and conflicting ideas and interpretations of what intelligence is specifically, but as far as the RAF was concerned, information was needed on the intentions and capabilities of the Luftwaffe and on the everyday real-time situation during air battles. Where Enigma's intelligence was quickly rendered out of date, the intelligence collected and disseminated by the Dowding System was groundbreaking, in that it provided a real-time picture of the battle as it was happening. This system was utilised by Fighter Command to collect and disseminate information that would provide a steady stream of consistently up-to-date intelligence, resulting in a clear image and understanding of the airspace over and around Britain. This was immensely valuable, as it would enable the timely scrambling of the RAF fighters and anti-aircraft artillery to intercept enemy aircraft before they even reached British shores.

In modern terms, the Dowding System was a command, control and communications system, used by commanders to follow and direct a battle from minute to minute.[7] The Luftwaffe had the ability to attack Britain from the direction of Norway all the way around to north-eastern France and could do so at any moment. Dowding needed an accurate idea of where Luftwaffe aircraft were and which direction they were coming from, as well as an idea of where his own aircraft were. He also needed a way of passing instructions and orders to his fighter squadrons, often at short notice – as soon as a radar contact was picked up at a coastal radar station, he needed to scramble fighters to intercept it as quickly as possible, in order to minimise damage and hopefully prevent the enemy from making it past the British shoreline. He needed a clear, unambiguous real-time picture of his battle space, and the gathering of information to meet this need was critical to British victory. Though the Dowding System and Fighter Control were technically operational units, they contained and were reliant upon intelligence-gathering elements. The system itself was what was important. No single part of it was of much use without all the other elements. The radar technology, the analytical processes, the procedures for dissemination and the communications network all needed to work efficiently together for the system, and ultimately the RAF, to be successful. This was a vast system, filled with highly skilled personnel from both the RAF and the WAAF, who worked long, busy shifts to keep the vital early warning system functioning twenty-four hours a day, seven days a week.

Radar stations around the British coastline detected incoming Luftwaffe aircraft as they crossed the sea on their journeys to Britain. The radar units themselves were set up around the coast at about thirty-mile intervals, to concentrate on the sea approaches of enemy aircraft. Inside these units, sometimes just caravans on cliff tops, were radar operators. These stations, along with the Royal Observer Corps, collected information on approaching aircraft, both friendly and hostile. The information was raw data, technical in nature and of no use to fighter pilots at this point in the process. It needed to be analysed and compared to other data in order to make any sense.

The information was sent from the coastal radar station to a Fighter Command 'filter centre'. Once received there, the data was carefully 'filtered' – a complex analytical procedure – and anomalies were removed to produce a 'track', a set of information which was then uniquely referenced, identified and categorised. The track contained various pieces of information, depending on which type of radar had produced it. The information could include a bearing, direction of travel, altitude and number of aircraft in the raid, for example. The filter centre was a vital cog in the Dowding System machine, as its personnel made sense of the information from the radar chain and promptly disseminated it to Fighter Command operations rooms, at various levels – to headquarters at Bentley Priory, Stanmore, and to group- and sector-level operations rooms. The disseminating was carried out using a web of telephone communications operated by the General Post Office.

Operations room personnel would record the data from the track on a huge map of a particular area – this process was called 'plotting'. At Fighter Command HQ level, the map would depict the entirety of Britain. The intelligence was also plotted on much more detailed maps, in group and sector operations rooms. The country was divided into four 'groups', each responsible for the air defence of a specific area – 10 Group covered the south-west of England and Wales, 11 Group was responsible for London and the south-east, 12 Group for the Midlands and 13 Group for northern England and Scotland. Due to its location, 11 Group bore the brunt of enemy raids during the Battle of Britain and had the toughest job on its hands. Each group operations room displayed a large table-map of the area it covered and would update information on the air situation as it came in using wooden blocks and arrows. Every group was further divided into sectors, each of which had an operations room with a map of the smaller, specific area it covered. Orders to scramble fighter squadrons were given at group command but were communicated to pilots at sector level.

The Dowding System kept real-time information flowing constantly throughout the levels of RAF command – information which would lead to the scrambling of fighter aircraft to intercept the enemy raiders, as well as the implementation of other kinds of defence for Britain and its people, including air raid warnings being issued and anti-aircraft sites being notified. An effective early warning system, radar played a pivotal role during the Battle of Britain by allowing Dowding to use his numerically inferior forces with the tactical advantage of knowing where enemy aircraft were before they had even reached their targets. In each level of the Dowding System air defence network, members of the WAAF worked tirelessly towards this end.

The flow of intelligence in the Dowding System

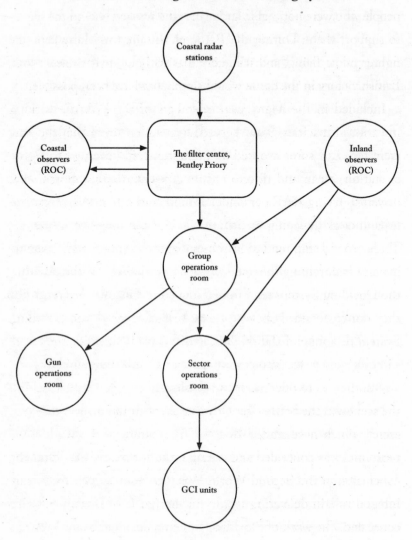

THE WAAF AND THE GREAT AIR BATTLE

Where the RAF pilots who flew their Spitfires and Hurricanes into battle are remembered as 'the Few', the men and women of Fighter Command who served on the ground are known as 'the Many'.

As with most major operations and organisations, there were a few people who were noticeable and many who worked behind the scenes to support them. During the Battle of Britain, the Many kept the fighter pilots flying, and it's likely that without their tireless work, British victory in the battle would simply not have been possible.

Included in the Many were members of the WAAF, working in various capacities. Some served as cooks, ensuring that the Few were fed, and some worked as domestic staff, keeping the fighter stations clean and tidy to ensure efficient running. Some were drivers, ferrying RAF personnel around, and others were secretaries and clerks, keeping records up to date and paperwork flowing. These ground staff tend to be remembered as support staff, sustaining and maintaining the operational units. WAAFs working within the Dowding System tend to be grouped in this category too – but they don't necessarily belong there. In fact, none of the Dowding System personnel do. Though they may have looked like they were carrying out clerical and communications work like secretaries and clerks, they were operational staff, directly engaged, albeit behind the scenes, in the battle. The Dowding System was a very well-kept secret, which necessitated that the true nature of the work of its personnel was concealed and remained so for many years after the conclusion of the Second World War. The result is that their truly integral role in delivering victory in the Battle of Britain was also concealed. The work of Dowding System personnel, many WAAFs among them, frequently culminated in the dissemination of information that was of vital importance to Fighter Command and to the British war effort and the outcome of the Battle of Britain, in that it led to the strategic movements of fighter aircraft and anti-aircraft defences in the heat of the battle. From the operations room at Bentley Priory, Dowding monitored the intelligence that

WAAFs were contributing from their radar stations around the coast, which was so critical to his decision-making for the infamous battle. Whether the work of the WAAFs in Fighter Command is classed as operational, intelligence or both, it certainly doesn't belong in the support category where it has historically been placed, confining the women involved to the outer margins of historical memory in the Battle of Britain and, to some extent, the Second World War. These WAAFs were privy to highly secret and sensitive information and could tell no one about their work. They took their vow of secrecy very seriously and many refused to talk about their work even after the war, which is a contributing factor in why their role in the Battle of Britain has been so misunderstood and has kept them missing from its history and our memory of it. Other factors which have kept them hidden are the fact that the system was quite complicated and used language that is unfamiliar to the uninitiated. Sometimes deliberately misleading language was used, stemming from the need for secrecy to be maintained. Radar devices were given strange names or acronyms and the WAAFs who operated them were listed as 'Clerk, Special Duties', which implied that they were doing office work with no direct link to the battle. As a result, the work of the WAAFs in the Dowding System has been misunderstood, and somewhat demeaned, but it was in fact a critically important operational component of Fighter Command's efforts during the Battle of Britain.

4

EARLY WARNING WAAFS: WOMEN IN THE DOWDING SYSTEM

WAAFS IN THE DOWDING SYSTEM

The well-known image of the Second World War operations room usually includes women in smart military uniforms pushing counters or wooden blocks around on a table with what looks like a casino croupier stick. The true definition of what these women, most of them members of the Women's Auxiliary Air Force, were actually doing and how important it was is much less well known. Mislabelled as 'support workers', which carries the implication that they might have been monitoring stationery supplies or making endless cups of tea, WAAFs employed in RAF Headquarters, group and sector operations rooms were engaged in vital, fast-paced work generating and disseminating intelligence that was of crucial importance to Fighter Command's limited number of pilots. And passing information to the operations rooms were the personnel on radar stations.

Air Chief Marshal Dowding knew that in order to effectively defend Britain against the impending Luftwaffe onslaught, he would need to know where the enemy planes and his own forces were at any given time. In view of the fact that the Luftwaffe was a larger force than the RAF, Dowding, and Britain for that matter, could not afford for the German aircraft to also have the element of surprise attack on their side. It was the Dowding System that would remove this dangerous element, and within it, the technology that provided the intelligence – RDF, or radar. The technology and the intelligence it yielded were useless if the information could not get to someone who could act on it with enough time to be able to do so. The human element of the system was what rendered radar intelligence at all useable. Human and machine worked together in synergy, collecting data, analysing it, processing it and disseminating it to the point that RAF commanders could use it to make decisions and give orders that would result in military action. The Dowding System was the most impressive and effective air defence system in the world, but without the people that filled the various roles within it, it would not have been able to accomplish anything useful at all. Members of the WAAF were at the very heart of the system, and many were spread out across it, working in each piece of the giant puzzle to provide as full a picture of the air battle situation as possible. It was vital that the Germans did not know that the system existed, and so it operated under conditions of extreme secrecy. WAAFs worked under considerable pressure in this highly secret world and the integration of the women's air auxiliary into the Dowding System was, arguably, one of the reasons it was so successful.

RADAR OPERATORS

The development of radar necessitated the introduction of a new trade within the RAF, as it was impossible to combine it with telecommunications due to the increasing complexity already existent within that trade category.[1] Realising the great importance of radar intelligence, the Air Ministry prioritised the training of a percentage of highly skilled operators to work on radar stations, and the increasing shortage of available men for this work caused the RAF to look to the WAAF. Robert Watson-Watt, the 'father of radar', believed that the 'anti-hamfistedness' of women made them ideal candidates for the work of radar operators. He was not alone in thinking this – women were thought to be suited to jobs where having 'nimble fingers' would be of benefit, and domestic skills such as making lace were thought to have given them the ability to do fiddly or intricate tasks. As the technology of radar and the system within which it functioned were evolving and developing, so too was the WAAF, as its members ventured into roles previously occupied by RAF personnel only. In peacetime, secret work was usually reserved for men, as it was believed that women would have a hard time keeping secrets and could not be trusted to do so. The shortage of available male personnel and tense conditions created by the imminent German invasion, however, necessitated a 'trial with female personnel' in radar work.[2] The Air Ministry was adamant in February 1940 that it could not spare airmen 'without seriously impairing operational efficiency' on RAF stations and that it was 'very necessary' to train WAAF personnel as RDF operators – though 'great care must be taken' to ensure that they were 'correctly selected to be employed in important secret work'.[3]

There were several reasons why women were unlikely or undesirable recruits for radar operation. For one thing, in the historical context leading up to the Second World War, it wasn't common for girls to be educated to a very high level in maths or the sciences, let alone in engineering or the technical trades. To be a radar operator required skills which women didn't commonly possess in 1940. Jean Mackenzie took a six-week 'experimental' course in radar, during which she wrote a diary. She confessed privately that while wiring up circuits in the lab, she and a friend agreed, 'neither of us has a clue'. When learning the intricacies of the Avometer and trying to work out decimals and fractions, she wished she hadn't been so hopeless at maths.[4] In many cases, by training to be radar operators, WAAFs were not simply learning how to operate equipment that they had never seen before – often they had to gain a more thorough understanding of basic maths and science in a very short space of time. Jean and her friend passed their course, finding their male superior officer to be as shaken as they were at the news because it wasn't generally expected that women could show aptitude in such subjects.

In addition to finding it difficult to believe that women could be capable of being radar operators, there was also resistance to them being present on radar stations at all due to the inherent danger of the job. Radar facilities were noticeable from above due to their tall towers and equipment arrays, which made them an obvious target for German bombers. Placing WAAFs on radar stations meant knowingly putting them in direct danger. It was certainly true that WAAF personnel were more obviously exposed to danger by working at RAF stations and facilities, which were important strategic targets for the Luftwaffe, than their colleagues in the WRNS and the ATS were. In some ways considering exposure to danger and combat to be one and the same, in accordance with not allowing women to serve as combatants on the front lines, the British authorities and the RAF were at first reluctant to put them in the path of Luftwaffe assaults by placing them on stations that were obvious targets. This argument, however, did not seem to hold much sway.

Women were in danger throughout Britain due to indiscriminate German area bombing, and the bombing of British cities undermined the geographical fighting front. It was a little more complicated than that, though. As members of a military auxiliary, WAAFs would be expected to remain at their posts during air raids, when civilian women were expected and encouraged to take cover and find safety. The front may have moved, but just because women were exposed to danger and death in their everyday lives, they were not automatically redefined as combatants. If the RAF employed women on radar stations, thus asking them to remain at their posts during air raids, it was, in addition to placing them in great danger, essentially intentionally placing them in the thick of the fighting which could be construed as making them combative. The combination of the lack of prior precedent for such an action and the ambiguous status of servicewomen with regard to combat caused reluctance in the Air Ministry and the RAF to placing WAAFs on fighter and radar stations. The pressing lack of male personnel to fill certain roles on these stations meant that eventually the British authorities had no choice but to swallow their misgivings regarding the combative status of airwomen, and the ambiguous stance of the Air Ministry towards this status served as justification for the employment of WAAFs on RAF stations just as it had as an argument against it. Other less obvious dangers came in the form of the sites themselves. Operators would sometimes work out of flimsy huts or caravans in fields and on cliff edges, as stations had to be close to the coast for the equipment to work. Sometimes the radar aerials moved around in high winds and there was always the risk of them crashing through the roof or of women being blown over cliff edges while trying to alter the positioning of the equipment. Again, though, the argument that WAAFs shouldn't work under such hazardous conditions did not hold, as women working in agriculture or munitions factories were at just as much risk of accident and injury, if not more. All of these women displayed great courage and ability, defying expectations and proving that they were capable of much more than even they themselves thought.

WAAF radar operator Joyce Millard is of the opinion that she and her WAAF colleagues were of a generation of women who served in the forces and proved that they 'could do many men's jobs', which they had 'not been given the chance to undertake before, just as efficiently'.[5] Indeed, the operators coped extremely well with the challenges of their roles. Barbara Davies was a Chain Home radar operator during the Battle of Britain through to the end of the Blitz. When a new RAF officer arrived at her station one day and asked to see the Commanding Officer or Flight Sergeant in charge, he was informed that Corporal Davies was in charge. When he discovered that Corporal Davies was in fact a WAAF member, he said, 'Never worked with bloody women, never want to.' After two weeks of working with her, he had totally changed his mind.[6] There are numerous accounts of WAAFs behaving calmly and coolly under pressure while fulfilling the duties of radar operators during the Battle of Britain. Mary Brewster passed her exams to become a radar operator and was posted to a very small and 'hush, hush' station on the point of a cliff which protruded into the English Channel. Almost a constant target, the station was machine-gunned by the Luftwaffe and the RAF posted a permanent machine gunner on the cliff above it to provide some protection. Despite this unnerving situation, Mary found the station 'very exciting' to be on, and when she left it, she and her colleagues had filled two walls with swastikas that represented enemy aircraft that had been shot down by the RAF as a result of the intelligence produced by the radar station.[7]

Peggy Haynes, a radar operator also posted on a station atop steep cliffs, found the location of her station 'a bit tricky in winter' but like Mary did not allow it to interfere with her operational capability.[8]

Inside their stations, WAAF radar operators would sit in a darkened room continuously scanning a cathode-ray tube, which would show approaching enemy aircraft. Once they had identified an aircraft, they would establish whether it was an enemy or a 'friendly' plane and collect as much data as possible from the blip on the screen.

At this point the technology produced 'raw' data, which was scientific in nature and didn't make sense to anyone not specially trained in the operation of radar equipment. The WAAF radar operator would sit at the receiving screen, wearing a headset and speaking into a mouthpiece through which she could directly communicate with plotters in a Fighter Command filter room.

Most radar stations used a watch system, meaning that twenty-four hours a day, seven days a week, WAAFs were watching the radar screens and enemy aircraft positions were being identified, plotted and reported to Fighter Command. Often radar was so effective that WAAF operators could detect enemy aircraft taking off in the Netherlands and would plot them all the way across the sea until they reached the British coast.[9] This gave the RAF the early warning that it needed to deploy fighters to intercept, and during the Battle of Britain German pilots often found that an RAF reception was waiting for them when they arrived in British airspace. The Luftwaffe pilots reported their surprise at the way the air was full of calm British voices, directing aircraft and not at all shocked or panicked at their arrival.

WAAFs were not able to fly as the Few did during the Battle, but they remained at the heart of the Dowding System – the very point of it, in fact – helping the RAF to intercept the enemy in the air without having to fly numerous costly patrols and lose men and aircraft in surprise attacks. One of the greatest contributions of radar during the Battle of Britain was the way in which it economised precious commodities. Planes and pilots were not as plentiful as the RAF would have liked, and up against the might of the Luftwaffe, every single one was important and valuable. Planes took time to build, and pilots took time to train, so if they could be conserved, this was a major advantage. WAAF radar operators seized the opportunity to prove their capabilities and performed with 'conspicuous success'.[10] Demonstrating their 'competency for the work', WAAF radar operators played a significant part in the success of Fighter Command in the Battle of Britain.[11] Such valuable work kept the Few flying and saved many lives.

Later, in 1941, radar was used not only to protect Britain and its aircraft but to locate aircrew who had had to bail out of damaged planes over the English Channel and the North Sea. By sending an SOS signal using their identification friend or foe (IFF) indicators to give a broader 'blip' right before baling out, crews could send radar stations their position in the sea so that the Air Sea Rescue Service could be mobilised to help them. Initially wary of using the IFF switch, afraid that it would alert the Luftwaffe to their location, some pilots visited radar facilities and the WAAFs explained to them how the technology could save their lives.

Some WAAF radar operators, including Joyce Millard, were tasked specifically with looking for SOS signals, which they would report in the same way as an enemy aircraft so that it was plotted, resulting in the scrambling of Air Sea Rescue craft rather than fighter squadrons. When a pilot experienced aircraft trouble, he might only have seconds to send an SOS signal. Often if a WAAF radar operator was alone on duty, she would not even be able to go to the bathroom, as leaving the radar screen unmanned could mean the difference between life and death for a pilot. Wing Commander Johnny Checketts's aircraft was shot down between Boulogne and Dungeness. He says, 'We had great confidence in the R/T operators in England and the fixing stations saved many lives, mine among them.'[12] Over the course of the war, some 13,000 men were plucked from the sea thanks to this work, many of whom were back on operations very soon afterwards.[13]

THE FILTER ROOM

In high-speed aerial warfare, the 'rapid transmission of reliable and essential information to all the operational centres concerned is a vitally necessary service'.[14] The raw data collected by radar operators needed to undergo processing and analysis. It was transmitted from the radar stations on the coast to the Fighter Command filter rooms. The purpose of these rooms was to produce an easily readable 'track', or a set of information on the incoming enemy aircraft, which was then sent to operations rooms where it was used to scramble fighter squadrons for interception and to order other forms of defence.

Incoming information was recorded by WAAF 'plotters' on a large grid-lined map on a table in the centre of the room, using coloured counters and wooden blocks. The information was then filtered to give only the basic and essential details of the aircraft in a given area. The work was analytical and demanded a high degree of concentration, and the process was designed to assess information, to remove anomalies and to combine overlapping or repeated information, therefore conserving resources. The resulting enemy or friendly track would usually include the most probable position, direction of travel, speed, height and strength of the contact, and tracks could be grouped into clusters.

Once the intelligence had been recorded, WAAF personnel would pass it on to the operations room, as well as to air raid warning officers, the Royal Observer Corps and in-land anti-aircraft artillery sites, if necessary. During the Battle of Britain and the Blitz, the central filter room at Bentley Priory was the 'linchpin' of the Dowding System, providing a real-time picture of what was happening in the British airspace to allow commanders time to effectively defend the country.

To the 'uninitiated', the filter centre looked 'anarchic', and the plotters needed 'very high levels of concentration and considerable skill, combined with the closest of teamwork'.[15] WAAF filterers dealt with a huge number of signals and needed to be able to think quickly and decisively for long periods of time and to act with confidence and courage, as lives, both those of the British pilots and those of the public, rested upon it.

In September 1939, it was tentatively proposed within the Air Ministry to trial using women in the filter rooms. If the experiment proved 'entirely successful', it was intended that three out of the four watches in a 24-hour period could be manned by WAAFs.[16] Due to the fast-paced nature of aerial combat, filter room plotters needed to be able to work at great speed. Though there were initially concerns that women might not be able to function adequately under such intense pressure, it was noted that WAAF plotters were generally 'very dexterous, quick and had very good situational awareness'.[17] In December 1939, the Air Ministry stated that WAAF personnel were 'eminently suitable' for employment as plotters and that the women recruited would be trained at Leighton Buzzard before being posted to operations and filter rooms. In each of these rooms there was to be a WAAF officer in charge of the WAAFs on each watch, in the position of assistant floor supervisor. In late 1939, it was realised that the women going to Fighter Command Headquarters in Stanmore had been 'specially selected as suitable for promotion to commissioned and NCO rank'.[18] There were, however, still misgivings in early 1940 on the commissioning of women, evident in the use of expressions within the Air Ministry such as 'swallowing' or 'gilding the pill', so undesirable was the idea.

Patricia Clark was a filter officer serving in 10 Group area during the Battle of Britain and the Blitz. She was commissioned, knowing full well that at this stage of the war her commission was still 'experimental'. She states that the RAF 'weren't at all sure whether women would be able to cope' around the plotting table and 'thought we would faint from fatigue'.[19] Plotter Claire Lorrimer was aware of the fact that there were 'still a great many who felt the weaker sex was incapable of replacing men in non-domestic tasks' and recognised that the only reason she'd been allowed to plot was because of the desperate shortage of manpower.[20] Also conscious that her male colleagues were 'dubious' of women being allowed to work in Special Duties was Edith Mary Kup, though she states that she was treated with respect by them.[21] Mary James, a plotter at Bentley Priory, knew that at first the authorities had been reluctant to use WAAFs as plotters, claiming that 'they did not have enough mental dexterity'. It soon became clear, however, that quite the opposite was true, and that the WAAFs were 'far more dextrous and speedy than the men', often receiving information on new raids while they were still plotting previously reported ones. Plotting was 'gruelling, demanding, technically challenging' and carried 'great responsibility for accuracy', and the WAAFs were more than aware that lives depended on their work. Even during bombing raids on their stations, WAAF plotters continued to work with 'quiet coolness'.[22] Dame Felicity Peake, who would in 1946 become the first director of the new Women's Royal Air Force, was sent to No. 60 Group Fighter Command as senior WAAF staff officer at Leighton Buzzard. In her time there, she observed that the WAAFs excelled in the skilled, intricate task of plotting and that they made very responsible officers. She felt that 'there were practically no limits to the capabilities and achievements of women in the Service' and praised the WAAFs for 'what a fine and responsible job' they could do when they filled roles 'hitherto thought capable only of being performed by RAF officers and men'.[23]

A NATIONAL SECRET

When WAAFs were recruited to work as radar operators or plotters, they were only initially told that they would be 'Clerk, Special Duties'. They would then be required to sign the Official Secrets Act before being told anything else about what they would be doing, ensuring that they could not legally share any information about it with anyone who was not authorised to know about it. Joyce Deane (née Morley) left school at aged eighteen and promptly joined the WAAF and signed the Act in 1940. Sent for Special Duties training at Leighton Buzzard, she learned to plot in a secret building covered with camouflage netting and life-size cardboard figures of lambs pointing skyward. She later discovered that the building, which she was not allowed to leave because the rest of the facility was so secret, was part of 60 Group HQ for radar. She found the secrecy both exciting and frightening and continued to work in very secret conditions throughout the Battle of Britain.[24] Claire Lorrimer was disappointed when she found out what Special Duties work entailed, as being able to speak French and German, she'd hoped that the secrecy surrounding her new role might result in her being dropped behind enemy lines. It was not long, however, before her interest was aroused by the work.[25] On the whole, secrecy within the Dowding System and Fighter Command was so rigorously and effectively maintained that some WAAFs did not know until after the Battle of Britain how the information they were plotting had been obtained. Joyce Deane dealt with the plots as they came in 'thick and fast', completely unaware of the existence of the radar chain until much later.[26] The intense secrecy surrounding Special Duties work was neither a deterrent to the WAAFs engaged in it, nor a reason they were unable to do it. On the contrary, they performed exceptionally well in these conditions. Despite any misgivings the RAF and British authorities might have had regarding WAAF plotters, they proved themselves to be indispensable and very capable of filter room plotting.

The women often found themselves working in difficult conditions, aside from the speed at which they were required to work. Claire Lorrimer remembers working in a converted cowshed before the 10 Group Fighter Command filter room had been built at Rudloe Manor. It was cramped and the electric light frequently failed so the WAAFs had to plot by candlelight, sometimes in freezing temperatures. Being transported to their secret location from their billets in a tarpaulin-covered truck, Claire and her colleagues were so bitterly cold in winter that they were given the unprecedented permission to wear trousers instead of skirts.[27] In conditions such as these, and often with bombs falling around them, the WAAFs' general attitude was to 'put your tin hat on and get on with it'. Gladys Eva and her colleagues at Bentley Priory knew how important their work was, even if they couldn't share it with their family and friends. Gladys recalls how on days when the weather was good the radar stations could pick up the Germans as they were taking off, so that she could plot their position all the way to Britain, where they would arrive to find that 'the guns were in and the spits were up'. The conditions under which she worked did not inhibit her ability to do her job effectively – like Mary Knight in the Blitz, she and her colleagues took the attitude that they 'just had to get on with it'.[28] Privy to information about the Battle of Britain that the general public did not have access to, WAAFs were under no illusions as to how important their work was. The atmosphere in the filter room could be extremely tense and Edith Kup remembers the summer of 1940 as a desperate, anxious time. She says, 'We were working very hard because our pilots were too.'[29] Many WAAFs personally encountered the 'Few' in their day-to-day work, often considering them as friends as well as colleagues. The women worked hard behind these courageous men, aware that not only were the pilots' lives often dependent in part upon their work, but in the particular instance of the Battle of Britain, so too was the fate of the country.

RISING TO THE CHALLENGE

Posted to the 10 Group Fighter Command filter room at Rudloe Manor, Eileen Younghusband worked in cramped and uncomfortable conditions, plotting with the knowledge that speed and accuracy were of paramount importance. While at Rudloe Manor, she was tasked with designing a map table with a distorted grid, as it would appear on a globe. Such a process required some special calculations and her ultimate success gained her a recommendation for a commission. Eileen worked with WAAFs who were pre-dominantly younger than twenty-one, which she believes to be strategically useful. In her opinion, having not yet reached the 'age of caution' made the women more capable of providing virtually instant information through instinctive action, which was necessary due to the fact that aircraft were constantly moving.[30] Plots were never more than five minutes old and there was a colour-coded incremental clock on the wall to ensure that the picture being created was as accurate and up to date as possible. To ensure that they were capable of such work, WAAFs were given psychological tests prior to being employed on Special Duties, based on the same ones given to prospective fighter pilots. The work was hard, and being quick and accurate was tiring, but despite the fears that women might not cope with it, there are very few recorded or remembered instances where this was true. On the contrary, many WAAFs found it to be very exciting and enjoyed the work despite the tremendous pressure it entailed, rising to the challenge rather than crumbling under it as had been expected.

In addition to realising that the country itself was in danger, some WAAFs had more personal reasons to ensure that they were good at their work. Petrea Winterbotham remembers her brother being out on a bombing raid one night when she was on duty in the filter room. Communications within the filter room were used strictly for work and she had no choice but to continue her plotting and go to bed that night with no indication as to his fate. Rather than shaking her ability to work, the knowledge made her more intent on being 'utterly accurate' because lives, including that of someone she loved, were at stake.[31]

Jean Hilda Mills recalls the 'electric atmosphere' while plotting during the Battle of Britain and 'rooting for our boys to come back'.

The victory at the end of the battle was, as far as she and her colleagues were concerned, very much a 'combined effort', rather than attributable to one specific group of people.[32] Despite the difficult physical and tense emotional conditions under which they worked, the filter room WAAFs in the Dowding System defied the expectations of the RAF and the British authorities, working hard behind the Few to provide them with the vital intelligence that would enable them to famously protect Britain from German invasion in 1940.

OPERATIONS ROOMS

Once radar intelligence had been filtered and plotted by the WAAFs in the filter room, it was then sent on to Fighter Command HQ's operations rooms, as well as to various sector operations rooms. In these spaces, more WAAF plotters would plot the positions of British and German aircraft on a large map, on a table in the centre of the room. Standing around the table, they received the information directly through the radio headsets they wore and used long rods to move wooden counters and arrows depicting the information they were plotting around the map. Above the table was a balcony, or sometimes a raised platform, where senior RAF officers were positioned, so that they could see the map in its entirety and make telephone calls when they needed to order planes up and the deployment of defences. The operations room was a busy, seemingly hectic place, but there was a kind of chaotic order to the work, which only the initiated could understand. The work was fast-paced – sometimes a WAAF plotter had not even finished a plot when the next one started to come through – and could be stressful during busy periods where a lot of raids were taking place at once. Fighter

Command HQ was kept up to date at all times, so that Air Chief Marshal Dowding could see a real-time air picture of the Battle of Britain across the country. The sector operations room controllers, almost always RAF officers, used the information plotted on their sector maps to strategically scramble fighter squadrons to intercept the incoming enemy aircraft.

Filter room plotter Claire Lorrimer believes that where WAAF plotters are remembered or recorded in history, it tends to be almost exclusively those in the operations rooms.[33] She is correct, and this is perhaps inevitable, due to the fact that the staff of the operations rooms were in direct contact with fighter pilots. The 'Few' have long been the focus of the history of the Battle of Britain, and it follows that the operations rooms might be better remembered because of their contact with the pilots and the way in which their decisions directly affected the course of the battle. Claire is also correct in her argument that the operations rooms 'could not have functioned so efficiently' without the filter room passing them a constant stream of accurate intelligence. The reality of intelligence history is that often a vast system involving thousands of people can remain hidden behind a more glamorous or action-packed 'front' organisation, as is the case with the Dowding System. The operations room is, along with the Few, an enduringly popular scene from the Second World War. The reality is that without the filter room and the radar operators functioning in a vast system behind the operations rooms and the Few, there would have been no intelligence to be acted upon. Whether they worked on radar stations, in filter rooms or in operations rooms, WAAFs were extremely efficient and often worked so fast and with such a high degree of accuracy that their male colleagues were removed from the plotting tables because they could not keep up when the work became busy. Most

WAAFs chosen for plotting were found to possess a quality that their male colleagues had not thought it possible for women to have – 'unflappability'.[34]

The competence with which they worked in the Dowding System did not go unnoticed by their male colleagues. Speaking generally about the WAAF, RAF Group Captain Tom Sawyer insisted that WAAFs be included in the commendation of ground staff who aided air operations. These women, who Captain Sawyer recalls 'did so much to help the squadrons and stations throughout the war, working long hours where necessary', were, in his opinion, 'a great asset to the RAF'.[35] RAF wireless operator Fred Wright agreed with the Captain, wishing to 'debunk the popular and inaccurate idea that this vital arm of the RAF was an expediency'. The WAAFs, he argued, were 'every bit as competent and conscientious in the execution of the duties offered them, and were able to show that they were equally expert in a wider range of jobs', including all of the work they carried out within the Dowding System.[36] One of the Few, John C. French, admitted that had the WAAFs not done their jobs efficiently, hundreds of his colleagues in Fighter Command would not have survived the war.[37] Lieutenant Colonel Thomas Wheler thought the women of the WAAF were 'magnificent to say the least – a true example of the unbeatable English spirit'. From higher-ranking RAF officers like Douglas Grice, who recognised that 'their accuracy in monitoring Mayday calls must have helped to save countless pilots', to the pilots themselves, including Flight Lieutenant Douglas Matheson, the work of the WAAFs in radar was appreciated. Matheson was especially grateful for their help when he found himself flying through London fog, surrounded by barrage balloons – large, tethered balloons filled with hydrogen and often connected to explosives, designed to ensnare and destroy

Luftwaffe raiders. Communicating with a local radar station, he received crucial vectors which enabled him to carry out a safe landing. He later spoke of the vital role played by the WAAFs who had guided him to safety, citing their contribution to the British war effort as 'second to none'.[38] Air Vice Marshal 'Johnnie' Johnson personally commended Joyce Millard, a nineteen-year-old WAAF radar operator who had been 'right on the ball when things went wrong'. Speaking on behalf of the Few, he announced that he found it a 'great comfort' that the WAAFs were, with 'great devotion', toiling on the ground to get British fighter aircraft into the air and watching over them to bring them safely home, sometimes badly shot-up.[39] However reluctant they had been to accept in 1940 that women could or should be admitted into secret work in the Dowding System, the men of the RAF appear to have accepted by the end of the Battle of Britain that without the WAAFs the entire system of controlled interception would have been impossible. Without the Dowding System and the WAAFs working within it, a British victory in the battle would likely also have been impossible.

The officers and airmen of the RAF were not alone in recognising the success of the WAAFs in radar work and the air defence system. On 8 August 1945, a communiqué was released by the Air Ministry, revealing the existence of radar and the role played by women in the Dowding System. It stated that since 1939, under the 'closest secrecy', over 4,000 WAAFs had played 'an important part in the air victories achieved by radiolocation [radar]'. During the Battle of Britain, they had been trained to use 'some of the most delicate and complicated instruments ever invented' and had 'carried out their duties with enthusiasm, often under uncomfortable conditions and sometimes under enemy fire'.[40] WAAFs had proven themselves to be 'completely interchangeable' with RAF personnel in radar work, and the experience of the Battle of Britain had shown that in some roles WAAFs were 'much more fully employable than was at first anticipated'. Indeed, in the case of WAAF signals officers, it was reported that they had 'done very well', and though they had been 'originally in the nature of an experiment', they had 'proved so successful' that they were called for in greater numbers and in more senior posts. Also an apparent surprise to the Air Ministry was the success of the WAAFs as wireless operators, transmitting intelligence to the relevant places. In this trade, the Air Ministry stated that airwomen had 'proved most satisfactory'.[41] Regarding their work in Fighter Command, the director of the WAAF received 'many messages telling her of the admirable behaviour of airwomen on active service'. In a message to these WAAFs, the director congratulated them in 'being able to show that they can follow, so well, the traditions of courage and devotion to duty of the Royal Air Force'.[42] An outstanding example can be found in Corporal Avis Joan Hearn, one of the only WAAFs to receive the Military Medal. In August 1940, she was working on the telephones in her unit, disseminating intelligence, when bombs began to fall around her. All of the windows were blown in and the walls began to fall. Despite the noise and the obvious danger, Corporal Hearn remained at her post reporting the course of the enemy bombers, aware of how much the RAF fighters and anti-aircraft artillery gunners were depending on her work being carried out fully and properly. She continued to telephone the result of plots calmly and with accuracy.[43] The unexpected coolness and courage of the WAAFs working on operational stations in the Battle of Britain undoubtedly saved many lives – those of fighter pilots and bomber crews but also of civilians who were saved by the timely air raid warnings made possible by the Dowding System.

Writing on the Dowding System in 1949, Churchill stated his belief that 'all the ascendancy of the Hurricanes and Spitfires would have been fruitless but for this system of control'. This 'most elaborate instrument of war' denied the enemy the element of surprise and enabled the RAF to defeat a superior fighting force.[44] The result was the indefinite postponement of Operation Sealion. On 31 October 1940, Churchill and his Defence Committee agreed that the threat of German invasion was now remote and that the RAF had achieved a critical victory in winning the Battle of Britain. If Britain had been occupied, it could not have been used as a base for the Allied air offensive against Germany, or the D-Day landings that led to the liberation of Europe later in the war. The Battle of Britain was not simply a territorial success local to southern England – it was one of the most significant military engagements of the Second World War. Victory in this decisive air battle was the combined result of the work of the fighting Few and the men and women in the back rooms of the Dowding System. The remarkable bravery and achievements of Fighter Command's pilots must never be forgotten. Neither, though, should the work of the Dowding System personnel, thousands of WAAFs among them. Their work has remained largely hidden behind that of the Few, cloaked in secrecy and missing from history. The revelation of their work was doubly groundbreaking. The triumph of the new technology referenced by Churchill in 1940 was, without doubt, in part to thank for victory in the Battle of Britain. The fact that women were operating it was equally as new, and these WAAFs played an integral part in securing victory. Speaking to the House of Commons at the start of the Battle of Britain, Churchill said, 'Let us therefore brace ourselves to our duties, and so bear ourselves that, if the British Empire and its Commonwealth last for a thousand years, men will still say,

"This was their finest Hour."[45] The WAAFs braced themselves to their duties and played a direct and central role in the victory that Churchill had hoped would come. For them and the service within which they worked, it was a fine hour indeed.

THE BLITZ

The Battle of Britain showed beyond any doubt that when used operationally in the Dowding System, radar could render enemy bomber fleets ineffective. Now incapable of gaining air superiority over the RAF by attempting to attack by day, the Luftwaffe shifted its tactics in October 1940, switching to night bombing in what became known as 'the Blitz'. Infuriated by his inability to launch Operation Sealion and by the RAF's bombing raid on Berlin on 25 August 1940, Hitler decided that if the RAF could not be defeated by daylight raids on strategic military and industrial targets, then Britain should be bombed into submission by night. This new sustained aerial bombing campaign focused not simply on strategic and industrial targets but on British cities and civilians too, in an effort to destroy British morale. The bombing was frequent and heavy and this change in tactics spelled a change in how British people experienced the war. The danger, which had until then been encountered by most in the pages of newspapers and over the wireless, was suddenly much less remote. Though dogfights between the Luftwaffe and the RAF had been visible throughout the Battle of Britain, the danger had been, for the most part, confined to the famous Few and their colleagues in the RAF. When the Blitz began, suddenly danger was everywhere and no one was safe. Hitler's plan was to destroy the will of the British public to continue the war, through terrifying and indiscriminate bombing of their cities and homes.

The Dowding System's clever and effective use of radar had given Germany no choice but to change its aerial warfare tactics, which was a definite victory for the RAF. In its continuing role as the protector of Britain, however, the RAF would have to make a tactical change of its own. As effective as Chain Home radar was by day, it was not precise enough to be able to consistently intercept enemy bombers at night. The Blitz presented the RAF with a new problem to solve and applied greater pressure, as civilian deaths and the destruction of cities began to rack up. What was needed was a way to be able to detect the presence of an enemy aircraft within a close enough range to be able to shoot it down in the dark. A radiolocation early warning system was desirable in aerial warfare by day, but for night warfare it was essential. A system that could function effectively by night did exist in September 1940, but it was still being perfected in secret.

GROUND-CONTROLLED INTERCEPTION RADAR

Chain Home and Chain Home Low radar intelligence could be used to position fighters with an accuracy of about five miles. The CH radar stations faced out to sea, so once enemy aircraft had crossed the coastline and were over land it was up to the Royal Observer Corps to track them by sight. While this worked by day, it could not work in the dark or in poor weather conditions, as visibility would be low to zero. If the RAF was going to be able to prevent bombs from killing and injuring the British public, as well as destroying infrastructure which would negatively affect the war effort, then it was vital that it find a way to intercept Luftwaffe aircraft before they were able to release their bombs.

Secret radar experiments were being carried out in 1940, eventually yielding what became known as ground-controlled interception radar. GCI used height-finding radar and plan-position indicator data on a display screen, which showed both the enemy targets and the interception aircraft. A GCI aerial was pointed at the target aircraft while it was still visible on the radar screen, the aerial controlling the beam. The beam was then directed outward and when the aircraft crossed it, a 'blip' would appear on the screen. The aerial controller would then shorten the beam to try to keep track of the blip, thus following its position as it moved over land.[46] The information on the enemy bomber would then be passed to the RAF via the Dowding System and fighters could be scrambled to intercept it.

As well as the aerial or beam having to be controlled manually, the height of an aircraft had to be measured and tracked so that RAF fighters could ensure that they were above the enemy bomber, from where they could successfully shoot it down. Both skills were tricky and required great concentration, producing vital intelligence that enabled the RAF to eliminate enemy bombers before they could wreak havoc and destruction. Involved in various capacities with GCI radar throughout the Blitz, guiding the Few into position, were members of the WAAF. Due to the fact that GCI was still developing, often the WAAFs involved in the system worked in less than desirable conditions, just as they had in the CH and CHL systems. Joyce Anne Deane was sent to Orby near Skegness, where she worked as a plotter during the Blitz. Based in a small trailer in the middle of a field, she found that her working conditions were very cramped, as the cathode-ray tube consoles were very large. Two airmen were beneath the hut in a shed and rotated the aerials manually by cycling on a fixed frame. The plan-position indicator

(PPI) gave instant plots, and the second tube provided height and range, though the information was often difficult to read as the blips would fade.[47] The WAAFs involved in this next generation of radar were working to track enemy planes and to guide RAF fighters into position from the ground, facilitated by the screens showing the relative positions of both enemy and friendly aircraft, which updated simultaneously. On the night of 14 November 1940, 437 Luftwaffe bombers devastated Coventry and not one of them was shot down. Between September 1940 and February 1941, no more than four enemy bombers were shot down per month. GCI units were deployed widely from January 1941, and in March, twenty-two enemy bombers were shot down. In April, the number rose to forty-eight, and by May it was ninety-six.[48] WAAF GCI plotter Eileen Younghusband did not realise the significance of radar at first. It was not long before she understood the part that GCI, and her role within 'that fantastic weapon of defence', would play in Britain's victory in the skies.[49]

As with the daylight CH system, the GCI version employed WAAFs in various different roles, all requiring them to sign the Official Secrets Act and to take it very seriously. Radar operators, still under the secretive title of 'Clerk, Special Duties', were required to pass a specific training course, emerging with the same qualification as the average electrician. Operators would either control the direction of the aerial and beam or would be tasked with measuring the height of incoming raiders. Both pieces of intelligence were desperately needed by interception fighters. As with CH radar stations, GCI units were vulnerable, perhaps even more so due to the newly developed and highly secret equipment they housed. GCI radar operator Joan Fleetwood Varley remembers being 'a bit edgy', despite the machine gunner permanently posted on the unit for defence. She was given instructions that if the unit was attacked, she and any other WAAFs within it would have to hold it for fifteen minutes while the RAF mechanics disassembled and destroyed the equipment, to keep it out of German hands.[50] There were machine guns and ammunition in the hut, and despite the insistence of the British authorities that female personnel should not be allowed to handle lethal weapons, Joan was instructed to hold the unit by any means necessary. If she and the other WAAFs had trouble defending the unit, they should telephone the nearby army barracks for assistance. Joan found this instruction amusing, because the army barracks was on the other side of the estuary, meaning that if the tide was out, there was no way for the army personnel to get to the unit to help. The nature of GCI meant that information was sometimes passed directly to pilots from the unit itself, bypassing the filter and operations rooms. To begin with, Joan and her WAAF colleagues did not speak directly to the pilots, as initially there was a 'very strong belief that pilots wouldn't believe instructions given by a woman'.[51] Instead, the RAF controller liaised with the fighter pilots, despite the fact that it was the WAAFs who had generated the intelligence first-hand. In uncharted territory, WAAFs were being asked to do things that they were not conventionally expected to do and yet were still not being taken seriously by the RAF as intelligence providers. So pervasive was this attitude that in 1940 Dowding wrote an order that under no circumstances were women to be allowed to talk to pilots in the air. Fortunately, this order became an 'historical idiosyncrasy'.[52]

Where sometimes information was passed directly to pilots from GCI radar units, in other cases it did undergo the filtering process, with WAAF plotters playing a key role. Claire Lorrimer worked as a plotter and was kept so busy that she often had only a few minutes' relief at a time.[53] Plotters were engaged in plotting the mass raids of German bombers on their way to major cities. GCI plots were much more detailed and accurate and the plotters had to work extremely quickly for the information to be of any use. During a mass raid, it was not possible to mark the position of every enemy aircraft. Instead, a plotter marked squared outlines of areas, with estimates of how many hundreds of planes were in the cluster. The WAAFs were very successful in fast-paced plotting during the Blitz, Claire Lorrimer believes due to their 'smaller fingers', and their success is evident in the fact that it was not long before plotters were almost exclusively WAAF personnel.

WAAFs were also employed as GCI filterers, filtering the information before it was disseminated. Eileen Younghusband worked in a filter room in the caves below Box village, just outside Bath. During her time there, Bath was subjected to constant bombing for three days and three nights. Several off-duty WAAFs were among the many fatalities and Eileen had the 'sad job' of notifying their parents. This heart-rending task stayed in her memory long after the war concluded and even caused her to feel anger when she heard condemnation of the RAF's raid on Dresden.[54]

Like Eileen, many WAAFs experienced loss in some way during the Blitz. WAAFs who were friendly with pilots often arranged dates with men they would never see again, which was, Claire Lorrimer says, 'sad but so commonplace' that it was 'accepted ... as par for the course'. Claire and her colleagues 'managed not to think too often about the daily and nightly loss of lives' and instead put as much effort as they could into whatever work they were doing to help win the war.[55] Though they often found loss upsetting, they did not allow it to inhibit their work, all too aware of the importance of what they were doing. Sherry Lygo Hackett recalls the moment when the German raiders flew over her GCI station on their way to Coventry, which was bombed ferociously shortly afterwards. Though the noise was deafening, Sherry and her colleagues were 'over' being frightened, because they knew their work was so important. Aware that 'something big was happening', she continued to work and a colleague announced that Coventry was ablaze. Noticing that the announcer looked as if he were in shock, Sherry was horrified to discover later that he was from Coventry, where his family were living. Though many WAAFs were encountering such danger and devastation for the first time in their lives, their awareness of what was at stake kept them from sinking into the hysteria that the RAF and British authorities had feared they would be prone to, and instead they continued to work effectively throughout the Blitz. This they did in total secrecy, some refraining from speaking about it until forty years after the war. GCI plotter Elizabeth Clifton knew that 'you didn't query things, didn't ask', and Eileen Younghusband realised that what she was doing was 'vital, worthwhile and important' – so important that no amount of fear or sadness should be allowed to inhibit the work in any way.[56]

With the development of PPI and GCI, the role of the controller became important to RAF fighters being able to intercept enemy aircraft in a timely fashion. This role, at first exclusively filled by RAF officers, was eventually opened to members of the WAAF. The apparent success with which WAAFs had served as officers during the Battle of Britain led to them being employed as supervisory officers during the Blitz, and a handful of these WAAF supervisors went on to undergo further training to serve as GCI controllers. Trained to report the courses of incoming enemy raiders and to plot those that RAF interception aircraft would need to take to meet them in the air, WAAF controllers like Joyce Deane learned to

factor in wind speed and direction and used a simulator to prac-
tise ordering and scrambling fighters before doing it for real. Joyce
found the training frightening, as the timing of giving the orders
had to be extremely exact.[57] So secret was this work that when they
were off-duty, WAAFs had their outgoing mail censored.

In 1942, WAAF squadron officer T. C. Legge became a controller
and Air Chief Marshal Sir Frederick Rosier said 'her easily rec-
ognisable and calm voice, combined with their faith in her known
controlling ability, had in the heat of battle given our pilots that
added boost of confidence'. She later became the first woman ever
to command an RAF station, setting an impressive and important
precedent.[58]

The WAAFs proved to be instrumental in the Dowding System
during both the Battle of Britain and the Blitz. As the Few fought
to defend Britain in the air, their female colleagues worked tirelessly to ensure that they had the information they needed to multiply
their forces and deploy them as efficiently as possible. Though they
remained firmly hidden behind the Few, the women were vital to
their victory.

5

THE LADIES WHO LISTENED: WAAFS IN SIGNALS INTELLIGENCE

It has long been accepted that during war, the interception by one side of signals and messages between the various forces of the other side is one of the most useful and reliable sources of information available. Reading other people's electronic mail, as it were, provided what was probably the most trustworthy intelligence on enemy intentions and capabilities, at the lowest cost – spies took time to train and deploying them could be very difficult, rendering the more traditional methods of espionage of little use. The Second World War, more than any other war before it, was dominated by communications intelligence. The interception of signals – both communications between human beings and electrical signals used for indirect communication – significantly affected military operations throughout the conflict. Developments and advances in technology meant that by 1939, radio communications were being used ever-increasingly, especially given the vast distances across which Allied and Axis forces were spread in what was truly a world war.

'SIGINT', short for 'signals intelligence', was the name by which intelligence gathering by the interception of signals came to be known in Britain, and it included both the actual interception of enemy signals and the deciphering and decoding of these signals

when they were not in plain speech or text. Electronic interception of signals pre-dated the First World War and was used by
the Royal Navy in particular from 1914 to 1918. The experience of the
First World War was a catalyst for the permanent establishment
of interception and decryption facilities in Britain and in 1919 the
Government Code and Cypher School was established. The use of
SIGINT had great implications in the Second World War, most
famously through the British decryption of German Enigma signals. The combined resulting intelligence from signals interception
and cryptanalysis across the British armed forces was given the
codename 'Ultra' and the final product was produced at Bletchley
Park, the headquarters of the GC&CS. The Enigma story and the
actual codebreaking have somewhat monopolised the history of
British signals interception, overshadowing the contribution of the
raw material itself. Though the value of Ultra intelligence is beyond
doubt, and the extraordinary minds at Bletchley Park are owed
much for their wartime code and cypher feats, their work would
not have been possible without the raw intercepted data.

Before the outbreak of war in 1939, radio signals from potential
enemies were being monitored by an organisation in Britain known
as the 'Y Service', a network of signals intelligence collection sites,
known as 'Y stations'. The Y Service was established during the
First World War and functioned again throughout the Second,
listening in to enemy communications in secret and sending their
contents to where they could be best used to the Allies' advantage.
The Y Service contained branches, each operated by a specific service or agency, including the RAF, the navy, the army, MI5 and
MI6. Over 600 receiving points existed during the Second World
War, distributed around Britain on land and at sea, carrying out
radio surveillance on the enemy.[1] Y Service operators received

German wireless messages and radio traffic in both plain language and Morse code. The traffic was meticulously recorded in its entirety and passed to Bletchley Park, where the GC&CS would decrypt and analyse it for operational use. The GC&CS was totally dependent on the Y Service to have anything at all to decode and while Ultra is remembered as perhaps the greatest secret of the Second World War, it would not have existed without the Y Service. In an embryonic state in 1939, the Y Service had by 1945 developed into a 'sophisticated and vital intelligence producing agency'.[2] The intelligence it produced contributed significantly to Allied victory and undoubtedly saved many lives.

Where wartime SIGINT is concerned, it is nearly always Enigma and the Bletchley Park mathematicians that are front and centre in the story. There were, however, other ways in which the Y Service contributed to Allied victory, one of which was the intelligence it provided throughout the Battle of Britain. Like the radar intelligence provided by the Dowding System, the Y Service provided details on enemy attack formations to Fighter Command. Where the radar system could tell where the enemy was and what it seemed to be doing, the Y Service could provide confirmation of Luftwaffe attack formation details and sometimes of their intentions. This was due to its ability to hear conversations between German pilots, speaking to each other and to their ground staff. Some of the intelligence collected by the Y Service was in plain German language and could be translated by the listener and passed to Fighter Command immediately. Encrypted information was recorded by the listener but would make no immediate sense and it would have to be sent to Bletchley Park for decryption and analysis. Once it was presented in a usable state, it was then sent to Fighter Command. The information gleaned could contain details of impending enemy raids and of the force likely to be used and sometimes of intended targets and personnel involved in the raids. Such information was crucial, as it provided Fighter Command with an accurate idea of the kind of RAF reception it needed to provide to successfully counter the enemy attack. The intelligence could be combined with the use of radar, which enabled RAF controllers to direct the interception of the raid in real time. In the Battle of Britain, the Y Service would prove incredibly useful to the British fight. One of the necessary qualifications for Y Service personnel was the ability to speak fluent German. In part due to the success of the WAAFs working in the radar network and in the filter and operations rooms of Fighter Command, and also due to the chronic shortage of German-speaking RAF personnel, the Air Ministry decided that women should be recruited for work in the Y Service. Just as WAAFs were present behind the Few in the Dowding System, so they were in the Y Service, producing important intelligence that would directly influence the course of the Battle of Britain.

At the outbreak of war, more and more Y listening stations were set up around the country, providing locations where the covert interception of German wireless signals and traffic could take place. Potential WAAFs were asked to indicate on their recruitment forms if they could speak any other languages and those who listed fluent German were spotted and noted immediately. WAAF recruits into the Y Service needed to be capable linguists. They had to be intelligent, quick thinkers and ideally possess the ability to use their own initiative and exercise responsibility. They needed to be able to concentrate for long periods of time, as it was vital to get everything they heard down on paper. Mistakes or omissions could cost lives. WAAF Commandant Jane Trefusis Forbes held special selection boards at the WAAF Directorate in London, to which potential

Y operators were called for an interview. The interview involved the testing of an airwoman's knowledge of the German language, though it did not necessarily follow that all fluent German speakers would make good operators. In addition to excellent German skills, the WAAFs also needed to have good hearing and the ability to understand German slang, which was not easily learned from text-books. For this reason, WAAFs who had spent time in Germany before the war were especially attractive candidates. It was also thought that due to the highly secret nature of their work, Y Service WAAFs ought to be commissioned as officers. WAAFs engaged on encoding and decoding normal RAF signals traffic were usually given the rank of code and cypher officers, and it was eventually decided, after some argument, that Y Service WAAFs should be granted the rank of sergeant. There were misgivings within the Air Ministry about the commissioning of women, even more so the meteoric promotion of raw recruits of the lowest possible rank. Despite these concerns, however, the Air Ministry authorised this automatic granting of senior rank to Y Service WAAFs, on the grounds that they were dealing with secret material.

Y Service recruits were sent for three months' Morse training at the London Radio School. Like the WAAFs in the Dowding System, they were sworn to total secrecy and could tell no one about their work. When posted to a Y station, they were not told where they were going and were instead handed a sealed envelope so that they could not discuss their postings with friends and col-leagues.[3] Sealed orders were only opened at the train station. Once they had reached their destination and started on duty at the Y station, teams of WAAFs worked in shifts to monitor enemy sig-nals twenty-four hours a day, seven days a week. They would sit with headphones on, waiting for German ships, aircraft or ground personnel to start making radio transmissions, and once these began, the women were tasked with writing them down in as much detail as was possible. Sometimes they could even hear Panzer divisions on the Continent talking to one another or to their superiors. Packages of this accumulated intelligence were sealed and sent to the Air Ministry and to Bletchley Park, to be analysed and disseminated for operational use. If a receiver could be spared, the WAAF operator on a listening post would listen into British frequencies too, so that both sides of the battle were recorded in an effort to make more sense of the German transmissions. The German transmissions could be heavily encoded and even thorough knowledge of the German language didn't always help – code words and call signs could be quite puzzling. Sometimes the WAAFs were able to provide the RAF with brand-new intelligence and often they were able to relay information that could corroborate or disprove what the Air Ministry had established from other intelligence sources.

Fighter Groups quickly realised the value of this intelligence and requested direct access to it. The Air Ministry responded to the request by creating a number of coastal intercept stations, known as 'home defence units', in an attempt to ensure complete coverage of all Luftwaffe transmissions from Denmark to Brittany.[4] These units were in constant communication with RAF West Kingsdown, which was the headquarters of the RAF Y Service, and with the naval branch of the Y Service, to ensure timely interception of the enemy wherever and whenever possible. Intelligence sent to Bletchley Park was disseminated to the various operational units that could make decisions based on it, resulting in the deployment of military forces to defend or attack. The plentiful intelligence that emanated from Bletchley – Ultra – was transmitted at high priority to RAF operational commands, often resulting in immediate orders that were transmitted by telephone or by word of mouth. This form of transmission, coupled with the reluctance of intelligence authorities to keep written records because there was a risk that they could be of use to the enemy after invasion, means that very few records of the impact of Y Service intelligence on daily operations survive. Combined with the required silence of those who worked in the Y Service, as well as the focus on Ultra and Enigma, this has left the story of the British monitoring of enemy signals incomplete, an essential piece of it missing. The story of the Y Service and their collection of raw intelligence material for Bletchley Park, and of the WAAFs within this service, is best told by former Y Service intelligence officer Aileen Clayton.

In 1974, RAF officer Frederick Winterbotham published a book entitled *The Ultra Secret*. For the first time, the secret of how the Allies had exploited information obtained from the cracking of German messages transmitted in the Enigma cypher was made public. Frederick was an RAF officer placed in charge of distributing Ultra intelligence to Winston Churchill and to Allied military commands in multiple theatres of the war. *The Ultra Secret* was a real revelation and for the first time the public were able to understand how what they had seen unfold on battlefields all over the world, on land, at sea and in the air, had been influenced by intelligence collected by unseen groups of people in back rooms, far from the battles. The Ultra revelation caused a sensation and was a point of major fascination for the British public. One thing *The Ultra Secret* did not do, however, was reveal the extent of how involved the Y Service and the WAAF had been in this mammoth intelligence effort. That job was left to a WAAF operator to do herself.

Just after the conclusion of the war in 1945, Aileen Clayton was approached by the RAF public relations department to write about her experiences in the service, but as secrecy restrictions remained in place, she was not given permission to do so until after *The Ultra Secret* had been revealed in 1974. It fell to Aileen to fill in some of the gaps in the story and this she did marvellously. It certainly helped that by that point radio eavesdropping was being used by many foreign governments, while newer technologies were giving rise to alternative clandestine surveillance methods, so her book was not considered to be giving too much away. Aware of the many gaps in the official records and the story as told by Frederick Winterbotham, Aileen wrote *The Enemy Is Listening*, the authorised account of the secret Y Service during the Second World War.

Aileen had lived in Germany in the build-up to the outbreak of war and had witnessed first-hand what she saw as the 'intrinsic evil' of Nazism. Armed with the ability to speak fluent German and a strong desire to 'have a hand' in the protection of world peace, she joined the WAAF in London and in July 1940 became the first of its members to be commissioned for intelligence duties. Until the spring of 1941, Aileen was the only intelligence officer in the Kingsdown Y Service network and was one of the first 'Secret Six' WAAFs in the Y Service. The others included the Honourable Mrs Geoffrey Pearson, who was deaf and therefore initially an unlikely candidate for the role of a wireless operator but who spoke good German, and Barbara Pemberton, who was later awarded the MBE for her service with the unit. Aileen's role entailed briefing the WAAF operators in the Kingsdown network on what sort of traffic to concentrate on each day and to decide which messages should be passed along to Bletchley. As neither of her RAF supervisors spoke any German, the coordination and compilation of immediate intelligence from radio traffic was what she called her 'headache'.[5] Under the command of an RAF officer, she was installed in a caravan at the top of a cliff, where she and her team of operators monitored messages transmitted by the Luftwaffe. RAF Y Service units kept a 24-hour watch, in six-hour-long shifts. Their work was so secret that a sentry was posted nearby in a tent, whose duty it was to guard the hut or caravan from visits by curious locals. During a shift, a WAAF operator would sit next to a radio set, listening to a specific frequency through earphones. The radio equipment WAAFs used was complicated and to begin with, experienced RAF wireless operators searched for frequencies, handing the headphones to German-speaking WAAFs once they had located them. Operators would sit through hours and hours of background noise and interference, straining to hear the enemy communicating and taking great care to write down exactly what they heard. If too many letters were missed, decryption of the message would be much more difficult, and on the front line of communications, the Y operators bore great responsibility in collecting the raw data that would later undergo decryption and analysis to provide potentially life-saving, battle-winning information. If the volume of radio traffic was normal, operators had plenty of time to be able to take down a message accurately. If there was an increase in the volume of traffic, this became much more difficult and stressful and aside from the time pressure, it could indicate that a major operation was about to begin. Sometimes, when traffic volume was high, operators would be 'double-banked', meaning that two operators would work on the messages rather than the usual one, to ensure that as much as possible was recorded. Over a frequency the operators would hear messages being passed between Luftwaffe pilots and between these pilots and their ground control stations. The messages were entered by the listening WAAF operator into a logbook, including the time of the recording, the radio frequency, the call sign used by the pilot, the message contents and, if possible, a translation of the message. This work involved a reasonably high level of responsibility, as messages that were of obvious tactical use had to be identified and prepared for immediate dissemination to a Fighter Group or to the Royal Navy via the Air Ministry, where the rest of the messages could be translated during any lulls in the traffic. The Y Service was one area of air intelligence that left the RAF little choice but to trust women with such a high degree of responsibility, in part because few RAF wireless operators had a thorough enough knowledge of German. The Y Service WAAFs became proficient not only at recording the radio traffic but also at breaking down the German code words and grid references used in the messages. Without these grids, the messages were of very little value and only a thorough knowledge of the German language could provide them. It was 'like doing crossword puzzles', Aileen Clayton says, and 'being young and enthusiastic, we felt we were playing a guessing game with the Luftwaffe'.[6] Though, as they had been with WAAF radar operators, the RAF and the Air Ministry were uncomfortable with WAAFs being placed in caravans and huts in vulnerable and dangerous locations to perform highly secret work, they had little choice but to allow it, in the interest of providing vital and otherwise unobtainable intelligence on the Luftwaffe order of battle.

Every day, the WAAF Y Service operators listened to German reconnaissance aircraft reports on weather and the strength and position of British convoys in the Channel. This information was gleaned in such a regular fashion as to earn it the name the 'milk train'.[7] As well as obtaining information on what the Luftwaffe was up to, it was also useful for the British military services to know what information the Germans were collecting on them.

With great skill, dealing with every kind of German accent, and despite atmospheric interference and complicated code words, the Y Service WAAFs managed to provide extensive information of consistent vital use in both defensive and offensive air operations. This included air-to-air instructions between German fighters and bombers during attacks on British airfields and convoys, orders from German bases for landings and information on the strength, equipment and location of Luftwaffe units. Occasionally, Luftwaffe pilots would report seeing British pilots stranded at sea after bailing out of damaged aircraft. Later in the war, this information could enable the scrambling of Air Sea Rescue units to help the downed pilots, saving lives and conserving valuable Fighter and Bomber Command commodities.

Some of the most vital information collected pertained to British shipping. Every day, Luftwaffe reconnaissance aircraft searched the Channel shipping lanes for British ships and used their radios to notify each other and their superiors when they spotted them. As soon as the Y Service heard that a British ship had been identified, an immediate warning was sent to the Royal Navy at Dover, and to 11 Fighter Group at Uxbridge, which would deploy RAF fighters to protect the convoy in the Channel. Without these warnings, convoys carrying vital supplies of food and fuel might not have made it to Britain, and in its isolated position, such an outcome could have spelled the end of its ability to continue to fight the war.

Y Service WAAFs were aware that every single message intercepted had the potential to aid the British fight and to frustrate German war plans. In July 1940, Aileen Clayton's team began to intercept messages indicating that the Germans were using civil aircraft with Red Cross markings for reconnaissance flights over the Channel. This was contrary to international agreement of the rules for war and the Air Ministry was notified immediately, resulting in a warning issued to the German High Command that such aircraft would not be granted immunity. Information like this was highly valuable and could not be obtained anywhere else. The Y Service was also able to provide Fighter Command with detailed knowledge of the Luftwaffe's central control system, so that it could be successfully countered. Unlike the RAF, Luftwaffe pilots flew on carefully pre-arranged plans which had been given at their flight briefings before setting off on raids. The Luftwaffe was on the offensive and knew of their intended targets, where, as the defenders, the RAF had no choice but to meet the enemy where they appeared. The WAAFs reported hearing the obviously furious enemy pilots complaining to their colleagues about how, when they arrived in British airspace, there were always RAF fighters ready and waiting to intercept them. They even went so far as to make note of and compliment the effectiveness of the RAF's organisation and tactics. The combination of the intelligence provided by the Dowding System and the Y Service meant that there was little the RAF did not know about the Luftwaffe's order of battle, which was undoubtedly a major factor in the British victory in the Battle of Britain – a victory in which these hidden WAAFs played an integral part.

Thankfully, Aileen Clayton was not the only Y Service WAAF operator to record her experiences. Becoming interested in Morse after her boyfriend, who was in army signals, taught her how to use it, Margaret Porter joined the WAAF and was trained for Y Service work. She remembers how difficult interception work could be, due to awful reception at times, which caused fading signals, and shifts in frequency, atmospheric interference and oscillation from RAF routine communications.[8] Y Service work was so secret that much

of the RAF did not know of its existence and Margaret and her colleagues could not ask them to refrain from using certain frequencies
without alerting them to it.

As with the WAAFs in radar and in the Dowding System, the
training for WAAFs in the Y Service could be difficult due to their
lack of prior knowledge in certain subjects. Yvonne Jones trained
for her Y Service work at RAF Compton Bassett, where six weeks
of intensive study included physics, chemistry and other subjects
she was not familiar with but found to be fascinating. The lack of
prior knowledge and difficult intensive training, however, rarely
impeded the WAAFs in carrying out their duties in the Y Service.
A watch room was, as Yvonne explains, a 'hive of activity', but many
of the WAAFs 'loved the excitement of it all' rather than finding it
too overwhelming. When leaving a watch, Yvonne often found that
though she was exhausted, she could leave 'happy in the knowledge
of a job well done'.[9]

Like Aileen Clayton, Vera Ines Morley Elkan was placed in a
position of considerable responsibility when she was asked to command the RAF Y Section unit in Montrose, Scotland. Intelligence
generated by her unit contributed to the sinking of four German
battleships and Vera was so successful as an intelligence officer that
she was sent to the Air Ministry for a special interview, at which she
was asked if she would be willing to be parachuted into Germany
to perform secret work. She agreed, telling her interviewer, 'I will do
anything to beat the Nazis.'[10]

WAAF operator Dalma Flanders thought her job with the Y Service a huge responsibility at the age of twenty-one and was pleased
to be so trusted. She recalls that the radio sets would frequently
give her and her WAAF colleagues electrical shocks, as they did not
appear to be earthed very well. Dalma found the work exhausting

and even scary at times, particularly when RAF pilots could be heard, having been shot and wounded, trying to land as quickly as possible. The weight of the responsibility of her job was not lost on Dalma and she knew how important it was that she performed as well as possible – she knew that lives depended on it. Speaking of more tangible danger, Dalma recalls being able to see the church tower at Calais on a clear day from her station at Capel, which was at the top of a hundred-foot-high cliff above the sea. In addition to the church tower, she could often see huge German guns, nick-named 'Big Berthas', which could be fired across the water. If this happened, she and her colleagues had fifteen seconds to take cover before the shell would land and burst. Completely unused to being in such a dangerous position, Dalma found this 'very upsetting at first', but like the WAAFs on the radar stations, she 'soon got used to even that'.[11]

Y stations needed to be coastal and on cliff tops or high ground in order to reach frequencies as far into enemy territory as possible. The danger inherent in the necessary location of the stations was a deterrent to the Air Ministry and the RAF when considering the use of WAAFs in signals interception. Writing in 1980, Aileen Clayton acknowledged that with extensive coverage of the war by the media in modern times, women are accustomed to the sights and sounds of it. In 1940 and 1941 they were not, and before they had 'become hardened or inured, violence of this dimension was new and very terrible'.[12] The British authorities were worried about the physical danger that WAAFs on Y stations would be subjected to, but they were also concerned with the mental strain that the stress of it might place on them. Personnel on Y stations lived and worked in a state of constant tension, knowing that they were key targets for Luftwaffe bombers. As the bombing continued, during the day and at night, WAAFs frequented the air raid shelters but never left their sets when they were on watch. Aileen states that she saw total 'devotion to duty' from the WAAFs at her station, who continued to give 'invaluable service' as they plotted incoming raids, even as they were overhead. She is adamant that despite the falling bombs and the loud firing of machine and anti-aircraft guns all around them, the WAAFs concentrated as best they could on their work and proved themselves to be more than capable in these adverse conditions.

No one would dispute the fact that during the battle of Britain the Operations Rooms were largely dependent on the WAAF, and any doubts that there might have been about women's reactions under battle conditions were dispelled for ever. I was to observe throughout the war that, on the whole, women are initially much braver under bombardment than men but their morale has a tendency to decline, whereas though many men are somewhat panicky at first they seem to pull themselves together and become gradually braver, so that in the end, there is little to choose between men and women.[13]

Aileen recalls one particularly violent day when there was more bombing than usual and one of the men in her unit 'cracked under the strain'. As the senior WAAF operator on duty, she was worried that if the men began to become hysterical, the WAAFs might follow suit, particularly as lack of sleep due to the heavy bombing was beginning to take effect on everyone. Taking a risk, Aileen slapped the man hard across the face several times. A clear example of the reversal of the stereotypical view of women as the hysterical gender, the move had the desired effect and calmed the hysterical man down, but unfortunately he was her senior in rank and Aileen was worried about the repercussions of her actions. But she heard nothing more regarding the affair, the implication being that she had acted exactly as an RAF officer might have in order to maintain control of the unit and keep the rest of the staff from slipping into hysteria.[14]

Y SERVICE WAAFS BEHIND THE FEW

Just as WAAFs were working hard behind the scenes throughout the Battle of Britain and the Blitz, so the WAAFs of the RAF Y Service were working behind the Few in various other major instances during the Second World War. A colleague of Yvonne Jones recalls the time when she suddenly found herself surrounded by senior staff and was told that it was imperative that she got everything down, quickly and correctly, from the frequency traffic she was monitoring. It became clear later that she had been listening to a German frequency during an attack on the famous German battleship *Tirpitz*, a heavy German battlecruiser and the sister ship of *Bismarck*.[15] *Tirpitz* had been tasked with attacking convoys that were carrying Allied supplies to Soviet Russia – these supplies were a vital lifeline for the Soviet Union as it fought the German Army on a front stretching 500 miles. On 13 November 1944, it was confirmed that *Tirpitz* had been sunk, permanently removing a grave threat to Allied shipping. ·

In June 1941, Vera Ines Morley Elkan was monitoring signals for the Y Service when, one day, she identified that she was picking up traffic between Panzers rather than aircraft. The messages appeared to indicate an intended German attack, but she did not recognise the place names being mentioned. She recorded them and asked her Polish colleague if she knew where the attack might be scheduled to take place. Her colleague confirmed that the locations mentioned in the traffic were in Poland. Believing it to be important intelligence, Vera reported the traffic to the Air Ministry, but the enemy action that it appeared to indicate was dismissed by her superiors as routine manoeuvres. The traffic continued and for three days the Air Ministry did not believe it to indicate anything other than routine manoeuvres. On 22 June, the Germans launched their invasion of the Soviet Union, which included an armoured advance from southern Poland. The attack was not anticipated, due to the fact that Germany had signed a non-aggression pact with the Soviet Union in 1939. It was this attack that had been mentioned in the traffic Vera had intercepted. Where the RAF and the Air Ministry had underestimated the ability of the WAAFs to work effectively in roles previously filled by men, in cases such as Vera's it was the male-dominated Air Ministry that actually made grave mistakes, rather than the WAAFs they were so worried about. Though the full value of their work in instances such as these may never be known due to the lack of surviving official records, these WAAFs were present behind their male colleagues, providing a constant stream of intelligence on the enemy in a calm and intelligent manner that, prior to their service, had not been expected of them. The intelligence generated by the RAF Y Service proved to be of indisputable value in providing a picture of the Luftwaffe's order of battle, its capabilities and its intentions, throughout the war. Another experiment conducted by an unsure Air Ministry and the RAF, the integration of WAAFs into the Y Service proved to have very successful results, just as the experiment with their sisters in the Dowding System had been so worthwhile. The full force of the Luftwaffe had attempted to bombard Britain, aiming to exhaust and eliminate the RAF as a threat. Aileen Clayton admits that without the 'small, indomitable band of young airmen' – the

Few – the battle would have been lost, the invasion of Britain inevitable.[16] Behind them, though, was a band of women listening to the Luftwaffe communicate as it attempted to deprive Britain of its freedom and ability to continue the war against Germany. This other few, the WAAFs, made an extremely valuable contribution to British signals intelligence and helped to keep the Luftwaffe at bay.

With both the intelligence generated by the Dowding System and by the RAF Y Service, dissemination was as important as collection. Information, however clear and accurate, is of no real use in war if it is not placed in the hands of someone who can use it to make informed operational decisions. The collection and collation of information was vital to aerial warfare in the Second World War, but it would become useless if this information could not be passed on to RAF Fighter and Bomber Commands in a timely fashion. As well as being involved in the collection of intelligence in the radar chain and in the Y Service, WAAFs were involved in the dissemination of it to the relevant operational units. RAF Y Service units sent their daily logs full of information to the Air Ministry by despatch rider – often a WAAF operator on a motorcycle – and then on to Bletchley Park. Later, an extensive network of telephone lines was installed at West Kingsdown, the headquarters of the RAF Y Service. If WAAFs at outstations thought information might be particularly important or time-sensitive, they telephoned it to West Kingsdown, from where it could be disseminated for immediate operational use – West Kingsdown would then telephone it to the relevant RAF Fighter Group, which would deploy air defences. No. 11 Group at Uxbridge were responsible for the defence of southeast England and bore the brunt of much of the Battle of Britain bombing. During the summer of 1940, Y Service WAAFs telephoned vital information straight through to No. 11 Group, rather than wasting valuable time passing it up the chain first. Upon them rested huge responsibility and their work that summer was vital to the outcome of the Battle of Britain. When intercepted messages came through that were enciphered and encoded, they would need to undergo deciphering and decoding at the Government Code and Cypher School. WAAFs at Y stations would ensure that the messages reached Bletchley Park safely, where their colleagues would assist in the next stage of the process.

The indisputably valuable contribution of Ultra intelligence to the Allied military war effort is often attributed solely to the code-breakers at Bletchley Park. It is a contribution, however, that the Y Service shared in, just as much as the Bletchley few. Approximately 10,000 people staffed the Y Service and of them, around 75 per cent were women, including the WAAFs. Aileen Clayton considered Churchill's words regarding the Few to be 'very true', agreeing that 'so very much was owed by so many to those few brave young airmen of the RAF'. Referring to herself and her WAAF colleagues as 'onlookers on the ground' watching the aerial battles, Aileen claims that she was 'perhaps more fully appreciative of their great courage'.[17] Though she may be right about the ability of the WAAFs to fully appreciate the sacrifices of the fighting Few, Aileen and her colleagues cannot and should not be referred to as 'onlookers'. Though they watched the aerial battles from afar, the WAAFs working in the Dowding System and in the RAF Y Service were directly involved in delivering victory both in the Battle of Britain and in the end of hostilities in 1945, risking their safety and sometimes their lives. Though they did not enter into physical battle, WAAFs worked in often uncomfortable conditions under constant and gruelling pressure, for long, exhausting hours. Their work demanded constant precision and accuracy, unbroken concentration and inevitable loneliness due to their inability to talk about what they were doing. All of this they bore with intelligence, initiative, focus and poise not initially expected of them, and without them and their work, Allied victory in 1945 would have been much more difficult to achieve. In a paper given at an Air Intelligence Symposium by the Royal Air Force Historical Society, naval intelligence officer Edward Thomas declared that the story of air intelligence in the Second World War is 'worthy to stand beside the most historic achievements of the RAF, to which it made a notable contribution'.[18] Despite the fact that they are missing from most historical accounts of wartime air intelligence, the WAAFs were an integral part of that contribution. Where victory in 1940–41 and in 1945 is commonly attributed in part to the bravery of the pilots and aircrews of the RAF, it must also be attributed to the work of the WAAFs working in intelligence behind them, hidden and overlooked, but vital.

6

AT THE PARK: THE BLETCHLEY WAAFS

THE GOVERNMENT CODE AND CYPHER SCHOOL

Intelligence collected by the Y Service was routinely sent to Bletchley Park. This unique codebreaking organisation is perhaps the most famous intelligence organisation of the Second World War and became the centre for British codebreaking for the duration of the conflict. Bletchley Park, a country house and estate in Buckinghamshire, housed the wartime Government Code and Cypher School. Established by the Cabinet in 1919, the GC&CS was tasked with studying the methods of cypher communication used by foreign powers and was asked to advise on the security of British codes and cyphers in an effort to prevent Britain's enemies from being able to break into its codes the way it was breaking into theirs.

The introduction of wireless communications cyphers at the beginning of the century rendered the study of the methods of enciphering and encoding used by other countries more important than ever before, and such study could yield far superior intelligence than traditional espionage methods were capable of providing in wartime. The GC&CS regularly broke into German communications encipherment systems, most famously the Enigma and Lorenz cyphers, as well as those used by the other Axis nations. An inter-service organisation, the GC&CS contained a Naval Section from 1924, an Army Section from 1930 and an Air Section from 1936.[1]

Once information from the Dowding System and the Y Service arrived at Bletchley, it would undergo multiple processes so that its significance could be fully understood and the intelligence could be exploited as much as possible. Intercepted communications could be both enciphered and encoded and two separate tasks needed to take place to get the message into plain language so that it made sense. With cyphers, single letters and numbers were replaced by other letters and numbers. Encoding, on the other hand, meant that a whole word or phrase was replaced by a different word or phrase, or perhaps by several letters or numbers – these were called code groups. For the latter, codebooks were needed for the decoding process – these were a sort of key, where the decoder could look up each encoded word or phrase to find out what it meant. Once a message had been deciphered, and, when necessary, decoded, the results were analysed and interpreted to provide as full a meaning as possible. The intelligence produced was classified as 'Most Secret Ultra', often shortened to 'Ultra'. When it was sent on to military commanders, they were not told where it had come from and Ultra's source remained a mystery to most of the men making operational decisions based on it.

Bletchley operated under levels of secrecy verging on paranoia, in order to keep the secret from Germany that Britain was reading its communications. Winston Churchill was presented with a daily summary of the most important intelligence accumulated at the GC&CS, and the Prime Minister placed great value on this gold-mine of information. Working under what were sometimes difficult conditions of extreme secrecy, there were many specially trained and skilled personnel involved in the processes carried out at Bletchley, and by the end of the war in 1945, over 10,000 people had worked at the park itself and in its several associated outstations. Contrary to what the commonly constructed image of Bletchley implies, only very few of the people who worked there were codebreakers, and a number of different tasks needed to be carried out in order to successfully break into enemy codes and cyphers besides code-breaking. Many of these tasks were carried out by women.

WOMEN AT BLETCHLEY PARK

It was clear that the wartime Government Code and Cypher School would require Britain's best brains if it were to succeed in its mission to crack some of the most complicated cyphers that had ever been used in communications. Naturally, the GC&CS turned to the genius of men, particularly mathematicians and linguists, many of them recruited from Oxford and Cambridge universities. The genius of mathematicians like Alan Turing and Gordon Welchman is well documented, and some of the country's best linguists, men like Alfred 'Dilly' Knox and Alastair Denniston, have also made their way into the history books, the memory of their contributions to Bletchley's famous codebreaking outfit for ever preserved. As with the RAF's Few, the work of these men should never be diminished and was irrefutably valuable. As is also the case with the Few, however, their work was a small part of a much bigger story and their flashes of genius would not have been at all possible if it weren't for the massive workforce behind the scenes, ensuring that the huge volume of data that came into the park was ready for them to work on. The nature and implications of their contribution rarely appropriately appreciated, thousands of women made up this work-force and it was because of them that the park ran as successfully and efficiently as it did.

The first recruitment drive for Bletchley yielded 146 people and of them, sixty-seven were women. By the end of the war, women constituted around three-quarters of the workforce at Bletchley.[2] At least 6,600 women made a 'direct contribution' to the deciphering of enemy communications.[3] Bletchley's personnel were a mixture of civilians and members of all of the military services. The latter group included women from the Women's Royal Naval Service, the Auxiliary Territorial Service and the Women's Auxiliary Air Force. Of the three, the contribution of the WRNS at Bletchley is perhaps the most well known today and there were more of them than there were from the other two services. Many of the WRNS members worked the famous bombes, the electro-mechanical machines used to break Enigma-enciphered enemy messages. The WAAFs, however, were also present in the GC&CS intelligence machine, carrying out an abundance of wireless work and assisting in the production of usable air intelligence. Though their work appeared mundane – resembling the kind of work that was expected of women working in offices at the time – it was extremely important, as it kept the information flowing through the vast system that was supplying the Air Ministry and the RAF with details they needed in order to fight the Luftwaffe most effectively.

WAAFs were usually selected for work at Bletchley Park on the same criteria as for the Y Service. Language skills were essential in dealing with German radio traffic and when called for an inter-view, prospective Bletchley employees were given a translation test. Sometimes the piece they were given to translate was deliberately technically difficult, using engineering terms that the interviewer was aware a woman probably would not understand. Interviewers were looking for candidates to use the knowledge they did have, as well as initiative, to make informed guesses – after all, they would have to do this when they were working with unfamiliar German code words in intercepted radio traffic.

If posted to Bletchley, WAAFs were not told where they were going and every effort was made to keep the location and purpose of the GC&CS secret until they had actually arrived there. Gwen Watkins was put in the back of a blacked-out van and the sergeant overseeing the transport to Bletchley even joked about blindfolding her. Feeling 'decidedly anxious', Gwen was made to wait at the main gate upon her arrival at Bletchley and, to her surprise, was then sent to an old vicarage in the neighbouring village. Forbidden to leave the premises and supervised by a WAAF officer, she was collected after a few days and given a pass to Bletchley and learned that in the time she had been at the vicarage she had been thoroughly vetted and granted security clearance.[4]

THE BLETCHLEY PARK PROCESS

Once intelligence had been collected by the WAAFs in the Dowding System and by the various Y stations around Britain, it was sorted into low and high priority material. For low priority, intercepts were sent to Bletchley via courier. High priority material, which was time-sensitive, was transmitted directly from the receiving station to Bletchley via specially designated communications lines. It was received at Bletchley in the wireless room, which was staffed predominantly by WAAF personnel. These women facilitated a much-needed means of communication between the GC&CS and the intercept stations, and women with qualifications and abilities in communications were highly sought after for this purpose. This was not just the case at Bletchley Park – WAAFs worked throughout the entire RAF system to staff a critically important communications network, using radio, telephones and teleprinters to convey information from station to station and keeping them in touch with one another at all times.

Telephonists manually connected calls all day every day, facilitating the immediate dissemination of intelligence at great speeds. Women were thought to possess certain attributes that made them ideal radio telephony (R/T) operators. The pitch of their voices, for instance, and the clarity with which they often spoke, could be useful when passing information to operations rooms and RAF stations sometimes situated hundreds of miles away, the locations of these stations often causing a lot of radio interference and resulting in weak reception. They also needed to be able to work at significant speed while retaining a high level of accuracy and were required to be able to pay acute attention for long periods of time, often through exhausting night watches. It was not unusual for women to have knowledge and experience of telephone work, as this was one form of work accepted as suitable for them in the 1930s and 1940s and many had worked in telephone exchanges before the war.

Less common, however, were women with a knowledge of Morse code, which was needed in potential wireless operators. Some women had learned Morse privately – Doreen Luke, for example, learned Morse with her father, a signals officer in the Home Guard, in 1941. When she saw that wireless operators were needed, she applied to join the WAAF at age seventeen and a half, without hesitation. When it came to training as a wireless operator, Doreen was at a distinct advantage, as Morse was the essential basic skill. Once they had mastered the fundamentals of Morse, prospective wireless operators had to build up speed and accuracy to pass their course. Gaining her 'sparks', a badge with a spark symbol worn on the sleeve of the WAAF uniform after passing the course, Doreen then had to build up technical knowledge of wireless work, including the intricacies of wireless sets, transmitters and receivers and the operating and workings of them. She also learned touch-typing and Morse slip reading, which enabled the sending of messages at a much higher speed than hand-operating with a Morse key.[5] Aware that inaccurate details could alter message meanings dramatically, with potentially dire consequences, WAAFs were trained to a very high level of proficiency in radio operation before being posted to Bletchley to work for real.

As well as radio operators, who used wireless machines to receive and send encoded intelligence, WAAF teleprinter operators manned a vital, interference-free dissemination network. Referred to affectionately as 'tele-princesses', they had to be alert, quick and accurate.[6] WAAFs were required to attain the speed of sixty words per minute and, on top of the speed element, they also had to learn to use codes. Gladys Warnes learned to read International Teleprinter Code, also known as Murray code, which enabled messages to be sent as a series of electrical impulses. Gladys had to use a perforating machine, which punched combinations of five holes which together formed a letter. 'We had to read it at a rate of at least five words per minute and type accurately without any erasures', she says, and 'we also used the teleprinter switchboard'. Then there were Morse slip readers, who fed and typed the messages in plain language.[7] The conditions that teleprinter operators worked in often made their jobs quite stressful. Carol West describes the noise in her room as 'deafening', with an 'unbelievable' amount of paper spewing out.[8] The rooms had blacked-out windows and the teleprinter operators worked in artificial light, resulting in their needing sun lamp treatment to stave off vitamin D deficiency and any associated health problems.

Bletchley operators dealt with a huge number of signals, day and night, and worked extremely hard to keep the intelligence flowing. Upon arriving in the teleprinter room at Bletchley, which she had only heard referred to 'RAF Church Green', with no mention of its real name, Doreen Luke did not realise that she was going to form an integral link between the WAAFs collecting intelligence and those who could put it to operational use. Messages were never carried to her department by hand and were instead conveyed automatically through a chute. Doreen says:

> We operators only knew that we were a lifeline to the outside world, the senders and receivers. In contact with all the theatres of war, all our forces all over the world, whether land, sea or air. A communication section that reached wherever, or whoever, all highly secret material came through Bletchley Park. We knew so much and so little.

Operators never knew with whom they were in contact and Doreen often wondered if the operators from whom she was receiving intelligence were in enemy territory. She and her colleagues prepared the messages they'd received in their encoded state and passed them to their Flight Sergeant, who would despatch them to the Cypher Section. When the intelligence had been decoded and analysed, it was typed up as a report, often by WAAF typists. The reports were duplicated so that they could be sent to multiple recipients when necessary and copies could be filed and indexed, becoming part of a library of intelligence at Bletchley that could be accessed at a moment's notice. Filing clerks often possessed near-encyclopaedic knowledge of where things were in the index, which was useful if a fact in a new intelligence report needed to be corroborated or disproved. The reports were then sent to communications WAAFs to be transmitted to the relevant recipient.[9]

In addition to actually using communications equipment, WAAFs were employed as wireless mechanics, tasked with keeping the ever-important dissemination machines in good working order. It was vital that these machines did not break down and if they did, that they were up and running again as soon as possible – they were the link between Bletchley and its intelligence-hungry customers, including the operational commands that needed accurate information upon which to base decisions. WAAF wireless mechanics worked throughout the RAF, sometimes even on aircraft, to keep wireless equipment functioning effectively. Vera Collins was called to an aircraft whose wireless system was not working properly. Her training and accumulated experience meant that she had a pretty good idea, even before looking at the aircraft's system, what was wrong, so she was able to solve the problem before the pilot had even made it back to the crew room at the station. 'I felt I had struck a blow for women mechanics,' Vera says.[10] During Doris Brewster's first duty as the duty wireless mechanic, a fault was detected on the airfield telephone system. 'I felt like a doctor summoned to an urgent case,' Doris recalls. She gathered her tools and made her way outside, where she spent several hours tracing wires across the airfield. She found and fixed the fault and was asked if she could take a look at the beacon mechanism, as it appeared to be malfunctioning. 'Eventually with the aid of my nail file, the red winking eye once again gave out its position to overhead traffic,' she says.[11]

In charge of the WAAFs working in the dissemination of

intelligence at Bletchley were their WAAF officers. Posted to Bletchley after her intelligence commission, Felicity Ashbee's 'vague and romantic ideas' about 'blonde spies and secret agents' quickly faded after her arrival in 1941. Learning eventually that her boss was the renowned cryptographer Joshua Cooper, the head of the Air Section at the GC&CS, Felicity was surrounded by 'people without proper names or even identities'. Her job was to go through piles of intelligence, mostly the conversations of German pilots and soldiers logged by WAAFs at the listening stations, to check for lapses in security or coding that might reveal key information, such as which station the aircraft were operating from. Felicity found it 'almost uncanny' that a WAAF operator sitting in a van in a British meadow could be listening in on German soldiers talking to one another in their tanks in Russia, especially when one was once heard saying to another, 'Look out! There's a Russian over there by that tree. I'm not sure if he's dead or alive!'[12]

Though they may not have been 'Cypher Queens', the name given by the WAAFs to the code and cypher officers who carried out the more glamorised work of decoding and encoding incoming and outgoing intelligence at the GC&CS, the WAAFs constituted the vital link between Bletchley and the political and military decision-makers in Whitehall and the army, RAF and Royal Navy commands, who were determining how to direct the day-to-day fighting of the war. Where the air battle was concerned, this meant feeding information to RAF Fighter and Bomber Commands. Intelligence from Bletchley, combined with the invaluable work of the Dowding System, helped the RAF to keep track of Luftwaffe activity during the Battle of Britain. It also combined effectively with intelligence from aerial reconnaissance, often resulting in successful inter-service operations. The German battleship *Bismarck*, for instance, was tracked using photographic intelligence from reconnaissance and Ultra and was successfully sunk by the Royal Navy and the RAF.

The work that the WAAFs were doing was groundbreaking. The women were using brand new and evolving technology, sometimes before any of their male colleagues had even seen it, to pioneer new techniques and methods of intelligence collection, analysis and dissemination. Most WAAFs were aware of the importance of the intelligence that they were working with, even if they did not know the details of it. Y Service WAAFs were also occasionally tasked with monitoring British pilots while they were airborne, to carry out security checks. These recorded conversations were included in the logs Felicity Ashbee was given to check and the results, she found, 'were not too reassuring'. On some days, she found that the RAF pilots were 'giving things away left right and centre', usually due to code words being easily compromised when used in close proximity with ordinary phrases.[13] For all the worry and fear expressed by the British authorities over whether or not women could keep secrets sufficiently to be employed in intelligence work, often it was the WAAFs who were discovering security breaches made by their male colleagues. Whether airwomen or officers, the WAAFs worked very hard and extremely efficiently at Bletchley Park, collecting and disseminating intelligence that was vital to the British war effort and protecting British communications against enemy infiltration.

IN THE SHADOW OF ULTRA – BEHIND THE BLETCHLEY FEW

What happened at Bletchley Park was one of the best-kept secrets of the war, and, overwhelmingly, the WAAFs did their part to help keep it. While working at Bletchley, WAAF Sergeant Carol West was picked up by the RAF Police for a minor offence. When she informed them that she could not give them the location of her workplace, she was met with 'total disbelief'. Her pass simply said 'Station X', the deliberately vague name given to the shadowy mansion and its gated-off grounds, and when she continued to refuse to reveal anything further, she was marched in to see an officer and was only released after he had made a phone call to her superiors.[14] Secrecy was paramount above all else at Bletchley. Not content with the fact that all employees had signed the Official Secrets Act, the GC&CS gave a series of ominous and intimidating lectures and warnings regarding secrecy, even implying that if staff gave away information on their work, even to each other, they could be shot. The vast majority of the women at Bletchley, including the WAAFs, understood the importance of secrecy and did not ask questions of each other or of their superiors. Some personnel were not aware of exactly what it was they were doing and it was common for personnel in one part of the facility to have absolutely no idea what was happening in any of the other sections and to have limited understanding of the bigger picture at the park.

WAAFs did not need to see the bigger picture, however, to realise the importance of their work, and few grumbled about the strict secrecy requirements and extreme compartmentalisation at the vast codebreaking facility. Most were content to work as efficiently as they could within their own small section and did not resent the fact that they knew very little about what happened outside of it – they understood that wartime necessitated special conditions and secrecy was just an accepted part of the job.

The WAAFs took their vow of secrecy so seriously that many of them refused to speak about their work even after they had received permission to do so decades after the war had ended. This secrecy combined with other issues to keep them out of the Bletchley picture, even once the story came out in 1974.

Despite the fact that by the end of the war the majority of the workforce at Bletchley Park was female, it was still considered a man's world. Men occupied all of the senior positions and while some women did become supervisors, they generally supervised teams of other women. Heads of section were men and there was very limited opportunity for promotion for women.

Until recently, the narrative of Bletchley Park has focused on the famous men who worked there – men like Alan Turing and Joshua Cooper. In a highly compartmentalised, fanatically secret organisation like Bletchley, it is unusual to think of there being any kind of a limelight, and though Frederick Winterbotham's Ultra revelation in 1974 did cast one, it only ever illuminated the senior male codebreakers. The women who worked there in their thousands remained, for decades after 1945, hidden behind a few famous faces. In recent years, the narrative has extended to include some women at Bletchley, but still the net tends only to be cast over single individuals like Joan Clarke, the cryptanalyst who assisted Alan Turing and who was, for a brief period of time, engaged to him. The civilian women and the WRNS operators at Bletchley have made some gains in the telling of Bletchley's story, but the WAAFs rarely feature in historical memory of this extraordinary organisation. Wherever they were being afforded opportunities to contribute to British intelligence, the WAAFs were doing so in a meaningful and effective way, surprising those who had not thought it possible for them to work in the difficult conditions they were faced with.

Working in Hut 6, the centre for the decryption of Enigma

messages, Bletchley codebreaker Asa Briggs admitted that his work was 'dependent' on the radio interceptions carried out at Y stations and on these reaching him in Hut 6 via the communications network.[15] Though they may not have personally cracked the Enigma codes, the WAAFs constituted the first link in the chain at their Y listening stations, plucking German messages out of the air and forming another link by working in communications to ensure that they got to where they needed to go.

Among its many uses, Ultra intelligence helped the British military to monitor German preparations for Operation Sealion in 1940, provided confirmation that Sealion had been abandoned, supplied information on German troop and aircraft movements, delivered constant vital intelligence during the Battle of Britain (including Goering's order to commence Operation Eagle), enabled British scientists to develop radar countermeasures by supplying information on Luftwaffe navigational signals and gave valuable intelligence pertaining to the Normandy landings in the form of assessments of German defences. Speaking of Ultra's impact on D-Day, General Dwight D. Eisenhower expressed his appreciation in a letter to the Chief of the British Secret Service:

> The intelligence which has emanated from you before and during this campaign has been of priceless value to me. It has simplified my task as a commander enormously. It has saved thousands of British and American lives, and in no small way, contributed to the speed with which the enemy was routed and eventually forced to surrender.[16]

Eisenhower highlights just one instance where British intelligence directly contributed to the Allied victory in the Second World

War, and in their collection and dissemination of intelligence that resulted in Ultra, the WAAFs were a significant part of this contribution. Despite the fact that Ultra's success was owing undoubtedly to the success of the Y Service and the WAAF communications personnel, the work of the men and women in Y interception and communications is generally missing from most tellings of the Bletchley Park story. The intense secrecy surrounding the Y Service is perhaps partly to blame, but Bletchley functioned under equally as intense secrecy and its story has been told. It's more likely that the romanticised flashes of genius exhibited by men such as Alan Turing have captured the attention and imagination of the world, just as the rare and inspiring exploits of the Few fighter pilots did in the Battle of Britain. Hidden behind them, the WAAFs formed an integral component in the Bletchley intelligence machine.

7

BEHIND THE BOMBER BOYS: WAAFS IN BOMBER COMMAND

RAF BOMBER COMMAND IN THE SECOND WORLD WAR

Much of the burden of the defence of Britain throughout the Second World War rested on the shoulders of the Royal Air Force. The RAF's fight was not, however, limited to simply defending Britain and its interests. It also bore the responsibility of taking the offensive fight to the enemy – a task which fell largely to RAF Bomber Command.

Britain's bomber offensive against Nazi Germany would consume huge amounts of resources – money and men – in order to accomplish its aim to seriously impair Germany's fighting ability. At its inception in 1936, Bomber Command was relatively small and ineffective, a mere fraction of the powerful and destructive fighting force that it would become over the course of the war. Even in 1939–40, it did not possess the ability to seriously damage Germany, its 280 aircraft carrying out mostly strategic precision strikes with limited results. Growing steadily in size and strength, by 1942, with Air Chief Marshal Sir Arthur 'Bomber' Harris newly positioned at its helm, Bomber Command's ability to wreak havoc in Germany had begun to increase.

To accomplish the aim of diminishing Germany's ability to continue fighting the war, Bomber Command carried out raids designed to destroy specific industrial and military targets. In May 1943, for example, the infamous Dambusters used Barnes Wallis's specially engineered bouncing bombs to breach several dams in the industrialised Ruhr region. Bomber Command also used the more controversial tactic of area bombing – mass bombing of large areas with the intention of destroying as much property and personnel as possible – in lethal raids such as Operation Millennium, the first 'thousand-bomber raid', in which 1,047 bombers attacked Cologne in a single night. By 1945, Bomber Command was using its more than 1,500 aircraft to destroy enemy fuel and oil targets, crippling German production and seriously affecting its ability to continue to fight. Over the course of the war, more than 1 million people kept Bomber Command functioning, including both air and ground crews. These personnel came from around sixty different nations and were eventually joined in the offensive against Germany by the United States Eighth Air Force. Their efforts were a significant factor in the Allied victory in the Second World War. As with Fighter Command's flying Few, it is the 125,000 aircrew of Bomber Command who tend to be the most remembered and celebrated today. Of this number, 72 per cent were killed, seriously injured or interned by the enemy as prisoners of war. Over 44 per cent were killed in service, which gave Bomber Command the highest rate of attrition of any Allied unit.[1]

RAF Bomber Command was a key Allied weapon with the ability to reduce Germany's war potential, but in order to be able to do so, it needed timely and reliable intelligence on where and when to deploy its forces. The command's main report in 1945, 'The War in the Ether', commented that without the 'extraordinary range and accuracy' of intelligence with which it had been provided, 'no worthwhile [offensive] effort could have been possible'.[2] After the decision was taken to begin the strategic bombing of the enemy by night in May 1940, the young men of Bomber Command frequently flew long distances at night, sometimes in bad weather, and against effective and efficient enemy defences. Operations staff and aircrews worked closely with intelligence staff, the latter providing detailed information that was of the utmost importance to the successful execution of a raid. This information might be on enemy defences, tactics, weather or marking techniques and it could quite literally mean the difference between life and death, or success and failure. The pilots and aircrews of Bomber Command, the now-famous 'Bomber Boys', have deservedly received much attention, and the way in which they continuously faced intimidating and terrifying odds to take the war to the enemy must never be diminished or forgotten. Those brave young men who gave their lives to this end averaged an age of twenty-three years old when they died, and without doubt, their sacrifice contributed significantly to Allied victory in 1945. They deserve to be remembered and celebrated. In recent years, the ground and support crews of Bomber Command have begun to be recognised and commended for the part that they played in the command's operations, which would not have been possible without their tireless work. There is, however, one more group that was vital to Bomber Command's everyday operations and ultimate victory, a group which is usually missing from most tellings of the story – the personnel who worked to keep vital information flowing behind operations. Within this group, obscured from view but critical to victory, were a number of women.

BOMBER COMMAND AND WOMEN

So far, where history has remembered women working with Bomber Command, it has tended to be the women of the Air Transport Auxiliary who take centre stage. The ATA was a civilian organisation which tasked service pilots with ferrying aircraft between factories or maintenance facilities and frontline squadrons of the RAF and the Royal Navy. Over the course of the war, the ATA would employ 168 women, including the famous female pioneer Amy Johnson and a number of American female pilots. Initially only allowed to fly non-operational aircraft and paid 20 per cent of what their male colleagues earned, the 'ATA Girls' proved themselves to be extremely reliable and effective, and in July 1941 a Hurricane fighter was flown by a woman for the first time. Over a year later, first officer Lettice Curtis became the first woman to take to the skies flying a four-engined bomber, and by the end of the war women were being paid the same as the men of the ATA, flying Spitfires and most operational aircraft around the country to be deployed in operations.[3] The women of the ATA were truly groundbreaking and should be remembered as a vital part of British wartime fighter and bomber operations. Likely due to the subversive and glamorous nature of their work, they have become a recent point of fascination in British aviation history, and whenever women are included in popular tellings of the tales of the RAF, it is usually the ATA Girls who make the cut. They were not, however, the only women carrying out vital work behind Bomber Command's operations.

Hidden behind the Bomber Boys – but integral to their success – were many members of the Women's Auxiliary Air Force, working to collect and disseminate intelligence behind major offensive bombing operations. Members of the WAAF worked in various different capacities to provide intelligence towards Bomber Command operations. Some were involved in photographic intelligence, working towards the identification of targets for Allied bombing raids and in the assessment of these raids after they had taken place. There were also WAAFs working in intelligence roles within Bomber Command itself.

INTELLIGENCE OFFICERS AND WATCHKEEPERS

WAAFs were present and active behind the scenes before, during and after Allied bombing raids took place. There were four distinct stages to an operation: planning; briefing the aircrews; carrying out the operation; and debriefing and interrogating RAF crews after they returned. Heavily involved in the planning stage, WAAF intelligence officers prepared essential information which would aid the aircrews in carrying out their operations as effectively as possible. Intelligence officer Joan Baughan, for example, was responsible for keeping up-to-date information on enemy defences, including fighter aircraft, gun sites, balloons and searchlights. Working underground, she was required to keep her own large map of north-west Europe up to date, showing the disposition of the entire Luftwaffe presence in the area with particular emphasis on the positions of German night fighters. Her information came from Bletchley Park, likely sent by her WAAF colleagues working in communications there, via the duty WAAF Flight Sergeant who took calls coming into the Intelligence Section. The first thing Joan did every morning was to call Bletchley for the current German night fighter statistics. She was also required to keep the 'Blue Book' – a book of information which was taken to Winston Churchill at the weekends – up to date, and kept her own large books of statistics pertaining to raids.

These contained numbers and types of aircraft on each mission, losses, bomb loads, routes taken to targets, with times and information from returned pilot interrogations. Information usually came to Joan in teleprinted form, sometimes on a sheet up to sixteen-feet long, and it had to be read and reproduced as an 'interception and tactics report' for operational use. Joan enjoyed the work immensely and was aware of how important her contribution was: 'We were all so happy, wrapped up in the work that had to be done, as well as putting our heart and soul into it. We did not leave a single stone unturned, in case it caused death and sorrow.'[4]

Another of the roles filled by WAAFs at Bomber Command was that of watchkeeping. Watchkeepers worked alone in the operations room, under the jurisdiction of intelligence officers. WAAF watchkeeper Audrey Smith spent the whole day receiving broadcasts over scrambler phones and taking down the information onto three-ply teleprinter paper. Copies of the recorded information were given to the Commanding Officer of the station and to other relevant personnel and the information was logged in a large book which became the watchkeeper's 'bible'. At one end of the operations room, a large blackboard covered the wall, displaying received information on each squadron, including aircraft letters, the names of the Captain and crew members, payloads, estimated times of departure, time spent over targets and return times. In addition, the positions of aircraft were plotted on the central plotting table. Audrey recalls a 'tremendous thrill and pride to do the job', aware that the briefings given to bomber crews would contain the information she recorded.[5] These briefings were vital to the preservation of the lives of the crews and their aircraft, and the WAAFs worked tirelessly towards their effectiveness.

SIGNALS AND MAPS

Also involved in pre-raid planning were WAAF signals personnel like Eileen Smith. Upon arriving at RAF East Kirkby, an operational Bomber Command station home to 57 and 630 Squadrons and their Lancaster bombers, Eileen and her colleagues were given a strict security lecture and discovered that they would be working in a 'tomb-like building' without any windows. Eileen's work included the preparation of call signs for the aircrews. These were codenames for the crew members, used to identify them over the radio in place of their real names, and were distributed prior to the commencement of an operation. Eileen also typed, checked and distributed statistical data and figures before raids, to provide the crews with as much information as possible. She took her work very seriously, aware that the lives of the aircrews, many of whom she personally knew, depended upon her accuracy and secrecy.[6]

Grace Hall worked in the operations room at RAF Mildenhall, the 'nerve centre to and from which all secret and vital information was issued'. Her work in signals involved receiving target information for the coming night and passing it on to the relevant RAF personnel who could plan and execute the raids based on it. The information would be broadcast on the scrambler phone by the RAF Group controller to all of the stations within the group. The first time that Grace broadcast the information over the loudspeaker, she 'received an immediate and interesting variety of telephone calls, including one offer of marriage from the senior flying control officer', who was not used to working with 'golden voiced' WAAFs.[7] Both Eileen and Grace worked in vital roles preparing for Allied bombing raids, under conditions of extreme secrecy and often in tense atmospheres, highly charged with pre-raid anticipation.

Also involved in pre-raid planning were the WAAF map clerks. When Edna Skeen joined the WAAF aged eighteen, she was posted to RAF Scampton. There she worked alone in a large room lined from top to bottom with shelves, upon which were thousands of maps of varying scales and covering most of the world. Edna was tasked with cataloguing them and keeping them in good order and had to 'be able to put her hand on any particular one at a moment's notice'. She supplied Bomber Command navigators with maps and charts for their raids, which meant that often she knew of their destinations before they did. Known as the 'Map Queen', Edna was on duty for twenty-four hours a day, sleeping when the bomber crews were out on raids, and often the medical officer supplied her with caffeine tablets to keep her awake. Due to the fact that there was usually only one map clerk on each station, she had to leave a note saying where she was if she had time off and was frequently recalled to duty because the information she could provide so swiftly and ably was so critically needed.[8] Enid Purser, also a map clerk, found the responsibility of being one of the first to know the target and route for the night 'rather awesome'. Before a raid, she would pin up red tape on wall maps in the briefing room and in the intelligence officer's room, depicting the route the crews were to take and supplying them with a full set of maps to cover the entire route.[9] These were handed to the navigator and the bomb aimer, to aid navigation to and identification of the target. The WAAFs of Bomber Command were not simply supplying intelligence regarding operations – they were actively involved in aiding and enabling the execution of raids. Navigation and target identification could be difficult, especially when adverse weather conditions, cloud cover and enemy defences interfered. The more information a crew had prior to a raid, the more chance they stood of being successful and coming back alive.

Some WAAFs worked to provide intelligence as Allied raids were in progress. As a radio telephone operator at a bomber station, Doris McCreight's routine was to report for duty in the control tower just before dark, from where she could see the Lancaster bombers ready for take-off. Behind her was a blackboard listing the names of the crews and their aircraft identification information, with estimated times for take-off and return. Doris would watch the Lancasters take off in rotation, and once RAF aircraft were a certain distance away from their base, air radio traffic silence was imposed to prevent enemy listeners from gleaning information on the raid. As RAF aircraft were returning to England following a raid, Doris's job was to search for their call-ins and reports of safe arrival, or to pick up an SOS signal if an aircraft had been downed or damaged. The RAF needed this information to be able to keep operations against the enemy running efficiently and to be able to economise valuable aircraft and trained crew. Doris was the first point of contact for returning and potentially injured or endangered British aircrews and she, like her colleagues in signals, took her work very seriously. She used two microphones – one for long range and one for local frequency. When an aircraft appeared over the British coast on its way home from a raid, it would contact Doris as it progressed into local frequency range and she would land it according to orders given by the control officer. Priority was given to aircraft with injured crew aboard. If aircraft were damaged during the raid by enemy anti-aircraft artillery, they would often limp home, their crews in need of emergency medical attention as soon as possible upon landing – it would often be the responsibility of WAAF personnel to arrange this and assist with ensuring the safe landing of the aircraft. 'There were always those who did not return,' Doris remembers, 'and I would spend the rest of the night listening out for a mayday call. When all hope was gone, it was sad to see the blackboard wiped clean.'[10] Doris was also tasked with delivering the 'flimsies' to the briefing room prior to an operation. These were the various radio codes and frequencies that were due to be used in the operation, printed onto very thin edible rice paper so that if crews were shot down, they could swallow this highly secret information to keep it out of enemy hands. Bomber Command's notoriously dangerous work and very high rate of loss meant that stations could be emotionally charged, and the aircrews came to rely on the personnel who they knew, to some extent, held their lives in their hands. Far from being distrusted, the WAAFs sometimes represented a tangible constant, upon which the bombers could rely in a job where they never knew who would return from raids and who would not. After each briefing, the aircrew on her station would touch Edna Skeen's shoulder and say, 'See you tonight,' a ritual that they considered to be good luck.[11] Involved in highly secret and sensitive work behind the scenes of what was potentially Britain's most important offensive weapon, the WAAFs proved themselves to be trustworthy and reliable in the various roles they filled in Bomber Command.

POST-RAID INTELLIGENCE

While some WAAFs worked hard towards the collection and dissemination of intelligence prior to and during RAF bombing raids, others focused on post-raid intelligence. As soon as an aircrew had returned safely, its members were escorted to the operations block, where they would be interrogated by an intelligence officer. It was the officer's job to draw information out of the crew by getting them to share their individual experiences of the night's raid. The airmen might possess knowledge that could be useful to the RAF, even if they weren't aware of it. Quizzing them after a raid could yield information on the level of success the raid had achieved, the operational consequences of this success (or lack of it), an idea of whether or not another raid was needed and British losses during the raid, for example.

Initially, the idea of using WAAF officers to brief and interrogate aircrews was unpopular. Returned aircrews were often exhausted and emotional, sometimes traumatised, having perhaps watched friends and colleagues sustain injuries or be killed. It was thought that men might have a difficult time processing these emotions in front of female colleagues, and that the women themselves might not be able to deal with the terrible things they were likely to hear. As Bomber Command's workload increased, however, and more and more crews were returning, necessity dictated that the RAF trialled WAAF interrogators, and they were found to be very effective. By piecing together the recollections of the bomb-aimer, the pilot, the tail-gunner, the navigator and the other crew members, a WAAF interrogator could write a concise and accurate report which provided a detailed narrative of the role of a particular aircraft in a raid. As expected, interrogations were often difficult, but rather than becoming upset by harrowing stories, the WAAF interrogators treated the aircrews with patience and sensitivity, piecing together information on bombing successes and the positions and numbers of shot-down planes, both enemy and Allied. The very attribute that the RAF feared might inhibit the WAAFs – an inclination towards emotion – often caused them to be better at their work, and this was certainly the case in interrogations as crews were grateful for their sensitivity and understanding.

The Allied bombing campaign relied heavily on air intelligence from bomb damage assessment reports, which provided information on the effectiveness of individual raids and on the aggregate effectiveness of the campaign in support of the RAF's overall strategy. Where photographic intelligence staff contributed bomb damage assessment reports from reconnaissance and interpretation, WAAF watchkeepers at Bomber Command contributed information to the overall assessment of the progress of the Allied bombing campaign, specifically in the form of up-to-date information on aircrew and aircraft losses. Ground raid reports generated by WAAF interrogators provided information on enemy positions, both en route and at the target, and on enemy anti-aircraft defences, fighters, attacks, airfields, lights and flares, smoke screens, decoys, dummies and observations of aircraft shot down. Often the resulting report was so detailed that it could be three to four feet long, earning it the nickname 'the toilet-roll'.[12] Through their work in intelligence, Bomber Command WAAFs helped to provide vital information on the course of the war and contributed to both the success of the Allied offensive and the Allied understanding of the war's progress.

OPERATION MILLENNIUM

Where the WAAFs were present behind the 'Few' of Fighter Command during the Battle of Britain, they were also present behind Bomber Command's famous pilots in some of the most well-known operations of the Second World War. Early wartime Bomber Command operations, both during daylight and at night, saw the

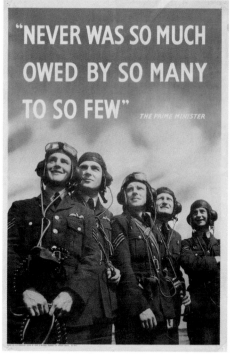

Convicted of being a spy for Germany in the First World War, Mata Hari was executed by firing squad and became the archetypal 'femme fatale', the spy seductress. © Pictorial Press Ltd / Alamy Stock Photo

The famous poster depicting 'the Few' – the pilots of the Royal Air Force who defended Britain against the Luftwaffe, as named in Winston Churchill's famous speech in August 1940.
© Ian Dagnall Computing / Alamy Stock Photo

Female pilots of the Air Transport Auxiliary preparing for a flight. © Popperfoto via Getty Images

Denise Miley, a WAAF radar operator, plotting aircraft at Bawdsey. © IWM CH 15332

WAAF personnel training in radar work. © IWM CH 7529

A Dowding System operations room, with WAAF plotters working busily at the central map table. © IWM CH 11887

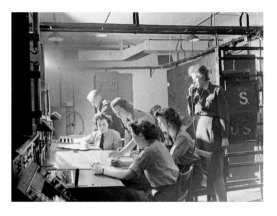

A WAAF operator working in the receiving room at Bawdsey Chain Home radar station. © IWM CH 15331

The Air Sea Rescue Service pull a downed pilot from the sea after being directed to his location by radar technology. © IWM CH 12389

WAAF plotters and officers in a Dowding System operations room. © IWM CH 7698

WAAF telephonists at work.
© IWM CH 10242

A WAAF Y Service flight sergeant collaborates with an RAF colleague.
© IWM CH 16682

A WAAF wireless operator receives a message in Morse code.
© IWM CH 7673

A WAAF intelligence officer interrogates a returned Bomber Command aircrew. © IWM CH 12687

WAAF and RAF map personnel at Bomber Command HQ.
© IWM CH 13707

Wing Commander Guy Gibson, distinguished RAF bomber pilot and leader of the Dambusters (617 Squadron).
© IWM MH 6673

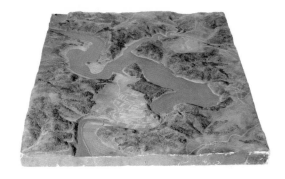

Model of the Eder Dam, one of the three targets for Operation Chastise, the famous Dambusters raid. © IWM MH 27710

King George VI visits the model of the Möhne Dam, prepared ahead of Operation Chastise to help with the execution of the raid. © IWM CH 9924

Working in photographic intelligence at Medmenham, Constance Babington Smith was the first person to identify the deadly V-weapons on aerial photographs. © TopFoto

At Medmenham, Millicent Laws plots the exact position at which each photograph had been taken on a map.
© Medmenham Collection

Jeanne Adams examines photographs and uses a set square to ensure the correct scale is plotted on maps. © Medmenham Collection

Sarah Churchill, daughter of wartime Prime Minister Winston Churchill, was a plotter and then a photographic interpreter. © Medmenham Collection

The Airfields Section hard at work at Medmenham. © Medmenham Collection

Famous wartime propaganda poster discouraging military personnel from speaking about sensitive and secret information around women.
© IWM Art.IWM PST 4095

Members of the WAAF serve tea to RAF aircrews. © IWM CH 8804

RAF sustaining an unacceptable rate of loss. As a result, with the appointment of Air Marshal Arthur Harris as Commander-in-Chief of Bomber Command in February 1942, British bombing tactics switched to mass area bombing and the destruction of certain civilian targets, as opposed to focusing on purely industrial targets. 'Bomber Harris', as he came to be known, presented Churchill with his proposal to 'put over the maximum possible force of bombers on a single and extremely important town in Germany with a view to wiping it out in one night, or at most two'. The objective being to 'cause a complete and uncontrollable conflagration throughout the target area', Harris planned to send 1,000 aircraft on each raid – an idea to which Churchill responded enthusiastically.[13] Code-named 'Operation Millennium', the 'thousand-bomber raids' were designed also to 'strike a severe blow to the morale of the German people in addition to causing unprecedented damage' to important industrial cities in Germany. Operation Millennium began with a raid on Cologne on the night of 30 May 1942, in which 1,047 aircraft took part. Of these, 868 hit the city, with a combined total of 1,455 tonnes of bombs.[14]

Following the raid on Cologne, RAF photographic reconnaissance aircraft flew over the city to carry out bomb damage assessment. The task took several attempts, as the fire cloud took days to disperse and expose the carnage and devastation below. The vast amount of damage done to the city was accompanied by the displacement of its civilian population. German records show that 469 people were confirmed dead and 5,027 were injured. Up until this point, all of the RAF's raids on Cologne throughout the war had killed a combined total of 139 people and injured 277. In addition, 45,132 people were bombed out of their homes and approximately 20 per cent of Cologne's population left the city.[15] This mass refugee exodus posed a great risk to the German authorities, striking a sig-nificant blow to morale across the country and boosting that of the British and of Bomber Command's aircrews. The raid gave the British the feeling that they were hitting back after the indiscrimi-nate Blitz they had endured at the Luftwaffe's hands. It is true that Bomber Command suffered its highest rate of loss of the war so far for a single operation during this raid, with forty-one aircraft and 198 aircrew lost (3.9 per cent of its total strength), plus fifty-eight crew taken as prisoners of war.[16] With more aircraft and men taking part than in any other operation, however, these figures are rela-tive. Operation Millennium was undoubtedly, to some extent, a success and constituted a 'major contribution to the survival and ultimate success' of Bomber Command, hinting at the beginning of the end for Nazi Germany.[17] Working at RAF Mildenhall, from where thirty-five aircraft had taken off to participate in the raid on Cologne, Grace Hall remembers the rejoicing when all of them returned safely.[18] WAAF intelligence officer Joan Baughan, on the other hand, remembers 'those poor dear chaps' and the heavy losses incurred and found the raid 'pretty tense'.[19] Both women and their WAAF colleagues were instrumental in the successful execution of the raid, providing intelligence to aircrews that assisted with the operation and guided them safely home.

OPERATION CHASTISE – THE DAMBUSTERS

In addition to being present in intelligence roles behind the scenes in the thousand-bomber raids, WAAFs were also present behind the famous 'Dambusters' raid, officially named 'Operation Chastise'.[20] The plan entailed a precision strike on three dams in Germany's in-dustrial Ruhr valley – the Möhne, Eder and Sorpe Dams – with the aim of destroying them to disrupt the vital supply of water in the region and damage German war production. What would today be termed a 'surgical strike', the raid would be very different from mass area bombing and required extensive preparation and planning. Though plans to take out the dams had first appeared in 1937, the RAF lacked a sufficient method by which to be able to do so. The dams being industrially important, they were well protected with torpedo nets to prevent underwater attacks and anti-aircraft defences, including guns, to protect against aerial attacks. By the spring of 1943, however, the RAF possessed both a suitable weapon with which to attack and the aircraft and crew capable of deploying it. The plan was to release a special bomb, designed by British engineer Barnes Wallis, that could 'skip' across the water, like a stone skipping across the surface of a lake. The bomb, codenamed 'Upkeep', was drum-shaped and had to be dropped from a height of sixty feet, at a ground speed of 232 miles per hour.[21] It would then skip across the water's surface, eventually reaching the wall of the dam, where it would detonate. Upkeep could not be carried by a normal aircraft and instead several Lancaster bombers were specially modified to deploy it. The raid would also require a specially trained crew and in late March 1943, 617 Squadron, codenamed 'Squadron X', was formed to carry out the task. Led by Wing Commander Guy Gibson and consisting of crew members from Britain, the US, Canada, Australia and New Zealand, 617 Squadron underwent specialist training to carry out low-level flying at night to drop their strange payload, all while navigating and avoiding enemy defences. The mission was dangerous and difficult. The approach to the dams would leave the Allied aircraft exposed, navigating hilly terrain with problematic obstacles in their paths. In order to successfully pull it off, in addition to their specialist training, 617 Squadron's crews needed a mass of information on the dams and their surroundings. It fell to the WAAFs to supply this.

Bomber Command intelligence officer Joan Baughan worked on gathering intelligence on the Ruhr valley area. This meant accumulating information on enemy defences and other elements that could cause difficulty for the aircrews. The Sorpe Dam, for instance, had steep inclines at each end of its reservoir and a church spire stood directly in the path of attack. Educating the aircrews with as much up-to-date information as possible could mean the difference between success and failure, and between life and death.[22] Edna Skeen's job was to provide maps of the Ruhr valley to the crews, which they could study to the last detail to familiarise themselves with the area over which they would be flying. Edna's work was so important that one week before the raid was due to take place, she was locked in her office and had to sleep and eat there. The crew might need to check the maps again at a moment's notice, and it was imperative that the details of the raid were kept secret. If she needed to use the bathroom, she was required to give the key to her office to Guy Gibson or the station commander, and at all times the two men needed to know where she was. Edna supplied 617 Squadron with maps right up until the night of the raid, when she watched the aircraft take off and thought to herself, 'This will make history and I have had a part in it.' For her role as a member of the intelligence staff behind Operation Chastise, she was awarded a Mention in Despatches and seven days' leave. She was also the first woman to be honoured in the war by her town, and once the raid and her place in it became public knowledge, she was presented with an inscribed gold watch and received a free local pass to cinemas.[23]

Vera Tassell was on duty as a watchkeeper the night of the Dambusters raid and remembers it as 'by far the most exciting and impressive' experience of her WAAF career. She had watched 617 Squadron training for their extraordinary operation, under intense security, and as the aircraft took off to carry out the raid, she wondered why the bomb doors of the aircraft did not seem to be able to close over the unusually shaped cargo it carried. When she went on duty in the operations room a short while later, the 'suppressed excitement' intensified with the arrival of the Commander-in-Chief of Bomber Command, Arthur Harris, in an unprecedented 'invasion' by the top brass. Vera recalls the 'dead silence' in the operations room, until the code word signifying the success of the attack on the first dam was brought in by a signals officer. Harris gave a 'slight grimace', which Vera presumed to be a smile, and he asked her to 'get Washington' on the telephone, which she duly did.[24]

Operation Chastise was extremely secret and the WAAFs involved behind the scenes, though carrying out work crucial to its success, did not all have access to the exact details of the operation prior to the night of the raid. Joan, Edna and Vera, for example, did not know exactly what was going to happen until it was taking place, despite the importance of their work to the aircrews' success. There was one WAAF operator, however, who 'knew all there was to know of the proposed raid'. The only woman involved in the detailed overall planning of Operation Chastise, intelligence officer Fay Gillon attended all of the briefings with the squadron and was heavily involved in their training.[25]

Most of the Dambusters' core team were recruited by Guy Gibson himself. Serving as a WAAF intelligence officer in RAF Scampton's resident unit, 57 Squadron, 21-year-old Fay Gillon was no exception.

Fay was working as a crew interrogator for Bomber Command when 617 Squadron arrived to begin training for the dams raid and soon after his arrival, Guy Gibson sent for her. Gibson's 'misgivings about the general inferiority of the opposite sex' were 'made even plainer' when he asked Fay if she could keep a secret and added, 'I don't often ask women this.' He had also been careful to check Fay's personal details and when he asked her about her husband, she surmised that he had chosen her because she would be unlikely to have boyfriends with whom she might discuss squadron matters. In addition, her husband was away fighting in Italy, so she had no one with whom she could discuss secret information.[26] Gibson assigned Fay an office next to that of the navigation officer, Jack Leggo, with whom she would become good friends, and had it decorated and furnished for her. He explained that her duties would be to liaise with the organisers of the flying training programme and with HQ 5 Group, as low-flying routes had to be cleared with them. The squadron needed to train at low altitudes, due to the height at which Upkeep needed to be dropped over the dams, and such low flying often caused problems and protests from the locals. Due to the highly secret nature of their operation, 617 Squadron were kept separate from the rest of the group and Fay became their essential link with the rest of Scampton, though she herself was cut off from the outside world once the training commenced.[27] Gibson informed Fay of the details of his intended practice flights and she passed them along to HQ 5 Group, who were 'not at all pleased that they were going to be flying around Lincoln Cathedral at a hundred feet'. Understandably, the locals were equally as unhappy, as the low flying upset cattle and caused other problems and discomforts. Fay's attempts to pacify the people around Scampton were made harder by the difficulty in justifying low flying without being allowed to explain why it was necessary. Recognising what a difficult and stressful job she had been tasked with, Gibson asked her to accompany the squadron on a practice flight over a group of dams and reservoirs in Wales in order to show her what it was all towards. Fay was the first passenger to fly with the Dambusters and found the flight, at sixty feet above the water, to be 'absolutely fantastic'.[28] On 14 May 1943, the Chief of the Air Staff signalled that Operation Chastise should proceed.[29] That night, Gibson ran a tactical exercise designed to be as close as possible to the real thing and Fay was again invited as a passenger. Prior to the flight, she helped to give out the Bomber Command codes and flimsies and observed the navigator laying out the maps and checking the compass. She describes her experience of the exercise:

A signal from the Wing Commander [Gibson] and all three of us simultaneously creeping down the runway and gathering speed. The terrific roar and power of the engines, then the last bump and we are airborne. Me clambering into the flight engineer's seat and watching eagerly and intently as we go rushing out to sea over Mablethorpe, and into the gathering dusk, gliding right down, practically into the drink. Dropping a smoke float to check the wind, and then a burst of firing from the WC's plane, followed by a burst from all three of us, missing each other by inches. Then, suddenly, the target, glistening in the moonlight. The voice of the Wing Commander coming over the VHF ... Then a huge explosion and a flash of light. Right on target. Then our turn. Mick doing a big circle to get into position, grim determination on his face, and Jack and I with our noses glued to the Perspex. Down, down, twenty feet more, ten feet more, five feet more, steady, steady on an altitude of sixty feet and the run along the water. 'Bomb's gone!' from Bob, and then pull up, up into the sky at full revs. (After landing and taxi) Then the crew bursting out with cracks and jokes and clambering out into the waiting bus. Looking around at their faces and noticing happiness and satisfaction on all of them. Wonderful, absolutely wizard. Back to the mess and a pint of beer and eggs and bacon for supper with the boys. Then the Wing Commander arriving with a beam of appreciation on his face. 'Bloody good show boys.'[30]

BEHIND THE DAMBUSTERS 'FEW'

The level of success of the Dambusters raid is the subject of a lot of historical debate. On one hand, it did not cause lasting damage to the dams as the Germans were able to carry out swift repairs. Squadron 617 lost eight out of its nineteen aircraft and 749 foreign workers in a labour camp were killed. On the other, the consequent widespread flooding and damage in the Ruhr valley resulted in the necessitation of repairs which were only achieved at great expense to other enemy projects. Even if only temporarily, the damage caused did disrupt industrial traffic and production, which could only aid the Allied cause.[31] One of the most positive outcomes for the Allies was the boost to the morale of Bomber Command aircrews and the British and Allied populations. The raid was described in the *Baltimore News-Post* as a 'spectacular feat' which resulted in 'Germany's greatest catastrophe of the war', and the London *Daily Telegraph* reported that it 'may prove to be the greatest industrial disaster yet inflicted on Germany in this war'.[32] Whatever the material consequences of the raid, the complexity of the task and the skill with which 617 Squadron carried it out was, like the work of Fighter Command's courageous aircrew, an inspirational piece of tangible hope to the Allied nations in 1943, and the story of Guy Gibson and the Dambusters is still widely known, told and celebrated today. Missing from this story, though, are the WAAFs like Fay Gillon, whose vital and valuable contributions to the famous raid have gone largely unnoticed, keeping them hidden behind the few men like Gibson and the aircrews of the 617 Squadron. The raid could not have taken place without them.

In a memorandum to the Cabinet on 3 September 1940, Churchill said, 'The Fighters are our salvation, but the Bombers alone provide our means of victory.'[33] Bomber Command's efforts were vital to victory in 1945, in that its continual bombing of Germany forced the enemy to expend and divert valuable resources and to effectively open a second front long before D-Day. The approval, planning and implementation of all of Bomber Command's operations were subject to many important factors, including overall strategy, operational conditions, priorities in the wider war and the selection of significant bombing targets, to name a few. Many of these individual factors were consistently affected by and reliant upon accurate and timely intelligence. The collection and dissemination of information and its incorporation into Bomber Command's operational planning proved critical to the war effort and to the eventual Allied victory in 1945. The contribution of the WAAFs in Bomber Command has historically been ignored, but in their secret and hidden roles, the WAAFs helped to provide the intelligence that was so necessary to the British and Allied offensives, directly affecting the successful execution of the Bomber Command operations that would help to secure victory in 1945.

8

A BIRD'S EYE VIEW: WAAFS IN PHOTOGRAPHIC INTELLIGENCE

THE HISTORY OF PHOTOGRAPHIC INTELLIGENCE

In 1938, German General Werner Freiherr von Fritsch expressed his opinion that 'the military organisation with the best aerial reconnaissance would win the next war'.[1] But aerial reconnaissance was not a new tactical tool in the 1930s. Indeed, by 1915, military maps prepared predominantly from aerial photographs were being used very effectively by both sides in the First World War. To begin with, aerial photographs contributed mostly to map-making. When Lieutenant Hugh Hamshaw Thomas joined the Royal Flying Corps in 1917, he began to produce maps of the whole of southern Palestine, which proved to be of 'decisive value' due to their information on Turkish fortifications and batteries. In the second half of the First World War, aerial reconnaissance was used successfully to map trenches, detect camouflage and mark the positions of gun batteries and poison gas generators. As camera equipment and photographic technique continued to develop, so too did the process of deriving information from photographs – a process which came to be known as photographic intelligence. By 1939, great changes had taken place in the field of military intelligence, largely due to such technological development. Though traditional methods of gathering intelligence had not been replaced, they were supplemented very effectively by photographic reconnaissance and interpretation, in the same way as signals and communications intelligence had been supplemented by the use of the telephone and wireless telegraphy. Photographic intelligence was deemed critically useful as another potential world war loomed, and it would provide vital information to the Allies that would save many lives and have a profound impact on the course of the war. Many of the personnel responsible for its collection, analysis and dissemination would be members of the WAAF.

THE ART OF PHOTOGRAPHIC INTELLIGENCE

During the Second World War, photographic intelligence provided a vast wealth of accurate intelligence at significant speed. Such intelligence was produced via the combined arts of photographic reconnaissance and interpretation. Aerial reconnaissance was carried out by RAF pilots, who often flew alone and unarmed over occupied countries, taking millions of photographs over the course of the war. The pictures meant very little to the untrained eye and were only operationally useful once they had been interpreted. Photographic interpreters spent hours poring over images that had been taken from great heights, using their own type of what WAAF operator Constance Babington Smith called a 'secret language' to make sense of them.[2]

In 1940, the RAF Photographic Reconnaissance Unit was based at Heston Aerodrome and the Photographic Interpretation Unit at Wembley. Due to heavy bombing, both sites were forced to move and the PRU made its new home at Benson near Oxford. Renamed No. 1 Photographic Reconnaissance Unit, it was equipped with specially modified Supermarine Spitfires, Bristol Blenheims, Lockheed Hudsons and de Havilland Mosquitos, which carried cameras rather than weapons, with the specific purpose of undertaking aerial reconnaissance over enemy-occupied territory. Such reconnaissance was deemed vitally important and aircraft were supplied despite the constant and desperate needs of Fighter Command, whose 'Few' were fighting to keep Britain free from German occupation.

The Central Interpretation Unit (CIU) moved in 1940 to RAF Medmenham, sited at Danesfield House in Buckinghamshire, which became the headquarters of Allied photographic intelligence for the rest of the war. From 1942 to 1943, the CIU expanded and was involved in the planning of virtually all Allied operations. From 1942, US service personnel were also employed at Medmenham, which was formally recognised in 1944 when the CIU was renamed the Allied Central Interpretation Unit. By VE Day, the print library held millions of photographs, covering the whole of Europe, the Middle East and the Far East, and photographic reconnaissance and interpretation was one of the largest and most significant sources of intelligence on enemy actions and intentions. The ACIU was populated by members of the British, American and Canadian forces, and despite the varied backgrounds of its personnel, all of them were completely integrated and the unit operated remarkably smoothly. Rather unusually, this total integration extended to women, and members of the WAAF formed a significant proportion of the highly skilled specialists at RAF Medmenham. The women ranked completely equal with their male colleagues and in some cases even served as their superiors. Despite this unusual level of equality, the WAAFs of the CIU have, much like their colleagues in the Dowding System, the Y Service and Bletchley Park, gone for the most part unnoticed in the history of the RAF and British intelligence. Integral to important contributions that the ACIU made to the ultimate Allied victory in the Second World War, the Medmenham WAAFs were among the first British personnel to know the details of significant Allied operations, including the Dambusters raid and the D-Day landings.

THE STRUCTURE OF PHOTOGRAPHIC INTELLIGENCE

Though RAF Medmenham was designed to be the Central Interpretation Unit for all three British armed services and the Allied forces, it was administered by the RAF and a large percentage of its officers were from the air force. It received all photographic images taken by Allied aircraft, both of enemy territory (used for intelligence purposes) and those taken over Britain (for 'purposes of construction, planning, camouflage and organising defences'). The CIU had 'almost identically the same objectives' as the Y Service; to provide the intelligence staffs with 'the best information about the enemy' that could be obtained, but through the medium of air photographs rather than signals interception.[3] It did this on a strict supply and demand basis, via a clear process. Demand came from its 'customers' – the Admiralty, the War Office, the Air Ministry, the Ministry of Economic Warfare (the Special Operations Executive), the navy, army and air force commands, the Supreme Headquarters Allied Expeditionary Force and various overseas commands, which would request photographic intelligence pertaining to their various interests. Through the joint efforts of the PRU and the ACIU, Medmenham would then supply information to their customers, sometimes also identifying information of importance that had not been requested and distributing it to the relevant commands and departments for operational use. Customers could request information to corroborate intelligence reports that they had already compiled from other sources, or in situations where they were unsure of what the enemy was doing and had no other way of attempting to find out. In addition to aircraft specifically equipped for aerial photography, every bomber and coastal patrol aircraft carried a camera, and photographic coverage was 'so total and so frequent that remarkably complete information could be deduced on many subjects'.[4]

THE RECRUITMENT OF WAAFS FOR PHOTOGRAPHIC INTELLIGENCE

With the Second World War approaching fast, the value of photographic intelligence was quickly realised and the Directorate of Intelligence created a special section, designed to prepare intelligence officers to carry out such work. Despite this, in September 1939 there were only eight capable officers.[5] The earliest establishment of the CIU (then called the Photographic Intelligence Unit) found that, like most other domestically based intelligence departments, it lacked men due to the demands of war. The chronic shortage of interpretation officers left the PIU with little choice but to recruit WAAFs, and by mid-1940, WAAF officers were serving at Wembley.

Though the WAAF administration was 'arrogantly despised' by some technical officers within RAF photographic intelligence, the WAAFs posted to Medmenham met with a different experience to many of their colleagues in other areas of air intelligence.[6] After the war, many of them recounted that they did not experience the usual 'old boy network' or 'glass ceiling' that women usually encountered in the British military and intelligence services, and found that rather their work was 'genuinely merit-based'. WAAF operator Mollie Thompson said, 'You did your job, you were capable and whether you were a man or a woman did not matter.'[7] This unusual situation is possibly due in part to the fact that many WAAFs at Medmenham were commissioned as officers. Some WAAFs, like Ursula Powys-Lybbe, served in the WAAF ranks first and were then recruited and commissioned as photographic intelligence (PI) officers. In other cases, where the need for PI officers was more urgent, women could be employed as civilians first. In 1940, four early recruits – Angus Wilson, Cynthia Wood, Mary MacLean and Honor Clements – joined as civilians and were eventually commissioned straight into the WAAF. Commissions were required for photographic interpreters because of the kind of work that the WAAFs would be doing. Upon their accuracy and ability rested the success or failure of a planned operation, as well as the lives of the men taking part in it.[8] It could happen that when a watch was being maintained on the German fleet, the 'disposition of the entire British Fleet would wait upon the word of a single junior photographic interpreter'.[9] Some experience, the Air Ministry thought, might endow WAAFs with the confidence and credibility to be able to make such decisions. Wing Commander Sidney Cotton, one of the 'fathers' of modern photographic intelligence, believed that women naturally possessed the necessary attributes for PI work, his reasoning being that 'looking through magnifying glasses at minute objects in a photograph required the patience of Job and the skill of a good darner of socks'.[10]

The WAAFs who came to work in PI came from very diverse backgrounds. Some had yet to reach eighteen years old and others, like Dorothy Garrod, were older than the maximum age for women's conscription, forty-three. Dorothy was an archaeologist specialising in the Palaeolithic period and the first woman to hold an Oxbridge chair as Disney Professor of Archaeology at the University of Cambridge from 1938 to 1952. From 1941 to 1945, she took a leave of absence from her university post to serve at RAF Medmenham. Unlike many other trades in the WAAF, PI work required a candidate to possess certain personal qualities that could not be taught in a training course, of which Dorothy had in spades. These included a good visual memory, the ability to sketch, attention to detail, a mind that naturally asked questions and an appreciation of the significance of objects, and students were required to become 'curious in the unusual'.[11] As such, WAAFs were given responsibility for decision-making in every aspect of gathering, analysing and disseminating intelligence at Medmenham.

THE PROCESS OF PHOTOGRAPHIC INTERPRETATION

As soon as a reconnaissance aircraft had landed, the film from its camera would be removed so photographic staff could develop it. The aircraft's pilot would often be debriefed and quizzed by a WAAF operator, so as to provide context and ensure accuracy of details when analysing the photographs. Interpretation of photographs could be easier and quicker if the location they depicted had been recorded accurately, and sometimes it was possible to issue initial intelligence reports from the basic combination of the camera negatives and reports from pilots. As soon as they had been printed, photographs were given to a team of WAAF plotters, who recorded where the reconnaissance flights, or 'sorties', had taken place. Working at a large table, they 'inked on to map sheets a whole series of overlapping rectangles, each representing an exposure, that looked like a pack of cards pushed over sideways'.[12] This work had the effect of speeding up interpretation, as it provided a very quick, simple view of the area covered by each print.

Photographs were then filed by date and within two hours of the aircraft landing, 'first-phase' intelligence reports had been produced from the prints. For each sortie, two sets of prints and their corresponding reports were produced and one was sent to RAF Medmenham with the negatives. The other set was sent to Nuneham Park, RAF Medmenham's satellite site, for additional analysis where necessary. At Medmenham, another team of WAAF plotters recorded the locations of sorties and the images and first-phase reports were reviewed to produce more detailed, in-depth intelligence. Within twenty-four hours of the aircraft landing, a detailed intelligence report and the photographs of a sortie had been produced and disseminated to the relevant Allied operational command or intelligence organisation. Photographic interpreters at Medmenham were trained to identify anything that looked as if it could be a possible threat. The threat would be assessed as to its type and then the second-phase report and photographs pertaining to it would be passed to third-phase interpreters. These were specialist, more focused interpreters who had detailed knowledge and experience of specific areas of industry or weaponry. In cases where threats were positively identified, regular reconnaissance sorties would be carried out over the area in question, so that they could be compared to monitor any changes or progress that the enemy was making on each particular perceived threat.

The full process of photographic interpretation

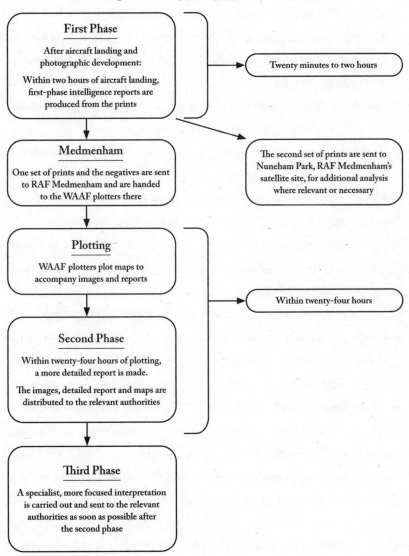

First Phase

After aircraft landing and
photographic development:

Within two hours of aircraft landing,
first-phase intelligence reports are
produced from the prints

Twenty minutes to two hours

Medmenham

One set of prints and the negatives are sent
to RAF Medmenham and are handed
to the WAAF plotters there

The second set of prints are sent to
Nuneham Park, RAF Medmenham's
satellite site, for additional analysis
where relevant or necessary

Plotting

WAAF plotters plot maps to
accompany images and reports

Within twenty-four hours

Second Phase

Within twenty-four hours of plotting,
a more detailed report is made.

The images, detailed report and maps are
distributed to the relevant authorities

Third Phase

A specialist, more focused interpretation
is carried out and sent to the relevant
authorities as soon as possible after
the second phase

Working in conditions of extreme secrecy, WAAFs at Medmenham provided intelligence on a vast array of subjects, including information on enemy airfields, troop movements, anti-aircraft artillery, shipping and U-boat production and movements, radar installations, camouflage and decoys, military installations, indus-trial work and development and the aircraft industry.

WAAFs also received requests for intelligence from the Special Operations Executive and the SIS, on potential landing, parachute-drop and pick-up locations and operations pertaining to the deployment of agents behind enemy lines. These requests were clas-sified as 'most secret', meaning that they came under no category and carried no serial number, and often photographic interpret-ers were not told the intended purpose of what they were looking for. When asked to locate areas that were open but surrounded by cover, it was often clear to them that they were looking for 'drop zones' and landing zones, where Allied aircraft could drop agents and supplies behind enemy lines or land aircraft to drop off or pick up agents. Medmenham also carried out constant surveillance of German airfields, railways and naval units and made frequent bomb damage assessment reports. It was this kind of surveillance that enabled the identification of around a thousand converted invasion barges in Channel ports and moving down coastal canals, intended to land German troops in Britain in 1940. This intelligence provid-ed the warning on 6 September 1940 that Operation Sealion was imminent.[13] Eventually, different sections were created at Medmen-ham for individual subjects, and the WAAFs there were involved in this work in a variety of capacities, all of them highly secret.

PHOTOGRAPHIC STAFF AND PLOTTERS

Pamela Howie was nineteen years old when she became a photo-graphic processor in the WAAF. After she had learned how to load film into an aerial camera, and had practised installing and retriev-ing it from aircraft in both daylight and in the dark, she was posted to RAF Benson. Pamela and her colleagues developed, printed and titled the many films from returning reconnaissance aircraft, and the work was not without risk. She developed metol poisoning as a result of frequent exposure to the chemicals used in the developing of photographs and had to be moved to a section at Benson that titled the prints for ease of interpretation and filing. The importance of photographic intelligence meant that it was carried out almost constantly and the workload of the WAAFs involved was heavy. Pamela found it 'very tiring and exacting', fully aware of the importance of total accuracy, and by 2.30 a.m. she often found herself 'working like an automaton'.[14] Also working in the photographic section of a reconnaissance station, Millicent Laws plotted the exact position at which each photograph had been taken on a map. This could be a difficult job, as the only guide that plotters had to work with was a trace that the pilot had made over his map to show his route, often drawn hastily and without much attention to detail. This wasn't the only difficulty the WAAFs endured at work – as active RAF bases, PR stations were vulnerable to enemy bombing. A landmine fell on the mess at the PR station at Heston, forcing Millicent and her colleagues to move to Benson. She remembers her officer training course, where the WAAF Air Commandant gave a final speech, in which she said that the WAAFs 'must have guts'.[15]

Once the first-phase plotting and initial report had been completed, a set of prints was sent to Medmenham, where they were plotted again by the WAAFs there. As the war continued, these WAAFs became overworked and an experienced plotter could average 500 image plots in five hours – the record was 900 images in three and a half hours.[16] Section officer Jeanne Adams recalls using a stereoscope to obtain three-dimensional visualisations of structures on images and a set square to plot in order to get the right scale.[17] As was the case with WAAFs learning to use complicated radar and communications equipment in the Dowding System and Y Service, some knowledge of mathematics and science would have proven useful, but few women had any experience or training in either. This lack of technical knowledge, however, hardly ever impeded the WAAFs in their photographic work. When they needed to, they sought help and, in some cases, made records and guides to help those learning behind them. In one such case, Ursula Powys-Lybbe wrote a 'Child's Guide in the Use of the Slide Rule', including illustrations, which taught other WAAFs a simple mantra – 'size, shape, shadow, tone and associated features'.[18] Despite the new challenges it presented them with and its demanding nature, WAAFs like Jeanne Adams found PI work 'fascinating' and 'very exciting', particularly because the photographs they were given to plot could be different every day. Jeanne says that at one point, she thought she could identify any port from Norway to the south of France 'at a glance'.[19] Aware of the crucial need for secrecy because of the importance of their work, the WAAF plotters kept their secrets very effectively, once again defying the expectations of their RAF superiors.

THE MODEL MAKERS

Another of the important uses of photographic intelligence was the construction of models, used for operational briefing purposes. The Model Making Section at RAF Medmenham was responsible for producing hundreds of scale models prior to some of the most famous military operations of the Second World War. Work on a model could commence eight to nine months before an operation was intended to take place. Several photographic sorties of the target area would be taken by reconnaissance pilots and these photographs were then studied stereoscopically for information pertaining to elevation. Detailed plans were produced on the construction of land form and topographical information, and measurements were taken to ensure that the model was perfectly to scale. From this study of aerial photographs, models were produced which showed alterations in ground levels and surface detail, making possible the 'meticulous planning and briefing' necessary for an operation to be successful.

Operations for which models were produced included the Combined Operations raid on the port of St Nazaire in March 1942, the attack on Bruneval radar station, attacks on the German battleship *Tirpitz* by midget submarines and Operation Torch, the North African landings.[20] The most famous operations for which models were produced, predominantly by the WAAFs, were the Dambusters raid on the Ruhr dams and the Normandy D-Day landings.

MEDMENHAM WAAFS AND THE DAMBUSTERS

In preparation for Operation Chastise, Medmenham's model makers were tasked with providing accurate information on various physical elements of the Ruhr valley dams and with constructing scale models of them. Regular sorties were flown over the dams, and Kathleen Mary Franck was among the WAAFs involved in producing the models for Bomber Command. She used linoleum to make tiny buildings and trees, which she found 'very, very fiddly'. Using maps to establish the scale, she and her colleagues found they could make the models quite easily, constructing them in sections. Working around the clock, they used the masses of aerial photography to get every detail as accurate as possible, even down to how the seasons affected the landscape, so that the pilots of 617 Squadron who would be bombing the dams would know exactly what they were looking for on the night of the raid. Kathleen and her WAAF colleagues 'knew the idea was to blow up the dams', and though they were not privy to any details of the operation, they were aware of the importance of the implications of its success.[21]

On the night of 16–17 May 1943, Guy Gibson and his squadron carried out Operation Chastise, the raid that earned them the name the 'Dambusters'. Elspeth Macalister was on duty and described it as 'one of the most exciting' nights of her life.[22] Jeanne Adams was equally as excited to see the water gushing from the Möhne Dam in photographs taken soon after the raid, and Susan Bendon was tasked with preparing an album of photographs showing the sequence of the raids for King George VI.[23] Photographic reconnaissance and interpretation was a unique form of intelligence work, in that the WAAFs were able to see the tangible results of their efforts. The Air Ministry had expressed concern that women would not be able to emotionally handle knowing that they had been involved in causing death and destruction to others, or seeing such horrors up close, but rather than sending them into an emotional frenzy as was feared, the knowledge that their work had led to Allied success appeared to bring them great satisfaction.

MEDMENHAM AND D-DAY

Following the Trident Conference in Washington DC in May 1943, the Allies decided to launch the invasion of German-occupied western Europe, codenamed 'Operation Overlord'. With more than 150,000 troops to land, Churchill admitted that Overlord was the 'most complicated and difficult' operation undertaken and it would inevitably necessitate a massive amount of organisation.[24] In preparation for the landings, the WAAFs at Medmenham were set to work gathering information from aerial reconnaissance photographs on possible airfields and beaches where Allied aircraft, parachute troops and vessels could land. WAAF officer Ursula Powys-Lybbe was seconded from Medmenham in the summer of 1942 to the secretive Theatre Intelligence Section in Somerset House, London, where specially selected photographic interpreters worked to provide intelligence in the planning of Operation Overlord. She was asked to submit preliminary reports on the selection and suitability of landing areas, which would then be assessed by geologists and other experts before a final decision was taken. Her contribution to the vast intelligence picture required was accompanied by information and effort from many different sources and though it appeared small in the grand scheme of things, it was vital. Photography was one of the most efficient providers of intelligence in planning the invasion, particularly when the Germans began to construct huge defences in preparation for the landings they knew were imminent. Their defensive 'Atlantic Wall' ran along the northern coast of France and the Low Countries and was photographed by Allied reconnaissance aircraft regularly. Photographs showed anti-invasion defences such as spiked 'hedgehogs', tripods and mines buried in harbours and beaches, and due to the volume of these in the Pas de Calais area, Normandy was chosen for the landings.

Two years before the landings would take place, photographic interpreters at Medmenham began recording extensive information on sea depths and tide levels throughout the year on France's northern coastline, on beach gravel and sand to aid decisions over tank and vehicle manoeuvrability, on locations for possible airstrips to be built after the initial invasion, on enemy defences, communications and transport routes in and around Normandy and on ports, harbours and estuaries.[25] The WAAFs at Medmenham examined photographs to construct models and maps, providing information that was critical to the success of Overlord – over 8.5 million photographs were produced for D-Day preparations alone.[26] Mary Harrison worked on the construction of models for the D-Day landings, though the names of the locations were removed from the maps she was given to work with, to ensure absolute secrecy. Mary found that the models were 'not the most exciting' because the areas she was modelling were very flat, but the attention to detail had to be exact – any detail could help troops to identify where they were and the route they needed to take into occupied territory upon landing.[27]

On the evening of 5 June 1944, Jeanne Adams was relaxing with friends in Marlow, Buckinghamshire, when a 'strange whooshing, rumbling noise' began, accompanied by the smell of petrol. The sky quickly filled with aircraft and gliders, and with 'total air superiority', thousands of fighters and bombers headed for the south coast of England to begin their massive aerial assault on targets around the Normandy beaches. Despite her insight at Medmenham into the preparations for Overlord, Jeanne was 'still unprepared' for this sight, as tight security had kept details of the timing of the invasion a secret. It was obvious that evening, though, that D-Day was nigh and Jeanne realised:

All those days and nights we had spent poring over the photographs – this is what it had all been for. Every beach, every port and every cliff on the Normandy coast had been plotted and modelled by us and here it was at last! It was the invasion that I like to think was the beginning of the end of the war. I shall never, ever, forget that evening.[28]

The Normandy landings took place the following day and, as Jeanne states, they spelled the first step towards the liberation of western Europe and the defeat of Nazi Germany. After the landings, General Eisenhower, the Supreme Commander of the Supreme Headquarters of the Allied Expeditionary Force, congratulated Medmenham's personnel on their production of hundreds of models for Overlord and explained that their work had contributed significantly to the success of the operation. The staff at the ACIU, he advised, could claim that 'theirs was a real contribution to the ultimate victory'.[29]

WAAF PHOTOGRAPHIC INTERPRETERS

Serving as second- and third-phase photographic interpreters, WAAFs at RAF Medmenham needed to be good at decision-making, sometimes in very short spaces of time. Reviewing photographs and first-phase intelligence reports, they had the responsibility of writing more detailed reports based on their findings, which would often result in tactical decisions and affect the future planning of the British commands – directly affecting the course of the war. Loss of life was a distinct possibility if an inaccurate report led to action. Information essential to Allied strategic planning was being constantly compiled at Medmenham, by WAAFs with certain specialisations. Some of these WAAFs were in the unique position of being able to serve as section heads, commanding staff that included members of the RAF. One such WAAF member was flight officer Mollie Thompson, head of Medmenham's Camouflage Section. An expert on camouflage, she oversaw both the surveillance of German camouflage attempts, which sought to cloak industry, transport and military installations to shield them from Allied bombing, and the effective deployment of British camouflage. Working with the Decoy Section, Mollie and her team provided Bomber Command with up-to-date intelligence on 'dummy' bombing targets, designed to deter them from real ones and directly contributing to the success of the Allied offensive bombing campaign.[30]

Second in command to the head of the Night Photography Section, Bernard Babington Smith, flight officer Loyalty Howard was also in a position of considerable responsibility. Interpreting photographs taken over enemy-occupied territory by bomber crews at night, Loyalty was looking for information on the enemy's night defences as well as carrying out 'detailed analysis of the position of aircraft at the time of bombing', including the location of fires started by night bombings.[31] In doing so, she noticed that bombs destined for the Krupp steelworks in the Ruhr valley were consistently dropping six miles from the target. Studying comparative sorties, Loyalty eventually concluded that Lake Baldeneysee had been drained. Bodies of water could be a useful landmark to bomber crews, as they appeared on maps and reflected light from the moon, which aided navigation and identification of nearby targets. The Germans realised that RAF pilots were using the lake as a 'watermark' – a sort of landmark – to help them to identify the Krupp steelworks nearby. They drained the lake, tricking Bomber Command navigators into using a bend in the river instead, which meant that their bombs were actually falling six miles off target.[32] Loyalty's successful discovery contributed to more accurate Allied bombing. The third in command of the section, Arthur Lionel Sockett, found her to be a 'very efficient' superior officer and was perturbed by the patronising behaviour that visiting high-level military officers exhibited towards her.[33]

As head of the Airfields Section at Medmenham, section officer Ursula Powys-Lybbe and her team focused their efforts on deciphering what the Luftwaffe was doing, both currently and in terms of future intentions. The construction and development of airfields and their associated buildings and communications equipment could indicate intended purpose and therefore revealed something about what the Luftwaffe was planning. A routine report on an airfield included details on the dimensions of the landing areas, the number, length and orientation of the runways, details of the serviceability of runways, the position of fuel-storage tanks, water supply and ammunition storage, communications and the number and size of hangars, workshops and accommodation for personnel. Ursula felt a 'tremendous enthusiasm' and an 'almost fanatical desire' to succeed in her work, 'blended with a deep anxiety as to the outcome'. Her anxiety stemmed mostly from the fact that as an older WAAF operator, she did not have the initial knowledge of the subject and had left education years before some of her colleagues.[34] WAAF operator Diana Cussons worked with Ursula in the Airfields Section and shared the same difficulties:

> We followed the elite of the German Navy and that was really so difficult. I am no mathematician but we were told to find out not only where they were but also to pinpoint them. It sometimes took hours to do this if all you had on the photos was a rocky speck on one side and a huge German warship on the other. You had to give where it was and if you had no indication from the pilot it was very time consuming. You came off duty mentally as well as physically exhausted.

Despite the unfamiliar and difficult work, Diana thought the team always managed very well and was fascinated by her work. It was, to her, the 'most wonderful thing to be really "in" the war'.[35] Ursula shared this sentiment, finding her work to contain 'never-ending excitement' and immense satisfaction.[36] The section had a tough job, particularly when the Air Ministry withheld certain information – which it often did out of concern that if photographic interpreters thought they knew what they were looking for, it might influence what they thought they were seeing. Having this information, Ursula believed, could have 'proved useful and time saving', but the section functioned very effectively nonetheless.[37] Inevitably, the Airfields Section's work often overlapped with that of the Aircraft Section, if an aircraft was spotted on an airfield and needed to be identified.

After passing the exams to become a photographic interpreter in January 1941, WAAF operator Constance Babington Smith used her spare time to study *Jane's All the World's Aircraft*, producing a report on Italian aircraft for her own reference.[38] To her surprise, her Squadron Leader asked to see the report, and upon reviewing it, he asked Constance to create the Aircraft Interpretation Section at Medmenham. The section's task was to identify new types of hostile aircraft and to provide as much information on them as possible, including the location of the sighting, the dimensions of the aircraft, the number being manufactured and what they appeared to be designed for.[39] This task was extremely difficult, as interpreters were working with the unknown and often had nothing to compare their images to. War acted as a catalyst for technological development and innovation, and brand-new or experimental aircraft would, of course, not look like anything else the Aircraft Section's personnel had ever seen. Most of the few WAAF section heads at

Medmenham were joined by an RAF officer of equal rank, who would act as the nominal head of the section even if their technical knowledge of its subject was lacking or completely non-existent. Constance, however, was unique in that she had 'sufficient strength of character, an extraordinary singleness of purpose together with total dedication to the task, mixed in with a modicum of determination necessary to be able to assume sole command of the new section', which she did until the end of the war. Under her command, the Aircraft Section was recognised as being 'of first class efficiency and reliability' and built up a comprehensive dossier on the state of the German aircraft industry, so that aircraft assembly factories could be destroyed before they became operational.[40] The personnel of the Aircraft Section at Medmenham worked extremely well together with Constance in charge and their achievements formed a vitally important contribution to the Allied war effort.

THE SECRET WEAPONS THREAT

In early 1943, reports of secret German weapons trials reached London, causing great concern because of a package that had arrived on the desk of British scientist R. V. Jones in 1939. Delivered anonymously to the British naval attaché in Oslo, the package contained a report that warned of German experimental work on remote-controlled rocket-driven gliders, being developed at an experimental establishment called Peenemünde.[41] The report was circulated to the three service ministries, but it was decided that it was a hoax designed by the Germans to distract the Allies, and the matter was disregarded. In addition to the new reports of enemy activity on suspected glider bombs in early 1943, a War Office briefing declared that for a rocket to be able to reach London from the

French coast, it would need to be launched from a 'sharply inclined projector about a hundred yards long'.[42] The evidence pointed to the threat having become significantly more serious, and it prompted the Chiefs of Staff to appoint an investigator-in-chief – Duncan Sandys.[43] The Air Ministry immediately instructed Medmenham to begin a search for anything that might be linked to Germany's secret weapons trials, and photographic intelligence was identified as being of paramount importance, as it alone could provide unbiased, irrefutable information on a threat that no one, save its creators, had ever seen. When a sortie flown on 23 June 1943 showed two actual rockets lying horizontally on road vehicles at the Peenemünde experimental site, Churchill ordered that PI be enabled by 'every means possible to make a maximum contribution' to the long-range secret weapons investigation, which was codenamed 'Bodyline'.[44] The photographic interpreters at Medmenham were instructed to look for anything that might pertain to a long-range projector, or a firing ramp, as per the War Office briefing.

After two rockets had been identified by the Bodyline investigation, Constance Babington Smith was briefed to watch for anything out of the ordinary on the incoming photographs of aircraft. Though she wasn't officially involved in Bodyline, Constance decided to investigate the photographs from 23 June herself. On them, she spotted 'four little tailless aeroplanes', which she says 'looked queer enough to satisfy anybody'.[45] The little aircraft were identified to be Messerschmitt liquid-rocket fighters, known as Me 163s, and were the only rocket-powered fighter to enter operational service during the Second World War. Resulting Bodyline interpretation reports concluded that the aircraft were probably jet propelled, due to the 'single fan-shaped marks … of an unusual kind' that appeared on the ground around them when they took off.[46] Having positively identified the Me 163s, Constance then looked at sorties prior to 23 June and noticed 'pale blurred little shapes' of the same description accompanied by similar probable jet marks on some of the photographs. Duncan Sandys had already informed the War Cabinet of suspicions that the development of jet-propelled aircraft was likely proceeding alongside work on rockets and Constance's find, largely attributable to her own initiative and ability, confirmed these suspicions to be true.[47] The interpretation report explained the science that enabled the identification of jet-propelled technology:

> As soon as the projectile leaves the rails the expelled gases strike the front wall face of the earthed-up rail which may be assured to be rounded. An eddy effect is thus set up which may account for the marks on either side of the launching point. As the projectile rises and gets further from the end of the rail, the gases are expelled directly towards the ground, making the mark in front of the rail. The localisation of this blast effect is perhaps explained by the fact that the acceleration may be very considerable.[48]

The early identification of the Me 163 meant that Allied aircrews could be briefed on how to counter it and enabled the Aircraft Section to locate other sites where the ominous little aircraft were being used.[49]

In November 1943, the Bodyline investigation was renamed 'Crossbow' and Constance Babington Smith was officially involved. It was a time of confusion for the photographic interpreters at Medmenham, in part because of the discovery of the 'ski sites'.[50] At the beginning of the month, London had received intelligence from an agent on the ground that a French construction firm had been working on eight sites in the Pas de Calais region of northern

France. The Bois Carré sites, as they came to be known, each had three long, narrow buildings that had the appearance of a ski-board lying on its side. Somewhat more alarmingly, they also each had a pair of rails inclined at an angle of about ten degrees to the horizontal, 'lined up in the direction of London'.[51] Initially unaware of the existence of these rails, Constance Babington Smith was tasked with looking for a very small aircraft which might be pilotless, as intelligence had warned of the existence of German pilotless aircraft. Once again studying the photographs which had yielded the knowledge of the Me 163s, Constance identified an 'absurd little object' on them, which appeared to be a 'midget aircraft' in a corner behind the hangars.[52] This she named the Peenemünde 20 – also known as the V-1.[53] Continuing her search for more of the Peenemünde 20s, Constance requested back covers of the area. By the end of November, ninety-five ski sites had been identified through aerial reconnaissance and interpretation, with rails pointing towards London, Plymouth and Bristol.

Douglas Kendall, who replaced Duncan Sandys as head of the investigation in September 1943, was convinced that the rails were intended to launch flying bombs. Constance searched a large volume of back covers for more evidence of Peenemünde 20s, and based on the fact that she'd found the first one by a building, she began to study buildings on all of the photographs she looked at. Buildings were the domain of the Industry and Army Sections at Medmenham, but Constance relied on her own initiative and intelligence to conduct the search. Still unaware of the existence of the Bois Carré launching rails, she was surprised to find on one of the photographs what looked like four long 'catapult' structures. She could tell that the structures were ramped upwards because there were shadows where they had been banked up with earth. Unaware of Kendall's report, she took the find to the Industry Section and was informed that the ramps were 'something to do with the dredging equipment' in the area next to the water, which was also depicted on the photographs.[54] The officer she spoke to was 'just a trifle impatient' at her suggestion that the ramps might be flying bomb related, but their explanation 'did not seem reasonable' to Constance.[55] She showed the photographs to Kendall, who recognised the ramps immediately. He urged her to continue her work and Constance requested the most recent cover of the area in the picture. The newest sortie revealed the very same ramps, but there was something else on this picture. On one of the ramps there was a 'tiny cruciform shape', a 'midget' aircraft that seemed to be in position for launching. Thanks to Constance and the team at Medmenham, it was confirmed the next morning that the most imminent enemy threat was at last 'established beyond doubt' – it was to be a V-1 flying bomb.[56]

The Vergeltungswaffe 1, or 'Vengeance Weapon' 1, carried an 850-kilogram warhead and was guided to its target by autopilot technology. It could travel at 400 miles per hour and was launched from a specially constructed inclined ramp.[57] The sound of a V-1 approaching was a 'dreadful' memory for WAAF operator Doreen Luke for many years after the war and caused her 'heart to throb with fear'.[58] Mary Knight was a child at Woodford County High School in July 1944 and remembers a teacher being posted as a lookout on the roof to watch for approaching V-1s. One morning the lookout heard the trademark noise of the flying bomb, which has often been likened to an 'old-fashioned motorbike without a silencer', and sounded the bell.[59] Perhaps the most alarming characteristic of the V-1 was the way in which its engine would suddenly cut out, signalling imminent detonation, leaving just a few seconds for those beneath it to attempt to take cover. Mary was injured in the scramble for cover, and bore a scar on her leg for the rest of her life, but was fortunate to survive the experience.[60] Upon detonation, a V-1 caused blast damage over an area of around 400 to 600 yards in each direction, a huge blast wave rippling out from the epicentre.[61]

In December 1943, Constance Babington Smith became the first Allied person to detect and confirm that the V-1 was the dreaded secret weapon for which Churchill had ordered the search. She was a 'pioneer interpreter' in more ways than one.[62] In her unique position as head of the Aircraft Section at Medmenham without an RAF nominal head beside her, she intelligently and conscientiously worked to locate the threat by going above and beyond what was asked or expected of her. By searching outside of the parameters of her own section, she located the V-1 in a position where the Industry Section had jurisdiction and questioned their incorrect assessment of the launching ramps despite their impatience and frustration with her. To locate a previously unidentified aircraft was a difficult task, but to do so against the conviction of another entire section at Medmenham required a high level of ability, knowledge and confidence. Possessing all of these qualities and many more, Constance, along with her team, contributed intelligence that saved many lives and directly impeded the German war effort. A total of ninety-six 'ski sites' were eventually identified, each capable of housing at least twenty flying bombs at any one time. It seemed likely to photographic interpreters that the possible target for launchings was around 2,000 bombs in a 24-hour period and that the Germans had originally planned a 'really heavy bombardment'.[63] By the end of December 1943, every single ski site had been destroyed by Allied bombing. As a result, the 'potential menace' of the V-1s that would have been fired from them at London, Birmingham, Portsmouth, certain Bristol Channel ports and the south coast of England was eliminated, and the first round of the battle against Hitler's secret weapons was a definite victory for the Allies.[64]

BOMB DAMAGE ASSESSMENT

Where Constance Babington Smith and her colleagues worked daily towards the defence of Britain, other WAAFs at Medmenham worked towards the Allied offensive. Myra Collyer was posted to Medmenham in July 1943 and was assigned to the Progress Section. Myra was one of three WAAF officers in the section, working for a time with WAAF section officer Sarah Oliver, Winston Churchill's daughter. The section's task consisted of producing bomb damage assessment reports following Allied bombing raids. Myra's job was to assemble photographs from reconnaissance sorties flown after raids had taken place, and Sarah would then draft intelligence reports based on what they showed.[65] Myra then typed the reports for distribution, and if the reports recommended that the area be bombed again, Bomber Command made use of them in resulting operations. Her constant exposure to secret information on Allied bombing intentions meant that when a raid was on, Myra was not allowed to leave the room and had to be escorted by an RAF officer if she wished to use the bathroom.[66] Bomb damage assessment was important because it affected Allied strategic bombing target identification, the Allied understanding of German industrial strength and the provision of assistance to bomber aircraft in navigating their way towards and away from targets on raids. In all three capacities, it directly affected the course of the war from both the Allied and Axis perspectives, as did the work of the WAAFs towards it.

Bomb damage assessment intelligence reports identified the damage done to an area by a bombing raid and then they also made recommendations as to whether or not the area should be bombed again. In the case of the Peenemünde experimental establishment, for example, a sortie flown the day after a bombing raid reported that four buildings had been damaged or destroyed, at least five fires were still burning, smoke was still issuing from various places and at least fifteen craters could be seen on the railway lines.[67] Depending on the quality of the photographs, it could be difficult to assess what damage a raid had actually resulted in, and WAAF photographic interpreters involved in this work were under tremendous pressure to be precise and accurate. WAAF operator Stella Palmer, a bomb damage assessment officer for Bomber Command, remembered being 'pressurized by the Station Commander to publish glowing reports of glorious successes', which was difficult if WAAFs found no trace of damage on the post-raid photographs. Stella found that if she reported that little to no damage had been done, she was accused of 'minimising the results' of a raid and no one believed the reports.[68] The worst part for her was having to inform bomber crews that they had not hit their targets, as she fully realised the great danger they were in and understood their hatred of having to worry about reconnaissance at the same time as carrying out their main mission. The photography actually increased the danger the crews faced, as the film carried by the aircraft was highly flammable, and it was not possible to discharge it from the plane once it was airborne. It was especially tragic for Stella when a crew would limp back with dead or wounded members, only to be informed that they hadn't even been close to the target. Stella was aware that for bomber crews, who risked their lives every time they went on a raid, it might be quite galling to be told by a woman who sat at a desk all day that they had not done the job properly. WAAFs in bomb damage assessment had to be accurate and decisive, contributing to major operational decisions through their work, with the knowledge that their decisions would affect the morale and the safety of the Bomber Command aircrews. It was hard work accompanied with a high level of responsibility and pressure to produce results – results which were not within their control. Nevertheless, they worked with efficiency and accuracy, a necessary and important support to the famous 'Bomber Boys' upon whom the Allied advance weighed so heavily.

A JOB WELL DONE

The work of the WAAFs in PI was vast and varying, and their work saved lives and aided the Allied war effort. An Air Ministry News Service bulletin in September 1944 read: 'These girls have done a fine job and have played a vital part in warning us of the enemy's intentions. If it hadn't been for their accurate and thorough work much valuable information might have been missed.' The bulletin refers to Constance Babington Smith, citing her as 'the first to notice unusual features' on the photographs of Peenemünde in May 1943 and as 'responsible for drawing the attention of the intelligence authorities to the speck of a miniature aircraft which was eventually proved to be a flying bomb'.[69]

During the D-Day landings, all photographic reconnaissance other than that pertaining to the Allied invasion and advance was temporarily halted. This lapse in gathering intelligence on the V-weapons gave the enemy enough time to successfully complete work on some of the sites, and on 13 June 1944, the first V-1 landed in Britain. Douglas Kendall recorded 6,184 deaths as a result of the V-1s that did fall over Britain. In addition, he recorded 18,000 injured and 750,000 houses damaged or destroyed. These statistics were the result of around a hundred V-1 launchings in every 24-hour period, for the duration of the V-1 attacks.[70] The enemy had planned to fire 2,000 V-1s per 24-hour period, and it was largely thanks to the early identification of the weapon and the sites where it was being manufactured that the German target was not achieved. Had the enemy been able to attack Britain with flying bombs at the rate it had planned to, it might have altered the course of the war. Many more lives would have been lost and homes destroyed, and it is arguable also that the preparations for D-Day may not have been possible. General Eisenhower commented:

> It seemed likely that, if the enemy had succeeded in perfecting and using these new weapons six months earlier than he did, our invasion of Europe would have proved exceedingly difficult, perhaps impossible. I feel sure that if he had succeeded in using these weapons over a six-month period, and particularly if he had made the Portsmouth–Southampton area one of his principal targets, Overlord might have been written off.[71]

In the fight against the V-1s and in the preparations for D-Day, photographic evidence proved to be one of the most important and reliable sources of intelligence. From a total of 1,715 personnel at Medmenham in 1944, 1,400 were RAF and WAAF officers.[72] The WAAFs within this number were recognised as having done extremely valuable work, displaying devotion to duty, initiative and imaginative thinking on a daily basis. As stated by Marshal of the Royal Air Force Lord Arthur Tedder, the contribution of photographic intelligence to the ultimate success of the Allied cause, and the part of the WAAFs within it, was 'quite incalculable'.[73]

9

BEHIND THE LINES: WAAFS IN THE SPECIAL OPERATIONS EXECUTIVE

THE SPECIAL OPERATIONS EXECUTIVE

While most WAAFs working in intelligence did so from inside Britain, a handful operated behind enemy lines in German-occupied territory. Created in July 1940, the Special Operations Executive was instructed by Churchill to 'set Europe ablaze' by conducting espionage and aiding, supporting and helping to develop resistance movements.[1] By 1945, the SOE's networks of agents spread across occupied Europe and the Far East, consisting of over 13,000 people. The circumstances of Hitler's war, Churchill argued, were unique and called for a unique response. M. R. D. Foot, the official historian of the SOE, described it as 'true to the tradition of English eccentricity', the kind of thing that 'looks odd at the time, and eminently sensible later', something that Mycroft Holmes or Captain Hornblower might have gone for.[2] Consequently, the SOE did not find many friends in the intelligence community, where organisations like MI5 and the SIS objected to the methods and approaches it employed. Its subversive nature, they claimed, was 'on par with the Nazis' and was ungentlemanly. Dubbing it his 'ministry of ungentlemanly warfare', Churchill argued that the British were not fighting a gentlemanly enemy and that it was necessary to revert to irregular warfare if the Allies were to stand any chance of defeating the Nazis.[3] The SOE's methods, however, were not the only thing bothering the traditionally minded British armed and security services. The SOE was also 'irregular' and 'unorthodox' in that it sent women agents into Nazi-occupied territory.[4] A large amount of the publicity that the SOE has received since the Second World War is due to this unusual fact. Prior to 1939, women had been limited to domestic roles at home and support-based roles in war. They had served as nurses on the front lines, but the idea of sending them into 'the most dangerous form of armed combat imaginable', without even the protection of a uniform to keep them from being shot if caught, was certainly irregular in 1940.[5]

The SOE was divided into sections, each one covering a specific country. The French Section, known as F-Section, focused on operations in occupied France. F-Section sent thirty-nine women to France during the war and of them, fifteen were members of the WAAF. F-Section's main mission was to prepare the French Resistance to aid the planned Allied landings, by training them, helping them to recruit and supplying them with arms, money and aircraft. Straying from the clerical and nursing roles usually filled by women in war, these thirty-nine women were, Churchill ordered, to be treated 'on a perfect equality with men'.[6] The SOE was designed to deploy agents behind enemy lines, with the intention of carrying out sabotage work – destroying transport systems, war production sites and other strategic targets and lending assistance to resistance movements, both in terms of morale and physical strength. The SOE also collected various forms of intelligence, including information on the location of downed Allied pilots and strategic bombing targets for Allied air forces.

VERA ATKINS AND THE RECRUITMENT OF WOMEN

The supervising officer of F-Section's female agents was Vera M. Atkins. The only female superior officer at F-Section, Vera was in a similar situation to her thirty-nine female agents. In September 1941, Colonel Maurice Buckmaster was appointed head of F-Section. Buckmaster promoted Vera (albeit informally) to deputy director of F-Section and eventually formally to the rank of intelligence officer. Vera was absolutely integral to the smooth-running of the section. She could speak French, German, English and Romanian and was fiercely anti-Nazi. Like the women she would supervise, Vera's social conscience inspired her to seek a way in which she could serve in a position that would enable her to constructively oppose the Third Reich. She often worked eighteen-hour days, in a multifaceted role. Vera helped to select agents, used her 'encyclopaedic knowledge' of wartime France to invent cover stories for them, was involved in their training, personally briefed them and saw them off at the airfield when they were deployed in virtually every case.[7] While her agents were gone, she personally handled their affairs and their money, often writing to their families regularly. When they returned, she debriefed them, and when, in 1945, 118 of F-Section's operatives were recorded as missing presumed killed, she conducted detailed investigations into what had happened to them. Vera was responsible for more than 400 agents, but she was most intimately associated with the thirty-nine women, 'her girls'.[8] She felt the strain of being responsible for them, stating that 'the realisation that they were going off on a very dangerous mission' while she would remain safely in Britain did bother her 'very much'.[9]

Vera personally pushed for the inclusion of female agents in F-Section, and after encountering resistance from most official directions, she was finally authorised to send women into occupied France in 1942. Pragmatic and realistic, she was fortunate in that Buckmaster shared her view that there were some tasks that women could perform better than men. She said, 'I've always found personally that being a woman has great advantages if you know how to play the thing right and I believe that all the girls who went out had the same feeling.' She believed that women were better at talking their way out of situations and delivering cover stories and that they were 'wonderful wireless operators'.[10] The average life of a wireless operator in France was around six weeks before they were caught. The German authorities became adept at tracking them down via their wireless signals and used mobile detection vans to follow the signals to their source. The high rate of arrest rendered the need for wireless operators pressing and constant. It became harder and harder to find able-bodied men to perform the task, as they were usually engaged in other war work. The wireless link between England and France 'had to be preserved at all costs' and was deemed vital to any potential victory, and so to preserve it, women were sent to France as clandestine wireless operators and couriers.[11] The lack of men to fill these positions was not Vera's only argument for recruiting women. Though the headquarters staff had 'misgivings', they had to agree with her that women were 'less suspect' and 'seemingly innocent' and could merge more easily into the areas they were sent to.[12] Vera maintained that the women who volunteered for SOE service in France were the sort of people who possessed 'considerable courage', as they were made fully aware of the risks facing them and still they chose to go.[13] Their chances of survival had been calculated at 'no more than 50 per cent' – a fact which was not kept from them. The thirty-nine women who were deployed were educated, necessarily patriotic and had various motives for volunteering. When Vera's biographer asked her what her 'girls' had in common, she replied that it was 'bravery'.[14]

From the SOE's headquarters in London, Vera carefully selected and recruited the women of F-Section, established that they had serious reasons to want to go to France and verified that they were suitable for the job. Recruitment could be difficult due to the very secret nature of the organisation – it was not possible to put out a general call for volunteers and instead women were specially selected and, if found to be suitable, they were asked to volunteer. The First Aid Nursing Yeomanry (FANY) provided around 3,000 women for work with the SOE and recruits trained in motor transport, coding, general duties and wireless telegraphy and served in various capacities, including as field agents. Another pool from which the SOE drew was the women's military services, the ATS, the WRNS and the WAAF. Recruits with special skills were earmarked by WAAF officers – particularly those who could speak fluent French and those trained in wireless operating. Women who had spent any time in France were deemed particularly valuable, as knowledge of French life would enable them to blend in inconspicuously with the French people once deployed. All of the women needed to be bilingual, intelligent, quick-thinking, courageous, patriotic, selfless and good at acting. The fifteen WAAFs selected possessed all of these qualities and were made fully aware of the risks involved, including the very short average life of a wireless operator in occupied France.

Once recruited, they were sent to the SOE's training school, where they learned to parachute jump, studied navigation and survival techniques, became adept in the art of deception, underwent simulated interrogations and received weapons, explosives and hand-to-hand combat training. Due to the fact that women serving in the British military services were barred by law from participating in armed combat, it was necessary for the WAAF SOE agents to be seconded to the First Aid Nursing Yeomanry prior to deployment in France. As the FANY was a civilian organisation, it did not have to abide by the rules which governed the military, and by belonging to it, the women could legally use weapons and explosives, just like their male colleagues in the SOE.

Vera visited the school occasionally to give lectures and was conscientious in reading the training reports that came through from Beaulieu to London regularly. More often than not, the reports gave the impression that the women were incapable of being agents and should not be sent. Together with Buckmaster, Vera ignored and overruled most of them. Agent Eileen Nearne was deemed by her trainers to be unsuitable to go to France but transmitted a good deal of useful economic and military intelligence over five months in the field, lasting a lot longer than the predicted six weeks before she was caught. Her sister, Jacqueline Nearne, was also reported to be unsuitable, but Vera ruled that she be sent to France anyway.[15] After she was parachuted blind into the Auvergne in 1943, Jacqueline served an astounding fifteen months undercover in France, recruiting circuit members, locating landing grounds for supply drops and assisting in agent landings. As Buckmaster recognised, Vera was right to select such a 'personality of truly extraordinary courage, force and charm', who had proven her trainer to have completely misjudged her.[16] The female agents were often misjudged in such a way. Once agents had been trained and were ready to deploy, they were driven to secret locations to board the planes that would take them to France by night. In almost every case, Vera shared the car ride to the airstrip with them, briefed them personally and saw them off. She carried out final checks for each woman, making sure that they carried no sign of having come from England, even down to the labels in their clothing. She then gave each one a gift, usually a gold or silver compact mirror, which they could pawn if they ran out of money in France. Once the women had reached France, Vera was almost always present in the signals room at Baker Street, waiting to receive their first transmissions. Each agent had a 'sched', or a designated time for transmissions, and she knew each one by heart.

Map of SOE circuits

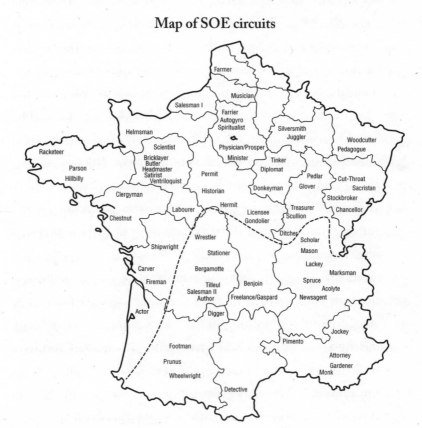

THE WAAFS OF F-SECTION

Of the thirty-nine women sent into occupied France by the SOE, a number were WAAFs. With many traits and much training in common, these women showed conspicuous courage in their dangerous, difficult work behind enemy lines.

Noor Inayat Khan

A direct descendant of Tipu Sultan, the eighteenth-century ruler of Mysore, Noor Inayat Khan was born in Moscow to an Indian Sufi teacher father and an American mother. Noor was educated in Paris and travelled to England in November 1940, where she joined the WAAF. Her background and ability to speak French brought her to the attention of the SOE, and she began training as a wireless operator in late 1942. In one of her training reports, a Colonel Frank Spooner wrote that she was 'not overburdened with brains' and seemed sensitive, jumpy and 'a bit unstable'. Still visible on the training report in her file is the word 'nonsense', scribbled by Buckmaster after he had consulted Vera Atkins on Noor's suitability – Vera decided that despite the negative reports, she should be sent to France.[17] In June 1943, Noor became the first female radio operator that the SOE sent to France, arriving in Paris to join the Prosper network.

An unlikely spy, given that she was the daughter of a pacifist Sufi preacher, Noor refused to carry a weapon or kill anyone, but she thought that to do nothing in the war would be paramount to allowing the Third Reich to inflict its evil on the innocent and that this would weigh on her conscience if she didn't play her part in trying to prevent it. Her fiancé was Jewish and the ideology of the Nazis towards Jews was 'fundamentally repulsive' to her.[18]

Noor spent her time in Paris transmitting crucial information to London concerning the locations of downed Allied pilots and more possible airstrike targets for the Allies. Noor's work led to the saving of thirty pilots' lives and the provision of explosives which would be used by the French Resistance to disrupt the transfer of torpedoes to German U-boats from the Parisian sewer system. Many members of the Prosper network were arrested around Noor, but rather than return to the safety of Britain as Buckmaster and Atkins urged, she chose to remain in Paris, at one point providing the only communications link between the French capital city and London by which to pass intelligence. She was aware of the importance of her work and believed that she should stay. The danger necessitated that she move frequently and the risk of capture was constant and exhausting. Eventually it caught up with her, and she was betrayed.

Trapped and arrested by the Gestapo, Noor fought so savagely against the arresting officers that it took multiple men to bring her in. In a deposition made before Atkins on 19 January 1947, Hans Kieffer, senior German intelligence officer in Paris, claimed under oath that Noor had been 'anxious above all not to betray her security checks' and gave them nothing of any use under interrogation.[19] She made no fewer than three escape attempts while incarcerated, and during one of them, two men, John Starr and Leon Faye, felt compelled to join her in it 'for no other reason than it was cooked up by a young woman who was obviously very brave'. They felt that 'as men, they should measure up to her courage by sharing the risk'.[20] She even earned the begrudging respect of the Gestapo, as evidenced in Kieffer's deposition, where he said she had 'behaved most bravely after her arrest and we got absolutely no new information out of her at all'. Josef Goetz, another Gestapo officer, agreed in an interrogation by Atkins on 3 September 1946 that Noor 'had not helped in any way'.[21] Enduring much harsher treatment than many of her captured comrades, most likely because of the dark colour of her skin and defiant escape attempts, Noor behaved with courage and dignity that contrasted starkly with Colonel Spooner's training report. Shot dead after horrific treatment by the Nazis, she gave nothing of any use away and saved many lives in her short career, also aiding sabotage that slowed down the German war effort.

Yvonne Cormeau

After she survived the Blitz bombing raid that killed her husband, Yvonne Cormeau joined the WAAF in 1941. Fluent in German and French, she was soon spotted and transferred to operations and intelligence and made it onto the SOE's radar. When asked if she would be willing to parachute into south-west France in August 1943, Yvonne agreed, saying, 'I thought this was something my husband would have liked to do, and as he was no longer there to do it, I thought it was time for me to do it.'[22] It was her way to 'fight back'.[23]

She trained as an SOE wireless operator alongside her WAAF colleagues, Noor Inayat Khan and Yolande Beekman, using a small wireless set secreted in a suitcase. All messages had to be enciphered, the cypher hidden in the false lining of the suitcase, and the information was then transmitted in Morse code. After sixteen weeks of wireless training, on the night of 23 August 1943, Yvonne was parachuted into south-west France, joining the Wheelwright network. She often had to double as a network courier as well as a wireless operator, travelling long distances to deliver information or supplies in person. Wireless operators needed to move frequently, to prevent the Germans from being able to track them via their wireless transmission signals. Yvonne was a very effective operator, lasting thirteen months and sending 402 messages, without a single mistake.[24] In addition to sending information to London, Yvonne could also receive it, so that information could be passed to the French Resistance groups that Wheelwright was working with. She was a vital link between Britain and the French Resistance and continued to operate efficiently throughout the war, passing intelligence between the two even after being shot in the leg while evading capture.

Yvonne also remembers how a German soldier stopped her at a roadblock and she managed to remain calm and ignore the pistol in her back, convincing him that she was a medical worker and that her suitcase contained an X-ray machine, rather than a wireless set. Yvonne was the second female radio operator to be sent to occupied France by the SOE and she spent thirteen long months sending information to Britain while constantly evading capture and arrest. After the war, she continued to use her linguistic skills as a translator at the Foreign Office and was awarded the Légion d'honneur, the Croix de Guerre, the Médaille de la Résistance and the Palmes Académiques.

Mary Herbert

At the outbreak of war in 1939, Mary Herbert possessed a university degree and could speak French, Italian, Spanish, German and Arabic. Her linguistic skills were very valuable and she worked as a translator in the Air Ministry in London until she joined the WAAF in September 1941. Mary was placed in an intelligence role and was the first WAAF officer to volunteer to join the SOE, after being sought out for her knowledge of languages. Mary trained as a courier and was landed by boat in France on 31 October. She joined the Scientist network, carrying messages, wireless sets, money and various other equipment between different locations and people. Couriers often covered long distances, sometimes by rail or car, and sometimes on foot or by bicycle – some even cycled over sixty miles per day. Mary also collected information on potential locations the network could use, as well as on potential recruits. Scientist was responsible for the destruction of a key radio station used by German Admiral Dönitz and his Atlantic submarine force, as well as a power station supplying Luftwaffe airfields and a set of transformers in Berlin which powered German anti-aircraft equipment and a radar establishment.

Mary had a relationship with fellow SOE member Claude de Baissac, who was in France as the leader of the Scientist network. In 1943, she became pregnant with de Baissac's child and initially hid the pregnancy. When de Baissac returned to London and took with him his sister, SOE agent Lise de Baissac, instead of her, Mary was forced to give birth to her child in a nursing home in Bordeaux. She named her daughter Claudine and the two moved to an apartment in Poitiers. Unfortunately, it was Lise de Baissac's name on the lease and the Gestapo, having discovered that Lise was an SOE agent, arrived to arrest Mary, assuming her to be Lise. They left little Claudine with Mary's maid, but the baby was soon placed in an orphanage by the French social services. Mary cleverly convinced her German captors that she could not possibly be an SOE agent – an agent would never have a baby while in the field, she claimed, and she only spoke French with an accent because she had spent some time in Egypt and spoke Arabic too. Her vast knowledge of French and Arabic made her story convincing and the Gestapo believed her, releasing her. The first thing Mary did was look for her daughter. Though it took a while, she eventually located Claudine at a convent and the two were reunited. Mary lost contact with the SOE, and after D-Day Claude and Lise de Baissac searched for her. They found her and Claudine, and the four returned to England, where Mary and Claude were married in November 1944. Mary became a French teacher after the war and was awarded the Croix de Guerre by France.

Cecily Lefort

When her husband urged her to leave France after the German invasion in 1940, Cecily Lefort travelled to England, where she joined the WAAF in 1941. Serving as a policewoman, Cecily was quickly noted for her ability to speak French and her knowledge of life in France, and she joined the SOE in 1943. After training as a courier, Cecily was flown into France on 17 June, where she joined the Jockey network. During her training, one of her instructors wrote in her file that she looked 'vague' and that though she 'could be relied on to be loyal', he doubted that she had 'enough initiative to achieve much'.[25] Once Cecily was in France, he was proven wrong. She worked hard to collect information that was to be transmitted to London and in particular was instructed to accumulate intelligence on suitable locations for aircraft to drop supplies for the Resistance and strategic bombing targets. Her work led to multiple successful instances of sabotage on railway lines, as well as damage to industrial targets. Another of Cecily's training instructors reported that she was 'inclined to blurt out things in a rather embarrassing way, which she probably would not have said if she thought first'.[26] Her instructors painted a picture of Cecily as a 'chatterbox' and were concerned that she was too 'talkative'.[27] Again, they were proven wrong. When Cecily was arrested by the SS in September 1943, the Gestapo failed to get any information out of her, and she refused to break even under interrogation. Of no further use to them, she was sent to Ravensbrück concentration camp for women, where she was killed, having never uttered an SOE secret to her captors.

Diana Rowden

Educated in Britain and France, and working in the latter during the early years of the war as a translator and journalist, Diana Rowden travelled to Britain in 1941 and joined the WAAF. Her language skills – particularly her fluent French – brought her to the attention of her superiors, and after being promoted to the rank of section officer engaged in intelligence work within the WAAF, she was recruited by the SOE in March 1943. Her love of France motivated her to return to the country and be a part of the efforts to free it from the Nazis' grip, and on 17 June she was flown by Lysander, joining the Acrobat network as a courier. Transporting information and supplies by bicycle and train, Diana helped to organise arms and ammunition drops and supplied information which contributed to the successful damaging of the Peugeot works at Sochaux, which had been making weapons for the German war machine. Unfortunately, not long after she arrived in France, Diana's circuit leader, John Starr, was betrayed and arrested by the Gestapo, placing the rest of the circuit in danger. On the run for several months, Diana was eventually captured when she was betrayed by a man posing as a fellow agent. After interrogation at the hands of the Gestapo, Diana was executed by lethal injection at Natzweiler-Struthof concentration camp in July 1944.

Yolande Beekman

Yolande Beekman was educated in Paris, London and Switzerland

and as a result spoke English, German and French fluently. When she joined the WAAF in 1941, she worked as a wireless operator and her wireless skills, combined with her trilingual ability and obvious French patriotism, caused her to stand out to the SOE. After her recruitment and training, Yolande was transported to France via Lysander on the night of 18 September 1943, where she joined the Musician network in St Quentin. This was an area of industrial importance to the Germans and provided several strategic targets for the SOE to sabotage. Yolande disseminated intelligence on the various strategic elements of these operations, assisting with RAF supply drops to equip the local Resistance against the German occupiers and contributing to the successful sabotage of 115 miles of railway and the St Quentin canal. The canal was being used by the Germans to transport parts for submarines, which were a constant menace to Allied shipping, and taking the canal out of action even for a short period of time would be useful. Musician used limpet mines to jam the lock by damaging the gates, and it was out of service for weeks, with almost 100 barges loaded with submarine parts sunk.[28] Unfortunately, through no fault of her own, Yolande was caught. She was badly beaten, and on 13 September 1944, she was shot in the back of the neck at Dachau concentration camp.

Anne-Marie Walters

With French as her first language, Anne-Marie Walters was an obvious candidate for the SOE. She had been educated in Geneva and moved to London, where she joined the WAAF in 1941. SOE recruiters were made aware of her ability to speak fluent French, and once she had passed all of the recruitment stages necessary, Anne-Marie was deployed to occupied France. In December 1943, the bomber aircraft transporting her to her network crashed due to fog and Anne-Marie was one of only two survivors. Less than a month later, she was airborne again and made it safely to France where she joined the Wheelwright circuit with fellow WAAF SOE recruit Yvonne Cormeau. Yvonne had been working as both the wireless operator and the courier for Wheelwright for some time and was becoming exhausted. Anne-Marie was sent to take over as courier, much to Yvonne's relief, replacing her as the link between the network itself and the various pockets of Resistance in the area. The network was working hard to amass arms and explosives ahead of the planned Allied invasion of Europe, and though they did not know when the invasion would take place, Wheelwright's members were excitedly collecting information and equipment that would enable them to carry out sabotage operations that would prevent the Germans from getting reinforcements to the coast easily or quickly. Anne-Marie worked to this end, carrying information and wireless sets in suitcases between different parts of the network, supplying wireless operators like Yvonne with the information that London needed for D-Day planning purposes. She also transported explosives in suitcases, ferrying them to targets such as the Toulouse powder factory.

Anne-Marie also worked on Allied escape lines, assisting downed pilots and escaped prisoners of war in getting over the Pyrenees and into Spain. It was especially important to get as many trained pilots back to Britain as possible, as they were a valuable commodity in Allied operations. She helped a number of prisoners from Eysses prison, who had staged a mass break-out, to escape – their number including one Sydney Hudson, who would go on to lead the revived Headmaster network, which Anne-Marie's WAAF SOE colleague Sonya Butt would work with as a courier. In addition, Anne-Marie also helped to train French Resistance members in using the weapons dropped by the RAF, calling upon her SOE weapons training. She was liked and respected by the Resistance and in June 1944 she took part in a battle beside them. Around 2,000 German soldiers attacked the 300 Resistance members at Castelnau-sur-l'Auvignon, and while the battle raged, Anne-Marie buried SOE papers and gave out hand grenades to Resistance fighters. In June 1945, Anne-Marie was awarded the MBE (Civil) in recognition of her 'personal courage and willingness to undergo any danger'.[29] From France she received the Croix de Guerre and the Médaille de la Reconnaissance française. After the war, Anne-Marie moved around, working as a translator, an editor and a literary agent. She died at the age of seventy-five in 1998.

Yvonne Baseden

Born in Paris, Yvonne Baseden moved to England with her parents in 1937 and joined the WAAF at age eighteen. Speaking fluent French, she was earmarked to help the Free French squadrons with the complicated technical English that they were struggling with. In 1941, she was commissioned as an officer in the WAAF and later, as a flight officer, she was sent to work at the Air Ministry in London. There she met WAAF colleague Pearl Witherington, who was already an SOE recruit. Pearl noticed Yvonne's ability to speak fluent French and her knowledge of French life and recommended her to her SOE recruiters. When approached quietly by the recruiters, Yvonne volunteered to join the SOE and was trained as a wireless operator. Parachuted into south-west France on 19 March 1944, she joined a new network codenamed Scholar. Yvonne had multiple wireless sets stored away in different locations and was conscious of moving constantly so as to avoid detection by the Gestapo. Like her WAAF SOE colleagues, Yvonne often had to go above and beyond, acting not only as a wireless operator for the network but also as a courier and weapons instructor too. She identified possible drop zones for agents and supplies and fed this information back to London for planning purposes. Yvonne was instrumental in guiding these drops, especially after D-Day, when huge amounts of weapons and personnel were needed to supply the Allies as they advanced into France and Europe. In one particularly large supply drop, Yvonne informed all of the arrangements and for the last twenty-four hours before the drop took place, she remained in the designated drop zone, guiding the aircraft, at one point in direct communication with the leading plane. That day – 26 June 1944 – thirty-six Flying Fortresses of the Eighth Army Air Force dropped 400 packages containing weapons and munitions to the waiting Resistance members, supplying them amply for their work in aiding the Allied push across France and the Continent.[30]

Unfortunately, a teenage network member was captured in possession of a wireless set and was beaten into giving up the names and probable locations of his colleagues, Yvonne included. She was arrested and taken to Dijon prison, where she was kept in an underground cell without food and water for days. She had her bare toes stamped on during interrogation and was badly beaten. Eventually, when it became obvious to her captors that she was not going to be of any use, she was taken to Ravensbrück, where she was subjected to brutal treatment and exhausting work. Unlike most of her captured colleagues, Yvonne was lucky and was released in April 1945.[31] Yvonne was awarded the MBE by Britain and the Légion d'honneur, the Médaille de la Résistance and the Croix de Guerre avec Palme by France. After the war, she lived in Northern Rhodesia and Portugal, and though she talked about her time with the SOE initially, she eventually expressed that she no longer had the desire to do so.

Maureen O'Sullivan

Educated in various European countries, Maureen O'Sullivan spoke fluent French when she moved to England. In 1941, she joined the WAAF and eventually SOE recruiters approached her. In the build-up to the Allied landings in Normandy, the urgent need for wireless operators and couriers increased, as vast amounts of information needed to be passed between the different parts of Resistance movements in France. Such pressing need meant that it became more and more common to deploy SOE personnel before they had completed their training. Maureen, nicknamed Paddy, was one such agent, and her training was incomplete when she parachuted into France on 22 March 1944 to join the Fireman network as a wireless operator. As Fireman lacked a reliable courier when she arrived, Paddy often doubled as courier and wireless operator, travelling vast distances to deliver information as well as receiving it from and transmitting it to London using her wireless set. As D-Day drew closer, she was constantly at her wireless, transmitting hundreds of messages that contributed to the cornering and eventual surrender of over 100,000 German troops who were attempting to retreat towards Germany in August 1944.

Paddy's cover was blown in June 1945 and she was posted to the SOE's Force 136 in Calcutta, where she would use the skills she had acquired to help encourage and supply indigenous resistance movements in enemy-occupied territory in the Far East. After the war, Paddy settled in England.

Lilian Rolfe

Born and raised in France, Lilian Rolfe found herself working at the British embassy in Brazil at the outbreak of the Second World War. In early 1943, she travelled to England to join the WAAF, her patriotism and eagerness to defeat the Third Reich evident in her determination to contribute to the Allied war effort. This, coupled with her ability to speak several languages, brought her to the attention of SOE recruiters, and in November that year she started training as a wireless operator.

In April 1944, she landed in France, a vital link between London and the Resistance and a valuable source of information on occupied territory. Involved with the Historian network, Lilian handled information that helped to prevent the transport of German troops to Normandy and assisted the Allied advance into France. Such information might include details of where supplies and weapons were needed to carry out important sabotage work and strategic information on German dispositions and the transport situation.

At the end of July, however, Lilian was arrested and the Gestapo found her wireless set. Wireless operators were considered particularly valuable by the Gestapo, which meant that they were usually savagely interrogated. Lilian resisted every attempt her captors made to break her and once they realised she would not give up any information, she was sent to Ravensbrück, where she met fellow SOE agents Violette Szabo, Denise Bloch and Cecily Lefort. Starved, beaten and worked to the point of exhaustion, the four women gave their lives for the Allied cause at the camp.

Muriel Byck

From a Jewish family and educated in Britain, Germany and France, Muriel Byck joined the WAAF in December 1942 and was approached by the SOE in July the following year. Her obvious drive to fight Nazism coupled with her fluent French and linguistic ability made her an attractive recruit, and she was trained as a wireless operator, proving very adept at the work.

Sent to France to help with the re-establishment of the Ventriloquist network, like so many of her colleagues, she doubled as a courier and assisted with the physical passing of information as well as electronic transmission. Muriel was also involved in the destruction of a vast amount of weapons, destined for German troops in northern France. Intelligence indicated that a local German weapons depot had been collecting arms and ammunition, amassing an arsenal that was due to be transported by train to the north. Saboteurs acted on this information, blowing up each end of the railway so that the trains would be stranded. London passed information to Muriel to inform the network that Allied forces planned to aerially bomb the weapons stash, and network members and locals were quietly warned to take cover. When the bombs dropped, the weapons were destroyed, preventing them from ending up in enemy hands.

Sadly, though not in captivity, Muriel died in France in May 1944, having contracted meningitis.

Phyllis Latour

Fluent in French due to her French father, Phyllis Latour joined the WAAF in November 1941 and trained as a flight mechanic. Her skills and experience as a mechanic likely came in very useful when she became a wireless operator with the SOE in November 1943. Phyllis's training was incomplete when she parachuted into France on 1 May 1944, and she joined the Scientist II network just a month before D-Day. Due to the fact that she was located in an area swarming with German soldiers, Phyllis had guards to protect her while she was sending messages, which she was doing pretty much constantly preceding, during and following D-Day. She was the link that made it possible for the network to arm the Maquis

Resistance fighters, organise guerrilla warfare against the German occupiers, sabotage transport links and destroy transport infrastructure so that the enemy could not move around easily. Phyllis also provided the Allies with information on German dispositions, which was of vital use in planning the Allied advance into the area. Speaking after the war, Phyllis remembered:

> I always carried knitting because my codes were on a piece of silk – I had about 2,000 I could use. When I used a code I would just pinprick it to indicate it had gone. I wrapped the piece of silk around a knitting needle and put it in a flat shoelace which I used to tie my hair up.[32]

When she was taken by the Germans for questioning, they did not think to check her hair tie, and they let her go. After the war, Phyllis moved to Kenya with her husband and spent time in Fiji, Australia and New Zealand. She celebrated her 100th birthday in April 2021, making her the last living female SOE agent of F-Section. Phyllis did not discuss her wartime work with her family, and her children only found out that she had worked for the SOE when they discovered information on the internet in 2000.[33]

Marguerite Knight

Born and brought up in Paris, Marguerite Knight joined the WAAF in Britain and was recruited by the SOE in April 1944. After only a couple of weeks of training, Marguerite was parachuted into France on 6 May, a month before the Normandy landings. She was desperately needed as a courier for the Donkeyman network and worked hard to disseminate intelligence for the Allied cause. In August, an American 'Jedburgh' team – a three-man team of Allied operatives sent to assist with the Allied advance into France after D-Day – landed to assist with Donkeyman's operations. This was dangerous work, as the Germans lingered in many of the towns and the Resistance found it very difficult to glean information on their strength, positions and intentions. Marguerite volunteered to cycle into the towns, where she could blend in inconspicuously, carry out reconnaissance and return to Donkeyman with reliable and current information on the German presence nearby. She was very successful in this work and carried out more of the same for the Special Air Service and the advancing Allied armies, also surveilling the countryside and paying particular attention to transport options.[34] Marguerite narrowly escaped capture when she was betrayed, but she managed to escape and travel back to England.

For her work transporting and delivering valuable intelligence to the Allies, Marguerite was awarded honours by Britain, France and America, including the MBE, the Croix de Guerre and the Presidential Medal of Freedom.

Sonya Butt

After growing up in the south of France, Sonya Butt joined the WAAF as soon as she was able to. After coming to the SOE's attention when she enquired about becoming a WAAF interpreter, she was recruited as a courier, at just nineteen years old. Just nine days before D-Day, Sonya was parachuted into France to join the Headmaster network as a courier, though she often doubled as weapons trainer for the Maquis. Moving around a lot to transport information and supplies, Sonya quickly earned the respect of the Resistance members she worked with and contributed to her network's sabotage work in aid of the Allied landings and advance into France.

After D-Day, Sonya worked for the American Army, collecting intelligence on the German forces in the area. Having been a courier, she possessed a huge amount of knowledge on the region, and the Germans within it, and she continued to risk her life by travelling to places still held by the enemy to report back to the Americans on their position, strength, intentions and capabilities. The intelligence she provided was of great use to the Allies as they pushed into France to take it back from the enemy occupiers. Sonya also worked as a weapons instructor in France, after one of the male agents dropped with her was shot in battle. After the war, Sonya married fellow agent Guy d'Artois. Guy's military career took the couple to Japan, and he served in the Korean War before they were able to settle down in his native Canada. They had six children, and Sonya died at the age of ninety in 2014.

Pearl Witherington

Born and raised in Paris by British parents, Pearl Witherington worked in the British embassy before the German occupation, when she fled to Britain, arriving in July 1941. Pearl and her sisters sought roles in which they could contribute to the Allied war effort and they found work with the WAAF and the Air Ministry. Pearl worked for the latter, until she learned that her fiancé had become an escaped prisoner of war and was in France. Desperate to return to France and to him, she joined the SOE and trained as a courier. Pearl's training reports were unusually positive, compared to those of her fellow female agents. Her instructor noted that she was 'probably the best shot, male or female' that he had seen yet and that, 'though a woman', she definitely possessed leaders' qualities and was 'an excellent student for the job'.[35]

On 23 September 1943, she parachuted into France and joined the Stationer network. For around eight months, she organised supply and agent drops and communicated with London regarding the network's activities and the local area. But in May 1944, the head of Stationer was captured by the Germans. The network was forced to reorganise and split in half, becoming Wrestler and Shipwright. Somewhat unusually, Pearl served as the leader of Wrestler – the only woman in the SOE to serve as a network head. An SOE training report prior to her departure had described Pearl as not being 'leadership material' and recommended that she be employed in a 'subordinate' role.[36] This report soon proved to be totally unfounded and inaccurate. Under her new codename 'Pauline', she became responsible for the organisation and training of around 3,000 members of the Resistance, and though at first it was difficult for the men to take orders from a woman, they soon came to respect and admire her. Don Farrington, who fought under Pearl near the time of the D-Day landings, recalls with obvious respect the way in which she was 'absolutely livid' with one of his colleagues for kidnapping a German soldier. When the colleague in question asked Farrington what to do, he replied, 'You do nothing at all – you see Pauline!'[37] Pearl's fighters worked hard to sabotage road, rail and telegraph links ahead of D-Day, while she organised over twenty drops of weapons and personnel into France, collecting the relevant intelligence behind these operations and ensuring that it got to where it needed to go.

After the war, Pearl was recommended for the Military Cross but was found to be ineligible to receive it on the grounds that she was a woman. Instead, she was offered an MBE (Civil). She rejected this award, due to the fact that she did not consider her work in France to have been 'civil' in nature. She was granted a military

MBE instead, which she accepted, and was advanced to CBE many years later.

Pearl's attitude highlights a common issue with female SOE agents and post-war decorations and awards. France was quick to decorate the women, acknowledging their courage and contributions to the Allied war effort. Britain, on the other hand, was not. If they were offered anything at all, the female agents were given civil awards and decorations. Pearl found this to be unjust and said, 'I do consider it to be most unjust to be given a civilian decoration … Our training, which we did with the men, was purely military and as women we were expected to replace them in the field.'[38] This inequality was taken to the extreme with Pearl, in the case of her 'parachute wings', which she was awarded in April 2006 after six decades of waiting. Parachute wings were a badge awarded to military parachutists, depending on the number of jumps completed. As a woman, Pearl completed three training jumps and a fourth which was operational. Her male colleagues, however, conducted four training jumps and their fifth was operational. Parachute wings were only awarded after a total of five jumps. Pearl considered this a great injustice, and it could appear as a deliberate attempt to bar women from being eligible to receive a military award.[39] The British government was begrudging with its awards and medals for female SOE agents, despite having asked them to risk their lives in service to their nation in such an extraordinary way. Though their work and contributions were recognised in the medals that were given, the nature of what they did was misconstrued in the 'civil' classification and, as in Pearl's case with her parachute wings, sometimes withheld altogether. This was likely deliberate, as recognising the women's contributions as military in nature meant admitting to having deployed them in a military or combat capacity, which was not only taboo in the 1940s – it was illegal.

SOE'S WAAF TRAILBLAZERS

The level of resistance to employing WAAFs in intelligence work on the home front in Britain was minimal compared to the resistance to sending them into occupied territory as agents. Though the British authorities and military services were hesitant to allow women into the secret world at home, the fact that much of what they were doing resembled secretarial duties and clerical work eased the situation somewhat, and perhaps made it slightly easier to accept. From the start of the conversation about sending women to France, Whitehall was completely opposed to the idea, as were the male-dominated government bodies and intelligence services. The SOE really was unique in suggesting that women be deployed behind enemy lines, where they would be in constant and very real danger. The Geneva Convention, Vera Atkins's superiors pointed out, made no provision whatsoever to protect women if they were caught, because they were not, and had not before been, considered as combatants. When, in 1942, Vera received unofficial permission to send the women, it was reportedly 'after much heart searching discussion at the highest levels'. The idea was opposed to every tradition of the British intelligence community, which had what Vera considered to be 'old fashioned ideas about women and danger'.[40] Society was still adjusting to the new political rights and social habits of women, who were increasingly voting, working outside the home and acting in a much more liberal way than they had before. The war further catapulted women into roles they had not previously occupied, but to the authorities, agents behind enemy lines was a step too far. Despite the resistance to sending them and the fact that most of the WAAFs who served with the SOE received negative, derogatory and, at times, damning reports from their instructors during their training, all of them served with immeasurable courage and dedication and made significant personal sacrifices. For some of them, those sacrifices included their freedom and, ultimately, their lives. Even under torture and intensive interrogation, they kept their secrets from the Gestapo with dignity and resolve. Vera Atkins's firm belief that the women would make suitable agents was proved right, and the part that they played in accumulating and disseminating important intelligence that ultimately saved lives and provided significant assistance to the Allied fight was greater than anyone could have imagined it would be. Maurice Buckmaster later spoke of the 'magnificent work carried out by members of the WAAF in occupied France', against both the odds and the expectations of almost everyone who knew they were being sent behind enemy lines.[41] Indeed, the misgivings of the headquarters staff, never shared by Vera, 'vanished as the mist before the sun' when the successes of the women F-Section sent to France came to light.[42]

Among the first British women to be sent behind enemy lines as agents, the women of the SOE set a precedent for women in military and security services for decades to come. In 2017, Lieutenant Colonel Tara Opielowski of the US Air Force named them as 'trailblazers', whose trials and obstacles led to greater involvement and freedom of career choice for women in security and military organisations. They were, she says, an 'untapped resource', an effective weapon against an enemy who totally underestimated them.[43] They remain an inspiration to women in similar roles today. First Lieutenant Harriet Randolph cited them as a personal inspiration, because they defied stereotypes and accomplished great success against expectations.[44]

Master Sergeant Sanya Bell identified how the women of the

SOE effectively had to fight two wars at the same time.[45] One, alongside their male counterparts against the Nazis. The other they fought for credibility, equality and fair recognition of their success within their own country. Their individual personal files contain scathing training reports, memorandums claiming that they should not be sent and an array of papers suggesting a strongly negative overall attitude towards them from the largely male staff training and assessing them. Though these men may have had legitimate reasons for their doubt, the women of F-Section more than proved these ideas wrong with their astonishing success in the field, just as Vera Atkins had hoped and believed they would. They were sent because they were needed, due to a lack of available men.

Ultimately, Vera was proven right to believe in them, and far from seductresses who would lead men astray, they made a positive and significant contribution to the D-Day landings and to the war effort in general on behalf of the Allies, and all remained loyal to their country, even when it meant losing their lives. The negative attitudes that the women encountered are understandable, given the historical context in which they lived. As Major Meredith Doran recognises, it is natural for forerunners, the first to do something out of the ordinary, to have to fight harder. It is a 'cross they bear', having more to overcome and to prove than those who will follow.[46] Though F-Section's women broke the mould, they had to wait decades for the rest of the world to catch up with them and for attitudes to change towards them. For being allowed to go to France and break so many moulds, they had Vera to thank. She was their superior officer, but in many cases, she was also their friend, sharing in their struggles through her own personal experience. Vera was right to believe in her courageous, trailblazing WAAFs, all of whom remain a tremendous inspiration today.

10

KEEP CALM AND CARRY ON

WOMEN AND EMOTIONS

In the same way that fear of gossip caused reluctance in the Air Ministry and the RAF towards using women in intelligence work, so too did the belief that they might be 'ruled by their emotions'.[1] As Air Commandant Dame Felicity Peake explains in her memoirs, a woman was initially not allowed to serve in the support staff of her husband's squadron, as it was felt that 'her emotions might get the better of her if she knew the times when her husband was in danger'.[2]

Where many WAAFs had husbands, significant others, brothers, cousins and friends in the RAF to worry about, many others were very young and had never been away from home before, and their inexperience was no secret. Ena Smith remembers falling asleep on her first night in the WAAF to the sound of 'snivelling'.[3] The RAF worried about such inexperience and supposed emotional fragility in its women's auxiliary. It believed that women were not psychologically suited to war work and worried about their emotional reactions to danger, destruction and killing, all of which intelligence WAAFs would likely be faced and involved with on a daily basis. WAAF plotter Jean Hilda Mills remembers being treated with apprehension and recalls how her male colleagues were worried that she and her fellow WAAF members would 'go into hysterics if things got tough'.[4]

RAF stations were obvious targets for the Luftwaffe and senior officers worried about the ability of the WAAFs to handle the constant exposure to danger. Though he later stated his 'conversion' on record, Group Captain Bouchier initially 'resented the appearance of girls' on fighter stations especially, as he 'did not think they would cope during raids'.[5] Grace Hall recalls how Fighter Command would initially 'have nothing to do with' WAAF interrogators, and as such she was sent to Bomber Command instead.[6]

Despite these popular beliefs and concerns, the WAAFs were not the distraction or strain that the RAF had feared they would be. Once again, they defied female stereotypes and the expectations of their male colleagues and the air authorities, a far cry from the hysterical wrecks they were expected to be.

EMOTIONAL REACTIONS TO WARFARE

Before 1939, when the special conditions of war invoked employment of women in the military services, they had largely been shielded from the full horrors of war and warfare. Having lived in a world without television and war journalism, most women were not confronted with the horrors and atrocities associated with war, their only glimpse into such things being the return of the men from the battlefields of the First World War. The RAF was concerned that the psychological burden of coming face to face with the effects of war for the first time might be too heavy for women to carry. Overwhelmingly, the WAAFs defied this expectation, not by failing to become upset by what they saw and experienced, but by continuing to work effectively despite how they felt. When Air Commandant Dame Felicity Peake was posted to RAF Biggin Hill in May 1940 as second in command of the WAAF section, she was twenty-six years old and already a war widow. In the first bombing raid on the station, she took cover in a trench, leaving it before the all-clear had sounded to find her airwomen. On her way to the trench that she suspected they might have taken cover in, she passed a girl lying by the road:

> I went towards her and a voice from somewhere told me not to bother; she was dead. She was the first dead person I had ever seen. I remember thinking I must have a good look at her as I might have to get used to this kind of thing. I was relieved that my reactions were, at least, controllable.[7]

Air Commandant Peake's reaction was evidence of her suitability to WAAF leadership, and she went on to be in command of the WAAF section. Having never been faced with the distressing sights of war, many WAAFs like her surprised even themselves with their ability to carry on and do what was needed. Myra Collyer was given the task of typing up letters that had been smuggled out of prisoner-of-war camps, to look for any factual information that might be of use. With one letter she found two photographs. One showed an Australian man bent over with a samurai sword raised above him, and the next photograph showed the same scene, but the man's head was now in the basket, detached from his body. Myra remembers crying when faced with such an 'absolute horror', quite unlike anything she was used to dealing with, but she carried on working effectively in spite of the incident.

Working for air intelligence overseas, Molly Sasson came face to face with the brutal effects of war. In November 1944, she was attached to a detachment unit of the Allied Military Government

for Occupied Territories. She was the only German interpreter in
the detachment and they travelled through north-east Belgium into
Germany via the Netherlands. It was a dangerous area, even though
it appeared that Germany had lost the war. As the Allies advanced
into Europe and the German Army retreated, Molly's detachment
was tasked with following Allied troops and bringing law and order
to the area as the Irish Guards and Royal Artillery fought ahead of
them. After German towns and villages had been occupied by the
Allies, the detachment would go into them and carry out its work.

'Needless to say,' Molly remembers, 'we were confronted with the
true horror of war, death, destruction and misery ... We encountered
teenage boys dressed in uniform, quite dazed and bewildered without
orders.' Any German individuals who tried to protect their towns and
villages from bombing by negotiation of surrender were shot by local
Nazi leaders, just as the British Liberation Army was approaching.
'Terrified, lost and orphaned children were severely traumatised at
being exposed to terrible scenes of badly injured, dying parents and
relatives,' Molly says. 'There was total chaos amidst the bombing,
with devastation, death, hunger and misery. The population seemed
stunned with disbelief at our arrival wherever we went.'[8]

Molly's tasks varied and there were many of them. As an interpreter with intelligence training, she helped to interrogate suspected war
criminals, and German soldiers of intelligence value were held and
interrogated too. Sometimes this was carried out under fire from both
Allied and German aircraft, and there was always the possibility that
snipers could be lurking nearby. Molly also encountered two schools
filled with many corpses and the remaining people seriously wounded.

One evening, she had no choice but to ride a 250cc motorcycle to another town, alone in the dark. The road was notoriously
dangerous, with groups of SS troops hiding in the woods. Molly

broke down twenty miles into the journey and did her best to think through what she should do, refusing to panic. She decided to walk with the malfunctioning motorcycle, thinking it a better plan than staying put. Her situation was serious and she knew it, but she had to make a decision and act rather than sitting down in a heap to await rescue or attack. Thankfully, an American Army truck came along and took Molly and her motorbike to where they needed to go. Molly was most upset to discover that another despatch rider, a staff sergeant, had been found floating in the river, having been decapitated. Thin wires had been stretched across the road by the enemy, to decapitate Allied motorcyclists. 'How grateful I was', Molly says, 'that my motorbike broke down where it did.'[9]

The things Molly saw and experienced, first-hand, could not easily be faced or forgotten, and she had to make decisions and carry out actions alone, without help, in difficult and dangerous situations. This she did, most effectively, continuing in the role she had been given without being overcome by her emotions as had been feared. Many other WAAFs followed the same example.

FEAR OF DANGER

Work on an RAF station carried with it inevitable exposure to danger, most commonly from enemy air raids. As strategically important targets for the Luftwaffe, many RAF stations suffered constant raids and extensive damage, and the risk of injury or death was 'never far away'. The WAAFs were generally 'always aware of their close proximity to war and its dangers', and though they were inevitably frightened during raids, the overall consensus is that they did not allow fear or anxiety to interfere with their work.[10] In fact, quite the opposite appears to be true. Some WAAFs said after the war that while they were frightened before and after a raid, they were rarely afraid while it was actually in progress.[11] WAAF plotter Edith Kup recalls that she and her colleagues had been trained 'not to show our feelings and to keep control' and that 'calmness reigned amongst the frenzied activity' on her station.[12] Air Commandant Dame Felicity Peake wrote after the war:

> I dwelt on the CO's remarks about the WAAF plotters during the raid, who had continued with their duties as if it was only an exercise. I thought of Flight Sgt Turner who continued to man the telephone switchboard in the Operations block as though she had lived in a perpetual earthquake all her life and was quite used to the intermittent, nerve-shattering blasts. I thought of them all, those who had had to work during the raid and those others who had had to sit and wait. I wondered how many of them had felt as I had, scared stiff, but even more scared of showing it. I felt very proud of them.[13]

Far from being too nervous to work effectively, some WAAFs were given awards for bravery. Three airwomen at Biggin Hill were the first servicewomen to be awarded Military Medals after the station was bombed in 1940. One of them was plotting supervisor Elspeth Henderson, who had managed to maintain communication with the Group HQ at Uxbridge on the one telephone line that had not been damaged and only ceased working when she was knocked over by a bomb which came through the roof.[14] Jean Mary Youle also received the Military Medal. Her citation reads:

> In August 1940 Sergeant Youle was on duty in a Station telephone exchange when the Station was attacked and bombed by five enemy aircraft. Part of the building containing the telephone exchange

suffered a direct hit and other bombs fell in very close proximity. The telephone staff were subjected to a heavy rain of debris and splinters and to the noise of the concussion of exploding bombs. It was solely due to the cool bravery of, and superb example set by, Sergeant Youle that the telephone operators carried on with their task with calmness and complete efficiency at a most dangerous time for them. She has at all times set an excellent example of coolness and efficiency to all.[15]

For some women, it was death and destruction that had inspired them to join the WAAF in the first place. Mollie Thompson travelled by train one day to London from Kent and came upon the site of a bombing raid. Observing the 'extraordinary almost theatrical scene of carnage and horror', she was 'deeply affected', feeling frustrated that she could do nothing about it. She resigned from her job immediately and joined the WAAF, training as a photographic interpreter in 1940.[16] Doreen Luke joined the WAAF aged seventeen and a half, having seen the 'horrors of war' close-up when she had observed soldiers returning to England after the evacuation of Dunkirk. She remembers:

Many of our friends with whom I went to school and had danced and flirted with in happier days were killed. Some of them were brought home to be buried in our local cemetery. I read their names, see their faces in my mind, and then read the terrible words 'killed in action'. I remember them as handsome young men, full of fun and vitality. Yes, it was time for me to go, away from home, join the WAAF and do my best to help end this dreadful war.[17]

Far from being put off war work or rendered incapable of it because of fear of death and destruction, the WAAFs were fuelled by the danger posed to their country to 'do their bit', working effectively alongside their male colleagues as the bombs fell around them. In some cases, women were less afraid of the danger posed by the enemy than they were by other threats. Radar operator Rosamond Grant Renton Barclay remembers walking back to her billet after a night watch and realising that she was being followed. Her route taking her through fields and woods, she was 'quite frightened and apprehensive' and realised that the man following her was a soldier. Facing him, she 'sounded very fierce' and told him to go home, hoping that the fact that she was an officer, and he was not, would help. Rosamond describes the experience as 'really horrible', and it is notable that the RAF appeared to be more worried about the WAAFs becoming hysterical during bombing raids than it was about women walking home from work in the middle of the night through deserted fields and woods. Often WAAFs took responsibility for their own safety and that of their colleagues – at Rosamond's billet, a WAAF officer routinely stayed up until 3 a.m. to make sure that the women got home safely.[18] In the case of the WAAFs, the RAF's fears regarding the emotional capability of women during times of danger were not realised.

FEAR FOR LOVED ONES

As WAAF operator Aileen Clayton points out, as women the WAAFs had the 'extra worry of what might befall' their menfolk.[19] Where the RAF saw this as a potential hazard to the efficiency of operations, concern for the safety of airmen actually seemed to improve the efficiency and effectiveness of the WAAFs, as they were aware that lives, including those of loved ones, depended on their accuracy and ability. The intelligence provided to aircrews could be responsible for 'that split second of prior knowledge' that 'might make all the difference between life and death', which was a major incentive for the WAAFs to try to block out their worry and work as effectively as they possibly could.[20]

Eileen Younghusband acknowledges the strain that fear for brothers, fiancés and husbands placed on WAAFs but remembers that despite their anxiety, the women in the filter room continued working, 'their discipline and devotion to duty' faultless.[21]

There were many occasions where WAAFs lost friends and relatives among fallen aircrew. Joan Baughan, a Bomber Command WAAF intelligence officer, lost her husband and as a result went 'limp and cold' after heavy raids and high losses.[22] She felt particularly upset after an Allied raid on Nuremberg in March 1944, after which ninety-six bombers were reported missing. She says, 'My heart always went out to wives, mothers and girlfriends. Having been through it myself, my feelings were especially strong, I think.'[23] Again, the RAF worried that if the worst happened and a WAAF operator did lose a loved one, they might be unable to continue in their work. In most cases, quite the opposite proved to be true. Joan Baughan continued in her work very successfully, her determination renewed by loss. When Muriel Gane Pushman received a telegram informing her that her boyfriend, who had just proposed to her, had been killed, she noticed after reading it that her best friend was crying next to her, also having received a telegram informing her that her brother had been killed. Putting aside her own feelings and grief, Muriel comforted her friend and escorted her home on compassionate leave, recognising that other WAAFs depended on her ability to cope.[24]

Though, as Eileen Smith acknowledges, it was inevitable that the WAAFs on RAF stations would experience strong and often conflicting emotions, there is nothing to suggest that their feelings kept them from being able to do their jobs well.[25] Edith Kup remembers that, from the lowest ranks to the highest, the women took the view that they were 'together against the battle' and 'took a pretty poor view of hysterics'.[26] Pam Beecroft remembers admiring the self-control of Air Commandant Dame Felicity Peake when her fiancé was constantly 'in the thick of battle', just as Commandant Peake had so admired the airwomen under her supervision.[27] Again, rather than being defeated by loss, women used it as incentive to fight back against enemy aggression on behalf of their country. Eileen Younghusband's cousin was killed and his death affected her greatly.[28] At nineteen years old, she joined the WAAF 'in the hope of replacing him', her intense patriotism fuelled by his death. The WAAFs overcame their fears and their grief, aware of the importance of their work in providing accurate and important intelligence to the aircrews fighting in the skies.

TEA AND SYMPATHY

Where the RAF was worried about the negative effect that emotion might have on the work of the WAAFs, emotional sensitivity arguably made them more effective at times. This is particularly true where WAAFs had to deal with aircrews who had good reason to return from operations tired and distressed. Flight Sergeant Alf Lorimer remembers appreciating the 'silence with a smile' from the WAAFs as he would queue for egg and chips prior to leaving on an operation, and upon returning was grateful that 'they seemed to know that there were times for talking and times for silence'.[29]

Edith Kup remembers debriefing returning crews, aware that sometimes they'd had a terrifying time and would come back 'in an emotional state'.[30] Joan Baughan often 'wanted to cuddle' incoming crews prior to interrogation, as they 'looked dreadful' and she could 'see all the horror of war on their faces'.[31]

Grace Hall never forgot a 'particularly grim' situation where one of the pilots had asked her to accompany him to the cinema after the day's raid. This he had done 'in defiance' of an RAF superstition that it 'wasn't done to say what you would do when you got back'. When the crew returned, minus the pilot, they brushed past Grace and refused to speak to her. She later discovered that they had last seen him baling out over a field in Germany, where men below waited with pitchforks. Though she was understandably distressed by this and the many other tragedies she encountered, Grace was of the opinion that it was a 'must' to 'keep a stiff upper lip at all times' and did her best to keep to this 'code'.[32]

Similarly, Jaqueline Witherington, the sister of WAAF SOE agent Pearl Witherington, worked at RAF Mildenhall debriefing returned aircrews, and though it could be tough work, she was never deterred from the job by the 'shattering' stories she heard.[33]

Speaking specifically of the returning Dambusters, Fay Gillon found it 'very embarrassing and awkward' having to interrogate them after they returned from the famous raid so exhausted and having watched some of their fellow crew members 'go down'.[34] Despite the fact that they clearly felt for the crews, the WAAF interrogators had no choice but to try to collect vital intelligence from them immediately after a raid had taken place. Though Fighter Command had initially opposed the idea of employing women as interrogators and did not allow it until it became absolutely necessary, it appeared that women were actually better at crew interrogations than either had ever thought possible. WAAF interrogators were always aware that the crews were tired, emotionally exhausted and hungry and did their best to gather intelligence as quickly and carefully as possible by asking direct questions and taking efficient notes while the raids were fresh in the airmen's heads. Though, as Grace Hall says, these WAAFs carried out their work sometimes with 'heavy hearts', they retained hope that downed crews might have been captured rather than killed, drawing information out of crews to try to gain an idea of where they might be being held by the enemy.[35] Far from being emotionally overwhelmed and incapable of the work, Grace was 'totally committed' and would not have changed her job for the world.[36]

Being emotionally sensitive to aircrew was not the disadvantage that the RAF had feared it might be. When a young Australian airman on her station went missing in action, his best friend sought solace in Grace Hall's company. He 'stuck' to her for days, following her silently and 'looking utterly lost'. Grace was aware that it was not appropriate for him to be behaving in such a way and discovered that it was upsetting the other airmen to see the young man in such distress. She invited him to a party in the WAAF officers' mess and the women 'chivvied him and he pulled himself together a little'.[37] Rather than falling apart themselves, the WAAFs were often able to give the airmen on their stations an emotional boost and were sensitive to the emotional states and needs of the war-weary men. They were able to empathise and exercise discretion, which was often valuable to aircrews. One of the reasons the RAF had been reluctant to use women in interrogations was the worry that men might feel embarrassed 'opening up' to them about their experiences. Indeed, Edith Kup found that aircrews often gave her a 'very edited edition', especially after very traumatising trips, and knew that it was up to her to get the real story with as many of the facts straight as possible. When one day a crew returned very early with no explanation as to why, they told Edith a 'fairy story', their sergeant 'beginning to sag' as they talked. Sensing that something was wrong, Edith told the sergeant to lie down until it was his turn, and when he did, they could not rouse him. When the sick bay crew attempted to lift him, they found that he was 'as stiff as a board', and the doctor reported that he had been 'literally scared stiff'. Through her interrogation Edith discovered that the young man had 'gone berserk with terror' on the flight and the crew had been forced to return. They had not initially wanted to reveal this to Edith, in an attempt to guard the man's dignity. They were very grateful that she kept it quiet and asked her to sit with them for breakfast regularly after that, until they themselves went missing in action shortly afterwards.[38]

Similarly, Grace Hall was on her way to interrogate a returned crew when she 'fell over a prostrate figure' on the ground next to the hangar. The figure was a teenage airman who had safely returned from his first operation and who had been 'bowled over by his first tot of rum', which the WAAFs often issued to all returning aircrew to calm their nerves. The men in his crew gently raised him to his feet and guided him away, appreciating Grace's discretion.[39]

One thing that the often-traumatised crews were most grateful for when returning from raids was the thoughtful provision of tea and refreshments by the WAAFs. Flight Sergeant Alf Lorimer was always glad to see them ready to welcome him home with a smile and a cup of tea, coffee or rum.[40] 'Our reception was warm,' he said, 'I appreciated that the pleasure shown was mixed with compassion, as many WAAFs knew the aircrew casualty rate.'[41] Similarly, Air Vice Marshal Joe Cox remembers the WAAFs having tea, coffee and sandwiches ready for returning aircrews, always with a smile.[42] The men of the RAF clearly appreciated the WAAFs for their 'thoughtfulness and cheerfulness' and for being a 'morale booster' after difficult missions.[43] Though it might appear as if gender divisions were being reinforced by highlighting the WAAFs for their smiles and their sandwiches, the WAAFs were still defying stereotypes and expectations placed upon women by using their emotional sensitivity to positively affect RAF operations and effectiveness.

PERSONAL RESPONSIBILITY IN WAR

From the outset, it was hoped and intended that women serving in military auxiliaries would do so as far as possible within the boundaries of existing gender definitions. In Britain, men fit into the 'fighting' category, where women were more associated with peace and non-combatant support. This binary division was dominant in British society, so that it became highly uncomfortable if women stepped outside of their accepted role by taking, or assisting in the taking, of lives. All sorts of lines were blurred by war, and though it was generally accepted that women could not serve as combatants in any of the auxiliary services, some of them worked in grey areas. Most famously, the British Army's Auxiliary Territorial Service placed women on anti-aircraft gun sites. These women could set the guns up to be fired, working as radar operators, height finders, spotters, predictors and locators, but they could not pull the trigger. Instead, they had to step aside while a man took over to fire the weapons. This was controversial, as it placed at least some responsibility on the women for the shooting down of enemy planes and the killing of their crews. These ATS women were stepping outside of their 'natural role' by becoming, even in part, 'life-takers'.

WAAFs in intelligence work were, in some ways, in a similar position. Aileen Clayton describes an incident in her Y Service career where one of the German pilots on the 'Milk Run' had become familiar, to the point where the WAAFs looked forward to him coming on air. Known by his call sign 'AmselEins', the pilot assumed that his communications were being heard by the British and would chatter to them in English, even making jokes. 'But war makes the most savage demands,' Aileen remembers. Her team was eventually instructed to advise No. II Fighter Group when AmselEins was operating, which inevitably led to his position being targeted by a flight of Spitfires. He was shot down, unable to get out of the aircraft as it plummeted towards the ground in flames. Aileen and her team listened to his final descent. 'He screamed and screamed for his mother and cursed the Fuhrer,' she says.

> I found myself praying: 'Get out, bale out – oh, please dear God, get him out.' But it was no use, he could not make it. We heard him the whole way down until he fell below reception range. I went outside and was sick. Only then did I realise that I was in part his executioner; only then did I realise what I had done to that young pilot. I thought of the sad letters I had written when I was in the Casualties Section in Record Office, and I knew that tomorrow a German mother's heart would break.[44]

It was clearly distressing for Aileen to realise that she had had a hand in the death of the German pilot, but this realisation did not make her incapable of continuing in her job. Quite the opposite, in fact – rather than being put off the work, she vowed instead to do her 'utmost to end this carnage as soon as possible' by continuing to work towards Allied victory.[45]

Mary Harrison worked at RAF Medmenham and was involved in the making of models for the thousand-bomber raid on Cologne. Her clear awareness of her active role in the mission is illustrated in her poem 'My Hands', which she wrote after she had seen photographs of Cologne after the raid:

> Do you know what it is like to have death in your hands
> when you haven't a murderer's mind?
> Do you know how it feels when you could be the cause
> of a child being blind?
> How many people have died through me
> From the skill in my fingertips?
> For I fashion the clay and portray the landscape
> As the fliers are briefed for their trips.
>
> Do these young men in blue feel as I do
> The destruction
> The pain.
> Let me cover my eyes as you cover the skies
> Let me pray it can't happen again.
> Don't show me the pictures you take as you fly,
> They're ruins and scape – little more.
>
> Is all this part
> Of the madness we choose to call War?
> If there is a God up above who listens at all
> Does he know why this has to be?
> Did he give me my hands just to fashion the plans
> That my own land may always be free?[46]

Similarly, Medmenham WAAF operator Kathleen Mary Franck remembers seeing a piece of film after the Dambusters raid which showed a car trying to get away from the surging water leaking from one of the dams. The car was engulfed by the water and Kathleen wondered about the German family inside of it.[47] Empathy did cause emotional distress in some WAAFs. Aileen Clayton encountered two survivors of a German bomber that had been shot down, who had been adrift in a dinghy in the Mediterranean for four days. She says: 'They looked so very young – mere children – which reminded me of my brother, and they were obviously very scared and bewildered. I wanted so much to put my arm around them and say – "Don't be afraid. No one will harm you. For you now the war is over."'[48]

As was common in WAAFs, Aileen did not allow her feelings to compromise her work, or her country: 'I knew that I must not show any sympathy, or chatter with them to reassure them because they had not yet been "processed" by the prisoner-of-war interrogation centre and I might compromise its work.'

Kathlyn Williams, a map-maker at Medmenham, said after the war:

> With our paintbrushes we had helped to kill people we did not know. At one point I had considered becoming a conscientious objector. With every target in my mind I had put my hands together and prayed that no children would be killed. In a discussion with a major from Sandhurst Military Academy, a kind and humane man, I was told that, 'You have to protect the things you believe in.' So I continued to paint. As a result I now have two medals and know that there are facts of life I shall never understand.[49]

Indeed, for many WAAFs, the knowledge that they were fighting to keep their loved ones safe from the evils of Nazism enabled or persuaded them to do things that they might not have naturally done under normal circumstances. Despite her sadness at having a hand in the taking of lives, Mary Harrison felt that in war it was 'teeth for teeth, eyes for eyes'.[50] This actually appeared to be the opinion of Britain in general. As Second World War scientist R. V. Jones points out, the British people had started the war 'morally opposed to the bombing of civilian populations', but after the indiscriminate bombing of British towns by the Germans, they had changed their minds.[51] Radar operator Anne Stobbs was warned in an interview by an RAF officer that Bomber Command was thinking less of defence and more in terms of 'dishing it out' to the Germans and that bombers were 'in the business of killing people'. The officer gave the interviewees the option to return to their previous roles should they wish to conscientiously object, but neither Anne nor her colleagues chose to, as they were aware of how vital their work was.[52]

Some WAAFs did not feel upset by the knowledge that they were involved in the taking of lives. Radar operator Gwen Arnold said:

It is strange how little we fretted about the reality of war and its horror. It did not worry me that each bomber carried a full load of bombs that would spell death and disaster somewhere. We had seen the ruins of British cities bombed by the enemy and we knew all about the British lives lost in the terrible raids of the early months of the war. To us the raids made by the Allies were just a necessary part of bringing the whole ghastly business to an end. We prayed for the safety of those nearest and dearest to us and for our country, but that was all. War was a necessary evil – to be lived through and won.[53]

Eileen Younghusband also found that she felt no remorse during the war and had 'only time to get on with the job', not feeling affected by it until long after 1945. As far as she was concerned, she and her colleagues were 'fighting for survival', and 'no one gave in'.[54] Similarly, Grace Hall considered that whatever she and her colleagues were responsible for, 'it had to be done at that time'.[55] Whether the WAAFs did or did not feel remorse at their involvement in the taking of German lives, they did not tend to display joy or satisfaction at it. Male RAF Bomber Command intelligence officer W. E. Jones says in his book that he would often 'crawl into bed, think of my wife and baby fast asleep 200 miles away and then think of Berlin hopefully blazing merrily and the bomb disposal squads dealing with unexploded or long-delay bombs'.[56] Despite their having arguably ventured to some degree into the realm of 'life-takers', there isn't much to suggest that the WAAFs actually hoped that their enemies would suffer.

Through their consistent hard work in their intelligence roles, the WAAFs proved themselves to be trustworthy, discreet and capable of keeping the nation's secrets. They also proved to be emotionally capable in the face of chaos, fear and grief. The Air Ministry recognised eventually that there was 'no evidence of responsibility weighing more heavily on women than men', and it was acknowledged that the experiment of using women in Special Duties or intelligence roles had been a 'resounding success'.[57] Their total dedication to duty did not go unnoticed. Grace Hall felt that at the beginning of the war, the WAAFs were 'novelties on trial', but that they were slowly accepted by their male colleagues, gradually dispelling their fears regarding loose lips and hysteria.[58] After hearing stories like those of the brave conduct of Jean Mary Youle, the Melbourne *Argus* reported in October 1943 that Britain's Blitz had produced its 'heroines':

Great deeds of bravery and endurance were performed in the Battle of Britain, not only by that gallant band of RAF pilots but also by the gallant women of the WAAF, who worked, lived and sometimes died beside the men of their service at fighter and bomber stations against which were directed the full force of the Luftwaffe's savage attacks. WAAF telephonists and plotters and clerks worked steadily on in operations rooms and control rooms though unbelievable noise and chaos with buildings literally falling about them. Many awards for bravery were won by members of the WAAF at this period, but the recognition which they prized most deeply was less tangible. It was the sort of thing that happened when one Sunday after a particularly heavy raid, with many casualties, the remaining WAAF were assembled for a rollcall and marched back to quarters. As they swung past (and who knows what an effort it cost to keep those chins up) the airmen on the station gave them a rousing cheer.[59]

Though they lost husbands, brothers, friends, fiancés and boy-friends on a daily basis and often faced danger, immense stress and discomfort, the WAAFs did indeed keep their chins up, defying expectations and rising above the hostility and reluctance of their male colleagues to work effectively towards the British war effort and Allied victory in 1945. They were not 'lethal women' and they did not break down under the pressure. Rather, they worked, lived and died beside the men of the RAF in service to their country, very much a part of Britain's finest hour.

CONCLUSION

THE JIGSAW PUZZLE OF BRITISH INTELLIGENCE

Members of the WAAF were present across the vast system of services and organisations that contributed to the overall British intelligence picture in the Second World War. As Aileen Clayton states, those at the head of the British fight between 1939 and 1945 were constantly 'piecing together bits of intelligence from various sources', in their attempt to understand their enemy and the war they were fighting. Reports from the Air Ministry, from intelligence gleaned by the codebreakers at Bletchley Park, from Y Service interceptors, from radar personnel and from the various other RAF sections and units formed pieces of what Aileen describes as a 'jigsaw puzzle'.[1] The more complete the picture, the more effectively Britain could deploy its air resources and fight the war – and the more chance it had of victory. The Air Ministry recognised that the details provided by the collection of intelligence were 'collectively of great importance' to the British war effort, especially in light of Germany's superior size and military strength.[2] Intelligence was a force multiplier and helped Britain to maximise its fighting potential while it was outmanned and outgunned. A vast mass of intelligence was collected, processed, analysed, disseminated and used to make operational decisions on a daily basis throughout the war, on a greater scale than ever before. Working across the jigsaw puzzle of RAF sections and units and actively involved in all of these processes were thousands of members of the Women's Auxiliary Air Force, every one of them a vital cog in the intelligence machine.

The WAAF had been designed in 1939 to 'economise manpower' by utilising 'womanpower', in order to release men from domestically based operational duties so that they could keep the RAF flying.[3] Over the course of the war, around a quarter of a million women served in the WAAF, and it is estimated that without their contribution, the RAF would have required around 150,000 extra men to function at the same level.[4] Due to the demands of war, specifically for pilots and aircrew, this would have been nigh impossible. WAAFs were successfully substituted for RAF personnel in many different roles, releasing men for combat and keeping the RAF functioning effectively.

The contribution of the WAAFs, though, was about much more than simply filling empty jobs, and releasing men for combat was not the extent of their accomplishments. These women worked tirelessly every day to provide information that saved lives and directly affected the course of the war. In many cases, they began at a disadvantage, having received little to no education in subjects that their new roles were based in – maths and physics, for example. They learned fast, worked hard and committed themselves fully to the Allied cause.

Some of them showed courage beyond measure and all of them faced danger on a daily basis, working hard as they did their best to remain unfazed by the bullets and the bombs. As Dame Helen Gwynne-Vaughan pointed out to the women of the auxiliaries in 1942, 'To serve in His Majesty's Forces is to incur a very grave responsibility which must be carried out though the cost be life itself.'[5] The members of the WAAF took this responsibility very seriously, and over the course of the war around 600 of its women were killed while serving. Gwynn-Vaughan warned that 'the critical moment may arise very suddenly, there may be no time to think. The right and courageous thing must be done instinctively.'[6]

In frequent displays of discipline, courage and loyalty to their country, women like Elspeth Henderson and Jean Mary Youle remained at their posts during bombing raids, and some RAF stations, including Fighter Command's essential station Biggin Hill, continued to function in part because of the courage of their airwomen.

Over the course of the war, members of the WAAF received 2,497 Mentions in Despatches, ninety-seven MBEs, ninety-three British Empire Medals (three of these were for 'special gallantry'), six Military Medals for bravery and one Empire Gallantry Medal (later superseded by the George Cross). Included in these were WAAFs involved in the collection and dissemination of intelligence. Telephonists Elspeth Henderson and Helen Turner realised the importance of information they had received needing to be passed on and remained at their posts in their burning building until it was almost too late to leave safely, and Jean Mary Youle acted in a similar fashion at her exchange. All three received the Military Medal, as did Avis Hearn, a WAAF radar operator who 'steadily passed on the course of enemy bombers with bombs and debris falling almost on her head'.[7] These women did what was asked of them and at times, much more. The WAAF had begun as an experiment – using WAAF personnel in intelligence roles even more so – and both experiments had irrefutably successful results.

The British government and military services expected women to buckle under the weight of being confronted with the effects of war and having to come to terms with their new, more direct involvement in the conflict, as well as being unable to refrain from leaking the RAF's secrets because of their supposed natural inclination to gossip. But the opposite was true. There is little evidence to suggest that members of the WAAF revealed secret information or undermined any operation through gossip or chatter, and on the contrary, there is a mountain of evidence to show that they were in fact very effective at keeping secrets, to the point where they didn't speak about their wartime experiences until three decades after the war ended. They were even involved in strategies to prevent secrets from getting out, in some cases being personally responsible for preventing security leaks.

It was expected that women would experience emotional reactions to the sights, sounds and experiences of war that they were being exposed to in a new way through their work in the WAAF. Of course, they did have emotional reactions, and in some cases it is clear that they were uncomfortable with the responsibility they knew they shared in the taking of lives through warfare. It was very rare, though, for them to be so overcome by their emotions that they were prevented from being able to do their work effectively. Painfully often, WAAFs lost loved ones – brothers, husbands, fiancés, boyfriends and friends – and carried on with their work with potent and powerful understanding of how important it was and what rested upon their success.

Indeed, they were often motivated by their fear, worry and grief to put a greater degree of effort into their work, well aware of the importance of their contribution to the British war effort and the potential consequence of the loss of the war.

The women lived with and overcame prejudice, endured social ostracism and sexism on a daily basis and smashed stereotypes with their clear ability to do what was required but not expected of them. They had no choice but to work hard to banish the stereotype of the subversive, lethal woman in the world of British intelligence.

THE POST-WAR TRAJECTORY

After the Allied victory in 1945, many WAAFs, particularly those in intelligence roles, found themselves redundant as far as the RAF were concerned. The end of hostilities meant that air intelligence efforts waned and the WAAFs began to be demobilised, starting with the service's married women. Many WAAFs welcomed the freedom of demobilisation, having lived under service restrictions for the duration of their wartime work. Others did not welcome it, as leaving the service meant that they returned to a life with no work, no regular income and the loss of their independence and precious camaraderie with their fellow servicewomen. This camaraderie was deeply valued by many WAAFs. Molly Sasson says:

> We all learned to work together, assist one another and care about each other. There was a good healthy competitive spirit that prevailed and I experienced only helpfulness and cooperation throughout my training. There was a bond of comradeship and loyalty, which permeated throughout my service career. All members of each course took their studies seriously, and there was a sense of mutual pride, shared in being members of our chosen service.[8]

Women in the WAAF had gained confidence and skills which gave them meaning and purpose. Many women left to find that the world had not changed as they had and found it very difficult to return to a life in which they were expected to marry and raise children and do little else. The Second World War had provided women with an opportunity to show what they were capable of, and in intelligence work, they had proven themselves to be more than up to the task. In some cases, such as in the Dowding System, they even came to be considered better at the work than their male colleagues.

Despite their proven capabilities and aptitudes, and the fact that they had become an integral part of the RAF's war-fighting ability, there was opposition to the suggestion of a peacetime regular service for airwomen. The WAAFs had overwhelmingly earned the respect and admiration of their male colleagues, only to find that their impressive wartime record had done little to earn them immediate change in terms of societal expectations and employment possibilities.

After much argument and discussion, though, a permanent female peacetime force was established, and after the passing of the Army and Air Force (Women's Service) Act in 1948, on 1 February 1949 the Women's Royal Air Force was formed. The WRAF was founded on the undoubtable success of the WAAF. It would, however, be many years before any resemblance of equality existed in the RAF. The WRAF was not formally merged with the RAF until 1 April 1994, and before this date women were not considered full members of the RAF.

In 1995, Flight Lieutenant Jo Salter became the first British woman to be declared 'combat ready' and went on to fly missions in Iraq as the first female operational Tornado GR1 pilot in the UK. In 2017, the RAF's ground-fighting force opened to women for the first time, making the RAF the first branch of the British military to open every role to female personnel. Though the WAAFs had more than proven the capability of women in the Second World War, it would be decades before military regulations and society officially and publicly recognised it.

The slow progress of the full integration of women into the RAF is matched by that of women in the British intelligence services, who were restricted largely to filing and clerical work for decades after 1945. The first woman to be promoted to the rank of director of a service branch, Dame Stella Rimington was appointed the director general of MI5 in 1992. When she joined the service in 1969, it was clear to her that 'a strict sex discrimination policy was in place in MI5 and women were treated quite differently from men'. She joined at the age of thirty-four, in possession of a degree and with several years' experience in public service at a higher grade than MI5 was offering.

Stella has been very open about sex discrimination in the security services, explaining the policy which dictated that men be recruited as 'officers' while women had their own career structure which kept them as 'second-class assistant officers'. Women were restricted to support work like filing and simple enquiries and were barred from 'sharp-end intelligence-gathering operations', meeting and controlling agents and recruiting sources.[9] Stella states that it was said that 'dangerous work was not for women' and that 'policemen would not take women seriously as colleagues', and she 'caused a stir' in 1971 when she returned to work after having a baby. These ideas, ingrained in the British authorities before and during the Second World War, had not been permanently altered by the work of the WAAFs towards British intelligence, and in the minds of the men of such authorities, little had changed.

Stella was promoted to be an officer in 1973. Her promotion did not, as she says, 'mark the opening of a floodgate', and there was no 'surge of female promotions' after hers, though things did begin to 'heat up' as sex discrimination began to appear on the political agenda and other women began to complain about discrimination in the security service. Director General Stella Rimington attributes her promotion to her determination, energy and ability to get things done, which made her 'difficult to ignore'.[10] The WAAFs making vital intelligence contributions in the Second World War displayed all of these attributes and more, and yet remained, for many years, ignored, hidden from the history of British and military intelligence.

BEHIND THE FEW

In part owing to their success as intelligence personnel, the WAAFs working in air intelligence have remained largely hidden in the shadows since the conclusion of the Second World War. Such intense secrecy and the proper adherence to security protocol often banish intelligence personnel to the outer margins of history, and it has only been in recent years that their stories and the true value of their contributions has begun to be recovered. This recovery remains difficult, in some ways, when it concerns women, who have often been 'missing from history' in so many ways.

When Jamie Seymour set out to try to discover what her mother Eleanor had really been doing with the WAAF during the Second World War, she hit roadblock after roadblock, owing to the fact that Eleanor had been involved in intelligence work. All Jamie had to begin with were the snippets of information she had gleaned from her conversations with her mother, and it was only after obtaining her wartime service record that she managed to confirm the basic details of her role.

WAAF wireless operator Betty Turner said in 2015 that, in her opinion, the WAAFs have 'absolutely not' received the recognition that they deserve for their work in the Second World War. Having worked in Bomber Command, Betty identified that it is 'just the Bomber Boys ... the boys that flew', who are remembered today. She speaks of her sadness about the fact the WAAFs remained, for a long time, missing from museums and media portrayals of the RAF and, in particular, Bomber Command. Though she thinks of the famous bomber crews as 'wonderful', she is keen to point out that 'everybody else behind those boys were wonderful too'. It is a particular sore point to her that where the WAAFs are recognised, which is seldom, they are portrayed as the 'love interest' of flight crews, a source of moral support and not much else.[11]

Betty is correct, in that the aircrews of Bomber and Fighter Commands have received much of the attention for their brave and heroic exploits, and it is not for this book to undermine their contributions or to suggest that they are not deserving of the attention they have received. The 'Few' were as important to the British war effort as Churchill deemed them to be, and their legacy is not only valid – it is a point of British historical pride. It is, however, time to redress the balance in historical memory regarding the WAAFs.

Far more than the 'love interest' for the men of the RAF, the women of the WAAF carried out crucial work that directly contributed to the victories won by the 'Bomber Boys' and the 'Few'. The radar operators of the Dowding System placed themselves in great danger in isolated coastal locations to collect information on incoming German aircraft, which they passed to their colleagues in Fighter Command filter rooms to record. WAAF filterers disseminated this information to operations rooms, where it was used to direct the 'Few' in battle, resulting ultimately in the British victory in the Battle of Britain, as well as saved lives and preserved aircraft.

Women worked to the same end during the Blitz, aiding British bomber crews in their offensive operations and helping to defend Britain against the relentless German onslaught by night. In the Y Service, German-speaking WAAFs collected first-hand information from German pilots and commanders, passing it to the Fighter Command hierarchy to utilise alongside information yielded by the Dowding System during the Battle of Britain and in the months and years that followed it.

At the Government Code and Cypher School, WAAFs worked alongside the famous codebreakers to ensure the continuous movement of intelligence to and from Bletchley Park, keeping the RAF and the Air Ministry informed and involved in the war at all times. After the Battle of Britain had been won and Hitler had failed to bomb Britain into submission during the Blitz, it was these WAAFs who disseminated Ultra intelligence to signal that Operation Sealion had been indefinitely abandoned.

In photographic intelligence, WAAFs worked to aid the discovery of and defence against the threatening V-weapons and jet-propelled aircraft, as well as assisting with Britain's offensive war in 617 Squadron's famous Dambusters raid and Bomber Command's 'thousand-bomber raids'.

WAAFs were also present in other intelligence capacities. Myra Murden, for example, helped to keep the maps in Churchill's underground War Rooms up to date, and her colleague Rachel Foster worked to disseminate incoming intelligence around this complicated labyrinth of subterranean rooms from which the War Cabinet directed the war in times of heavy bombing. Churchill took with him several WAAF code and cypher officers when he travelled abroad, and other code and cypher WAAFs were sent to work in British embassies overseas during the course of the war.

There were also WAAFs present in special intelligence capacities, where this research has focused on service intelligence. On these WAAFs, there is more work to be carried out, as there remains a gap in historical memory and in the history of British intelligence.

Wherever they were in the world, however isolated by location or by intense secrecy, WAAFs were urged to think of the service as a wider whole. This they did, thinking not only of their service but of their country and working effectively across the 'jigsaw puzzle' of British intelligence towards its war effort and eventual victory.

This list is not exhaustive but serves to highlight examples of the importance of the intelligence work that the WAAFs conducted behind the scenes during the Second World War. In part because of their work, air battles vital to victory were won, enemy planes were shot down before their bombs could drop, German ships were sunk before they could damage Allied shipping and naval forces, secret enemy weapons were annihilated before they could wreak war-altering havoc and enemy plans were severely disrupted and forced into abandonment. Lives were saved, resources were preserved, forces were multiplied and victories were won. Behind the few famous faces of the war, women of the WAAF worked, hidden but crucial, towards Allied victory.

APPENDIX

SCALE OF WAAF SUBSTITUTION IN ROLES RELATED TO INTELLIGENCE WORK[1]

WAAF Officers

Classification	Degree of substitution	Ratio of substitution (WAAF to RAF)	Notes
Code and cypher	100 per cent	1:1	Includes British Isles only (overseas code and cypher officers assessed separately)
Filterer	Approximately 50 per cent	–	
Intelligence officer	As needed	–	
Operations room	100 per cent	1:1	
Photographic	As needed	–	Specially assessed
Photographic interpretation	As needed	–	Specially assessed
Signals intelligence	As needed	–	Specially assessed
Signals radar	As needed	–	Assessed according to type of unit
Signals radar (supervisory)	As needed	–	Assessed according to type of unit
Signals special radar	As needed	–	Assessed according to type of unit

WAAF Other Ranks

Classification	Degree of substitution	Ratio of substitution (WAAF to RAF)	Notes
Clerk, General Duties (maps)	100 per cent	1:1	
Clerk, signals	100 per cent	1:1	(Except in special cases)
Clerk, Special Duties	75 per cent	1:1	
Clerk (watchkeeper)	100 per cent	1:1	
Central Interpretation Unit	80 per cent	1:1	Up to and including rank of sergeant
Radar operator	45 per cent	1:1	
Fighter Command R/T operator	100 per cent	1:1	
Telephonist	75 per cent	1:1	
Teleprinter operator	75 per cent	1:1	
Wireless operator	75 per cent	1:1	Up to and including rank of sergeant
Wireless operator (DF)	75 per cent	1:1	Up to and including rank of sergeant
Wireless operator (slip reader)	100 per cent	1:1	Excluding mobile stations

NOTES

PROLOGUE

1 Hansard, HC Deb, 20 August 1940, vol. 364, cc 1167 (Winston Churchill's 'Never in the field of human conflict was so much owed by so many to so few' speech).
2 Aileen Clayton, *The Enemy Is Listening* (London: Hutchinson & Co. Ltd, 1980), pp. 11–12.
3 Ibid., pp. 12–13.
4 Christopher Andrew and David Dilks, eds, *The Missing Dimension: Governments and Intelligence Communities in the Twentieth Century* (London: Macmillan, 1984), p. 1.

THE WAR, THE WAAF AND WOMEN IN INTELLIGENCE

1 Mary Knight, 'Second World War Memories', oral evidence recorded by the author, who is Mary's granddaughter, January 2016.
2 Catherine Butcher, *Edith Cavell: Faith Before the Firing Squad* (Oxford: Monarch Books, 2015), p. 183.
3 Royal Air Force, 'Our History', https://www.raf.mod.uk/our-organisation/our-history/ (accessed 30 August 2022).
4 Christopher Andrew, *The Defence of the Realm: The Authorized History of MI5* (London: Penguin Books, 2010), p. 60.
5 Tammy Proctor, *Female Intelligence: Women and Espionage in the First World War* (New York: New York University Press, 2003), pp. 147–8.
6 KV 1/35, MI5 World War I Branch Reports: F Branch, Prevention of Espionage 1914 1918, National Archives, Kew.
7 Security Service Archives, as referenced in Andrew (2010), p. 61.
8 KV 1/35, MI5 World War I Branch Reports: F Branch, Prevention of Espionage 1914 1918, National Archives, Kew.
9 Andrew (2010), p. 127.
10 Secret Intelligence Service, 'Our History', https://www.sis.gov.uk/our-history.html (accessed 27 February 2018).
11 AIR 24/646, Air Ministry and Ministry of Defence: Operations Record Books, HQ Fighter Command, National Archives, Kew.
12 Central Statistical Office, *Annual Abstract of Statistics 1938–50* (London: HMSO, 1951), vol. 88, Table 125.
13 AIR 2/8261, Women's Auxiliary Air Force: Personnel (Code B, 77/1): WAAF serving overseas: legal position, National Archives, Kew.
14 AIR 2/3036, Reserve and Auxiliary Forces (Code B, 66): Proposed formation of Women's Auxiliary Corps: consultation with the War Office, National Archives, Kew.

15 AIR 2/3036, Reserve and Auxiliary Forces (Code B, 66): Proposed formation of Women's Auxiliary Corps: consultation with the War Office, National Archives, Kew.

16 Leonard Taylor, *Airwomen's Work* (London: Sir Isaac Pitman & Sons Ltd, 1943), p. 2.

17 Denis Richards, *Royal Air Force, 1939–1945*, 3 vols (London: HMSO, 1974), vol. 1 (1974), p. 180.

18 Molly J. Sasson, *More Cloak Than Dagger: One Woman's Career in Secret Intelligence* (Ballarat: Connor Court Publishing, 2015), p. 24.

19 Ibid.

20 Ibid.

21 Squadron Leader Beryl E. Escott, *Women in Air Force Blue: The Story of Women in the Royal Air Force from 1918 to the Present Day* (Wellingborough: Patrick Stephens Ltd, 1989), p. 191.

22 Clayton (1980), p. 26.

23 John Frayn Turner, *The WAAF at War* (Barnsley: Pen & Sword Aviation, 2011), pp. 23–4.

24 F. H. Hinsley, *British Intelligence in the Second World War*, 6 vols (London: HMSO, 1979–90), vol. 1 (1979), p. 4.

CARELESS TALK AND KEEPING MUM

1   Clayton (1980), p. 29.

2   CEH14, notes pertaining to Mollie Thompson, Medmenham Collection Archive, RAF Wyton.

3   7463, interview with Petrea Winterbotham (oral history), Imperial War Museum Archive, London. Winterbotham was a plotter in the operations room at Bentley Priory throughout the Battle of Britain.

4   KV 4/227, Report on the work of MS (recruitment and operation of agents) during the Second World War, National Archives, Kew.

5   HW 14/36, Personal security form for all members of GCCS warning against careless talk and a security incident in Hut 3, National Archives, Kew.

6   Ibid.

7   Art.IWM PST 0142, Fougasse's 'Careless Talk Costs Lives' poster, Imperial War Museum Archive, London.

8   CAB 67/2/38, Memorandum from the Committee on Issue of Warnings against Discussion of Confidential Matters in Public Places, 13 November 1939, National Archives, Kew.

9   Jo Fox, 'Careless Talk: Tensions within British Domestic Propaganda during the Second World War', *Journal of British Studies*, vol. 51 (2012), pp. 938–42.

10 INF 1/264, Morale – summaries of daily reports, Home Intelligence Division (1940), National Archives, Kew.

11 Press Book 'Next of Kin', British Films Institute Special Collections, Thorold Dickinson Collection, box 7 item 7, as mentioned in Fox (2012), p. 958.

12 INF 3/229, Ministry of Information: original art work, anti-rumour and careless talk: 'Keep mum, she's not so dumb!' poster (figure of blonde-haired woman reclining, servicemen about her), National Archives, Kew.

13 INF 3/229, Ministry of Information: original art work, anti-rumour and careless talk, National Archives, Kew.

14 AMY 59, *Missed Date*, Second World War 'Careless Talk' short film with a rhyming commentary made to be shown to RAF personnel in 1943, Imperial War Museum Archive, London.

15 AMY 56, *Hush! Not a Word!*, Second World War 'Careless Talk' short film made to be shown to military personnel in 1943, Imperial War Museum Archive, London.

16 Government advertisement placed in *Picture Post* magazine, 27 July 1940, as featured in Fox (2012), pp. 936–66.

17 Ibid.

18 Fox (2012), p. 942.

19 INF 1/264, Morale – summaries of daily reports, Home Intelligence Division (1940), National Archives, Kew.

20 7463, interview with Petrea Winterbotham (oral history), Imperial War Museum Archive, London.

21 Adam and Charles Black, *The WAAF in Action* (London: Adam & Charles Black, 1944), p. 10.

22 Edward Wood, extract from a letter circulated to all 'V' Section personnel at RAF Medmenham in 1945, Medmenham Collection Archive.

23 'Shout and Whisper', Oral History Project Summary Document, entry for Olivia Davies, Bawdsey Radar Trust.

24 Marion Hill, *Bletchley Park People: Churchill's Geese That Never Cackled* (Stroud: The History Press, 2004), p. 130.

25 A1993098, Gwen Reading, Radar Operator in WW2, contributed 8 November 2003, BBC People's War Archive. Reading's family were told she was working on 'something to do with wireless'.

26 Ibid.

27 Any published before this, including those of Aileen Clayton and Constance Babington Smith, were written with official permission from the British authorities.

28 Richard Morris, *Guy Gibson* (London: Viking, 1994), pp. 156–7.

29 Max Arthur, *Dambusters: A Landmark Oral History* (London: Virgin Books, 2008), p. 155.

30 KV 4/227, Report on the work of MS (recruitment and operation of agents) during the Second World War, National Archives, Kew.

31 HW 14/57, Government Code and Cypher School: Directorate: Second World War Policy Papers, Staff Recruitment, Selection and Pay etc.

32 A2429561, Kathleen Godfrey, 'A WAAF at Bletchley', contributed 16 March 2004, BBC People's War Archive.

33 16900, interview with Vera Ines Morley Elkan (oral history), Imperial War Museum Archive, London.

34 7463, interview with Petrea Winterbotham (oral history), Imperial War Museum Archive, London. *The Ultra Secret* was the first popular account of the Ultra secret to be published in Britain.

35 VE Day Special Order to staff from Commander Travis, Bletchley Park Trust Archive, as quoted in Hill (2004), p. 129.

36 Hill (2004), pp. 129–32.

37 9106, interview with Gwendoline Saunders (oral history), Imperial War Museum Archive, London.

38 11885, interview with Jean Hilda Mills (oral history), Imperial War Museum Archive, London.

39 Muriel Gane Pushman, *We All Wore Blue: Experiences in the WAAF* (Stroud: Tempus, 2006), p. 46.

40 Ibid.

41 Anne Stobbs, *One-Oh-Eight Miller* (Marsworth: Bucks Literary Services, 1989), p. 28.

THE GREAT AIR BATTLE

1 Hansard, HC Deb, 18 June 1940, vol. 362, cc 51–64 (Winston Churchill's 'Finest Hour' speech).

2 Hitler's War Directive No. 16, http://der-fuehrer.org/reden/english/wardirectives/16.html (accessed 16 April 2018).

3 Joseph 'Beppo' Schmid, head of Luftwaffe intelligence, report submitted 22 November 1939.

4 Churchill's 'Few' speech.

5 Memorandum to the Cabinet by Winston Churchill, 3 September 1940, in Winston Churchill, *The Second World War*, 6 vols (London: Cassell & Co. Ltd, 1948–54), vol. 2 (1949), pp. 405–6.

6 Royal Air Force website, https://www.raf.mod.uk (accessed 18 April 2022).

7 T. C. Willbond, 'Understanding the Dowding System', Briefing Paper for the Association of RAF Fighter Control Officers.

EARLY WARNING WAAFS: WOMEN IN THE DOWDING SYSTEM

1 AIR 20/6427, Women's Auxiliary Air Force: Personnel (Code 77/1): Report of the Post War Manning Committee (Trades Sub-Committee), National Archives, Kew.

2 AIR 28/261, Air Ministry and Ministry of Defence: Operations Record Books, Royal Air Force Stations, Exeter, National Archives, Kew.

3 AIR16/8, WAAF operation training in plotting duties, National Archives, Kew.

4 Escott (1989), p. 183.

5 Joyce Millard, *Mayday Calling Mayday: A Story of Rescue* (Felixstowe: Bluebelle Books, 1995), p. x.

6 Video interviews with WAAF personnel who served in Fighter Command, Association of RAF Fighter Control Officers, Barbara Davies.

7 Daphne Bingham, ed., *Bluebirds Fly Past: Memories of the WAAF West Sussex Group* (Bognor Regis: Woodfield Publishing, 1999), p. 35.

8 Ibid., p. 84.

9 Gwen Arnold, *Radar Days* (Oxford: Isis Publishing Ltd, 2002), p. 128.

10 The Association of Royal Air Force Fighter Control Officers, 'Blazing a Trail for the Operational Employment of Women in the Royal Air Force', Briefing Paper (2012).

11 AIR 28/261, Air Ministry and Ministry of Defence: Operations Record Books, Royal Air Force Stations, Exeter, National Archives, Kew.

12 Millard (1995), p. ix.

13 Ibid., p. iii.

14 AMY 157, *RDF to Radar* film, Imperial War Museum Archive, London.

15 Video interviews with WAAF personnel who served in Fighter Command, Association of RAF Fighter Control Officers.

16 AIR16/8, WAAF operation training in plotting duties, National Archives, Kew.

17 The Association of Royal Air Force Fighter Control Officers, 'Blazing a Trail for the Operational Employment of Women in the Royal Air Force', Briefing Paper (2012).

18 AIR16/8, WAAF operation training in plotting duties, National Archives, Kew.

19 Video interviews with WAAF personnel who served in Fighter Command, Association of RAF Fighter Control Officers, Patricia Clark.

20 Claire Lorrimer, *You Never Know* (London: Hodder & Stoughton, 2016), p. 59.

21 13927, interview with Edith Mary Kup (oral history), Imperial War Museum Archive, London.

22 Mary James, 'The Big Picture', *Royal Air Force Salute*, 2010.

23 Dame Felicity Peake, *Pure Chance* (Shrewsbury: Airlife Publishing Ltd, 1993), pp. 132–3, 141.

24 A2121148, Joyce Anne Deane née Morley, 'War Memories: Plotting the Battle of Britain', contributed 9 December 2003, BBC People's War Archive.

25 Lorrimer (2016), p. 62.

26 A2121148, Joyce Anne Deane née Morley, 'War Memories: Plotting the Battle of Britain', contributed 9 December 2003, BBC People's War Archive.

27 Lorrimer (2016), p. 66.

28 Video interviews with WAAF personnel who served in Fighter Command, Association of RAF Fighter Control Officers.

29 13927, interview with Edith Mary Kup (oral history), Imperial War Museum Archive, London.

30 Eileen Younghusband, *Not an Ordinary Life* (Cardiff: Cardiff Centre for Lifelong Learning, 2009), p. 40.

31 7463, interview with Petrea Winterbotham (oral history), Imperial War Museum Archive, London.

32 11885, interview with Jean Hilda Mills (oral history), Imperial War Museum Archive, London.

33 Lorrimer (2016), p. 64.

34 Escott (1989), p. 185.

35 Tom Sawyer, *Only Owls and Bloody Fools Fly at Night* (Manchester: Crécy Publishing Ltd, 2000), p. 199.

36 Grace 'Archie' Hall, *We, Also, Were There: A Collection of Recollections of Wartime Women of Bomber Command* (Braunton: Merlin Books Ltd, 1985), p. 186.

37 Millard (1995), p. iii.

38 Ibid., p. v.

39 Ibid., p. vii.

40 Air Ministry Communiqué, 8 August 1945, as referenced by the Association of Royal Air Force Fighter Control Officers, 'Blazing a Trail for the Operational Employment of Women in the Royal Air Force', Briefing Paper (2012, acquired from the Association of RAF Fighter Control Officers).

41 AIR 2/8660, Women's Auxiliary Air Force: Personnel (Code B, 77/1): Substitution in signals trade, National Archives, Kew.

42 AIR 16/887, WAAF Historical Records, National Archives, Kew.

43 Frayn Turner (2011), p. 14.

44 Churchill (1949), p. 293.

45 Churchill's 'Finest Hour' speech.

46 The Institution of Electrical Engineers, ed., 'Seminar on the History of Radar Development to 1945' (London: The Institution of Electrical Engineers, 1985).

47 A2121148, Joyce Anne Deane née Morley, 'War Memories: Plotting the Battle of Britain', contributed 9 December 2003, BBC People's War Archive.

48 Video interviews with WAAF personnel who served in Fighter Command, Association of RAF Fighter Control Officers.

49 Younghusband (2009), p. 35.

50 28454, interview with Joan Fleetwood Varley (oral history), Imperial War Museum Archive, London.

51 Ibid.

52 The Association of Royal Air Force Fighter Control Officers, 'Blazing a Trail for the Operational Employment of Women in the Royal Air Force', Briefing Paper (2012).

53 Lorrimer (2016), p. 74.

54 Younghusband (2009), p. 47.

55 Lorrimer (2016), p. 104.

56 Video interviews with WAAF personnel who served in Fighter Command, Association of RAF Fighter Control Officers, Sherry Lygo Hackett.

57 A2121148, Joyce Anne Deane née Morley, 'War Memories: Plotting the Battle of Britain', contributed 9 December 2003, BBC People's War Archive.

58 Air Chief Marshal Sir Frederick Rosier, *Be Bold* (London: Grub Street, 2011), p. 158.

THE LADIES WHO LISTENED: WAAFS IN SIGNALS INTELLIGENCE

1 David Kenyon, *Bletchley Park and D-Day: The Untold Story of How the Battle for Normandy Was Won* (New Haven: Yale University Press, 2019), p. 24.

2 1682, Captain W. H. Wyllie, 'The History of Field SIGINT, 1939–45', Military Intelligence Museum Archive, Chicksands.

3 Clayton (1980), p. 29.

4 Ibid., p. 53.

5 Ibid., p. 23.

6 Ibid., p. 33.

7 Ibid.

8 7031, Margaret Porter, 'Memories of a WW2 WAAF Wireless Operator', Military Intelligence Museum Archive, Chicksands. Porter was a WAAF Wireless Operator at Chicksands Priory from 1941 to 1944.

9 2259, Yvonne Jones, RAF Chicksands Priory, 1941–45, Military Intelligence Museum Archive, Chicksands.

10 16900, interview with Vera Ines Morley Elkan (oral history), Imperial War Museum, London.

11 A2423143, Dalma Flanders, 'Intelligence WAAFs in Y Service', contributed 14 March 2004, BBC People's War Archive.

12 Clayton (1980), p. 42.
13 Ibid., p. 38.
14 Ibid.
15 Taylor Downing, *Spies in the Sky: The Secret Battle for Aerial Intelligence During World War II* (London: Abacus, 2012), p. 150.
16 Clayton (1980), p. 44.
17 Ibid., p. 58.
18 Edward Thomas, 'The Achievements of Air Intelligence', paper given at the Air Intelligence Symposium by the Royal Air Force Historical Society and the RAF Staff College at Bracknell, copy held by the Royal Air Force Museum, Hendon.

AT THE PARK: THE BLETCHLEY WAAFS

1   Hinsley (1979), pp. 20–22.
2   Hill (2004), p. 6.
3   Lee, John, '"Station X": The Women at Bletchley Park', in Celia Lee and Paul Edward Strong, eds, *Women in War: From Home Front to Front Line* (Barnsley, Pen & Sword, 2012), p. 159.
4   Tessa Dunlop, *The Bletchley Girls* (London: Hodder & Stoughton, 2015), pp. 95–6.
5   Doreen Luke, *My Road to Bletchley Park* (Kidderminster: M&M Baldwin, 2003), p. 23.
6   Sinclair McKay, *The Secret Listeners: How the Y Service Intercepted German Codes for Bletchley Park* (London: Aurum Press Ltd, 2012), p. 36.
7   Escott (1989), p. 187.
8   A2377460, Carol West, 'My Years at Bletchley Park – Station X', contributed 3 March 2004, BBC People's War Project.
9   Luke (2003), p. 35.
10 Escott (1989), pp. 188–9.
11 Ibid.
12 Felicity Ashbee, *For the Duration* (Syracuse: Syracuse University Press, 2012), pp. 51, 54, 57.
13 Ibid., pp. 59–60.
14 A2377460, Carol West, 'My Years at Bletchley Park – Station X', contributed 3 March 2004, BBC People's War Project.
15 Asa Briggs, *Secret Days: Codebreaking in Bletchley Park: A Memoir of Hut Six and the Enigma Machine* (Barnsley: Frontline Books, 2011), p. 80.
16 F. W. Winterbotham, *The Ultra Secret* (New York: Harper & Row Publishers, 1974), p. 2.

BEHIND THE BOMBER BOYS: WAAFS IN BOMBER COMMAND

1   International Bomber Command Centre, 'History of Bomber Command', https://internationalbcc.co.uk/history/the-history-of-bomber-command/ (accessed 28 April 2022).
2   Bomber Command's main report, 'The War in the Ether', October 1945, as quoted in R. V. Jones, *Most Secret War* (London: Penguin Books, 2009), p. 471.
3   Air Transport Auxiliary, Museum and Archive at Maidenhead Heritage Centre, 'Women Join and Do a "Man's Job"', https://atamuseum.org/women-join-and-do-a-mans-job/ (accessed 28 April 2022).
4   Joan Baughan, *The Inimitable Joan: The War Years* (Upton-upon-Severn: Square One Publications, 1996), pp. 54, 62–3, 66.
5   Frayn Turner (2011), p. 51.
6   Eileen Smith, *Why Did We Join? A Former WAAF Remembers Service Life in World War II* (Bognor Regis: Woodfield Publishing, 2003), pp. 68–9.
7   Hall (1985), p. 19.
8   Ibid., p. 53.
9   Ibid., p. 56.
10 Escott (1989), p. 188.
11 Hall (1985), p. 53.

12 W. E. Jones, *Bomber Intelligence: 103, 150, 166, 170 Squadrons – Operations and Techniques, '42–'45* (Leicester: Midland Counties Publications, 1983), p. 84.

13 Letter to all relevant Group, Costal Command, Flying Training Command and Army Co-operation Command units, as quoted in Martyn Chorlton, *Bomber Command: The Thousand Bomber Raids* (Newbury: Countryside Books, 2017), p. 26.

14 Operation Order No. 148 (issued 26 May), as quoted in Chorlton (2017), pp. 26, 86.

15 Statistics from Chorlton (2017), p. 87.

16 Ibid., pp. 87–8.

17 Ibid., pp. 6, 166.

18 Hall (1985), pp. 23–4.

19 Baughan (1996), p. 63.

20 AIR 14/844, Air Ministry, Bomber Command Registered Files, Operation 'Chastise', National Archives, Kew.

21 Imperial War Museum, 'The Incredible Story of the Dambusters Raid', https://www.iwm. org.uk/history/the-incredible-story-of-the-dambusters-raid (accessed 28 April 2022).

22 Baughan (1996), p. 67.

23 Hall (1985), p. 55.

24 Ibid., pp. 49–51.

25 Ibid., p. 50.

26 Morris (1994), pp. 145–6.

27 Tape interview with Fay Gillon, in author's own possession.

28 Ibid.

29 AIR 14/844, Air Ministry, Bomber Command Registered Files, Operation 'Chastise', National Archives, Kew.

30 Immediately after the practice operation, Gillon wrote down her impressions in a memoir she later called 'Dress Rehearsal'. This was published for the first time in Morris (1944), pp. 160–62. The Wing Commander whom Fay refers to is Guy Gibson.

31 Arthur (2008), pp. 1, 2.

32 *Baltimore News-Post*, 18 May 1913, and *Daily Telegraph and Morning Post*, London, 18 May 1943. Copies of both obtained from the Lincolnshire Aviation Heritage Centre.

33 Memorandum to the Cabinet, Churchill, 3 September 1940. Churchill (1949), pp. 405–6.

A BIRD'S EYE VIEW: WAAFS IN PHOTOGRAPHIC INTELLIGENCE

1 Allan Williams, *Operation Crossbow: The Untold Story of the Search for Hitler's Secret Weapons* (London: Arrow Books, 2014), p. 10.

2 Constance Babington Smith, *Evidence in Camera* (London: David & Charles, 1957), pp. 13–14.

3 AIR 40/1169, Central Interpretation Unit RAF Station, Medmenham: Organisation, control and functions, National Archives, Kew.

4 Ursula Powys-Lybbe, *The Eye of Intelligence* (London: William Kimber, 1983), pp. 10, 37–8.

5 Ibid., p. 20.

6 Ibid., p. 53.

7 CEH14, notes pertaining to Mollie Thompson, Medmenham Collection Archive, RAF Wyton.

8 Christine Halsall, *Women of Intelligence: Winning the Second World War with Air Photos* (Stroud: The History Press, 2017), pp. 28–9.

9 Paper on the attributes of photographic interpreters, 1945, Medmenham Collection Archive, RAF Wyton.

10 Babington Smith (1957), p. 66.

11 CEH18, notes pertaining to Diana Cussons, Medmenham Collection Archive, RAF Wyton.

12 Babington Smith (1957), pp. 65–6.

13 Powys-Lybbe (1983), p. 34.

14 CEH11, notes pertaining to Pamela Howie, Medmenham Collection Archive, RAF Wyton; Halsall (2017), pp. 119–20.

15 CEH34, notes pertaining to Millicent Laws, Medmenham Collection Archive, RAF Wyton.
16 Powys-Lybbe (1983), p. 42.
17 CEH50, notes pertaining to Jeanne Adams, Medmenham Collection Archive, RAF Wyton.
18 Halsall (2017), p. 50.
19 CEH50, notes pertaining to Jeanne Adams, Medmenham Collection Archive, RAF Wyton.
20 Powys-Lybbe (1983), pp. 61–2.
21 2419, interview with Kathleen Mary Franck (oral history), Imperial War Museum Archive, London.
22 CEH26, notes pertaining to Elspeth Macalister, Medmenham Collection Archive, RAF Wyton.
23 Halsall (2017), p. 148.
24 Churchill's speech on the evening of D-Day, 6 June 1944, https://winstonchurchill.org/resources/speeches/1941-1945-war-leader/the-invasion-of-france/ (accessed 1 September 2022).
25 CEH50, notes pertaining to Jeanne Adams, Medmenham Collection Archive, RAF Wyton.
26 Halsall (2017), p. 194.
27 22232, interview with Mary Elizabeth Harrison (oral history), Imperial War Museum Archive, London.
28 DFG9841, The Times, 5 June 2009, and CEH50, notes pertaining to Jeanne Adams, Medmenham Collection Archive, RAF Wyton.
29 Powys-Lybbe (1983), p. 62.
30 CEH60, notes pertaining to Mollie Thompson, Medmenham Collection Archive, RAF Wyton.
31 AIR 40/1169, Central Interpretation Unit RAF Station, Medmenham: Organisation, control and functions, National Archives, Kew.
32 Halsall (2017), pp. 141, 70.
33 CEH27, notes pertaining to Loyalty Howard, Medmenham Collection Archive, RAF Wyton.
34 Powys-Lybbe (1983), pp. 105–6, 46.
35 CEH18, notes pertaining to Diana Cussons, Medmenham Collection Archive, RAF Wyton.
36 Powys-Lybbe (1983), p. 49.
37 Ibid., p. 107.
38 Babington Smith (1957), p. 87.
39 Williams (2014), p. 91.
40 Powys-Lybbe (1983), pp. 135–236, 102.
41 Jones (2009), pp. 67–71.
42 Powys-Lybbe (1983), pp. 188–9.
43 At the time, Sandys was the Joint Parliamentary Secretary to the Ministry of Supply – in September 1943 Douglas Kendall replaced him as head of the investigation.
44 AIR 34/182, Interpretation reports: 'Crossbow' Peenemünde, National Archives, Kew.
45 Babington Smith (1957), p. 205.
46 AIR 34/183, Interpretation reports: 'Crossbow' Peenemünde, National Archives, Kew.
47 Babington Smith (1957), pp. 206–7.
48 AIR 34/182, Interpretation reports: 'Crossbow' Peenemünde, National Archives, Kew.
49 Ibid.
50 Ibid.
51 Ibid.
52 Babington Smith (1957), p. 218.
53 AIR 34/626, Peenemünde Zempin: wireless telegraphy, National Archives, Kew.
54 Babington Smith (1957), pp. 211–22.
55 DFG4818, notes pertaining to Constance Babington Smith, Medmenham Collection Archive, RAF Wyton.
56 Babington Smith (1957), pp. 223–4.
57 MUN 3854, annotated image of a Fieseler FI-103 V-1 flying bomb, Imperial War Museum Archive, London.

58 Luke (2003), p. 32.

59 Williams (2014), pp. 2–3.

60 Mary Knight, 'Second World War Memories', oral evidence recorded by the author, who is Mary's granddaughter, January 2016.

61 Williams (2014), pp. 2–3.

62 CEH4, notes pertaining to Constance Babington Smith, and DFG5003, *New York Times*, 6 October 1945, Medmenham Collection Archive, RAF Wyton.

63 Babington Smith (1957), p. 226. Figure from the Sanders Report: In the autumn of 1944, a mission was formed under Colonel T. R. B. Sanders of the Armament Design Department of the Ministry of Supply, with the brief to investigate Crossbow installations that had fallen into Allied hands and to prepare a report on them for the Prime Minister. The report was issued in 1945 (WO 106/2817) and gives official estimates of what each site would have been capable of firing had they not been flattened by Allied bombing.

64 WO 106/2817, Crossbow: Investigation of the heavy Crossbow installations in N. France: report by Sanders mission: vol. 1, National Archives, Kew.

65 CEH17, notes pertaining to Myra Collyer, Medmenham Collection Archive, RAF Wyton.

66 23845, interview with Myra Collyer (oral history), Imperial War Museum Archive, London.

67 AIR 34/184, Interpretation reports: 'Crossbow' Peenemünde, National Archives, Kew.

68 Halsall (2017), pp. 26–7.

69 Air Ministry Bulletin No. 15560 issued on 9 September 1944, quoted in Halsall (2017), p. 203.

70 Douglas Kendall, 'A War of Intelligence', unpublished account, Medmenham Collection Archive, RAF Wyton.

71 From Dwight D. Eisenhower's book *Crusade in Europe* (1948), quoted in Kendall, 'A War of Intelligence'.

72 Halsall (2017), p. 213.

73 Babington Smith (1957), p. 6. Foreword by Lord Tedder G. C. B., Marshal of the Royal Air Force.

BEHIND THE LINES: WAAFS IN THE SPECIAL OPERATIONS EXECUTIVE

1 Roy Jenkins, *Churchill* (London: Macmillan, 2001), p. 629.

2 M. R. D. Foot, *SOE in France: An Account of the Work of the British Special Operations Executive in France, 1940–1944* (London: HMSO, 1966), p. 12.

3 Marc E. Vargo, *Women of the Resistance: Eight Who Defied the Third Reich* (North Carolina: McFarland & Company, Inc., 2012), p. 13.

4 Foot (1966), p. 12.

5 *The Princess Spy*, BBC Timewatch, 2006, prod. by John Hayes Fisher, interview with Sarah Helm.

6 M. R. D. Foot, *SOE: The Special Operations Executive 1940–1946* (London: Pimlico, 1999), p. 74.

7 Gordon Thomas and Greg Lewis, *Shadow Warriors of World War II: The Daring Women of the OSS and SOE* (Chicago: Chicago Review Press Incorporated, 2017), p. 100.

8 Sarah Helm, *A Life in Secrets: The Story of Vera Atkins and the Lost Agents of SOE* (London: Abacus, 2005), p. xx.

9 9551, interview with Vera Atkins (oral history), Imperial War Museum Archive, London.

10 Roderick Bailey, *Forgotten Voices of the Secret War* (London: Ebury Press, 2008), p. 42.

11 Documents.12636, private papers of Squadron Officer V. M. Atkins, eleven boxes containing documents, photographs and objects, Imperial War Museum, London.

12 Ibid.

13 9551, interview with Vera Atkins (oral history), Imperial War Museum Archive, London.

14 Helm (2005), p. xxi.

15 HS 9/1089/4, Records of the Special Operations Executive: Personnel Files: Jacqueline Francoise Mary Josephine Nearne, National Archives, Kew.

16 Documents.12636, private papers of Squadron Officer V. M. Atkins, eleven boxes containing documents, photographs and objects, Imperial War Museum, London.

17 HS 9/836/5, HS 9/1089/4, Records of the Special Operations Executive: Personnel Files: Noor Inayat Khan, National Archives, Kew.

18 Shrabani Basu, *Spy Princess: The Life of Noor Inayat Khan* (Stroud: The History Press, 2008), p. 86.

19 HS9/836/5, HS9/1089/4, Records of the Special Operations Executive, Personnel Files, Noor Inayat Khan, National Archives, Kew.

20 Vargo (2012), p. 101.

21 HS 9/836/5, HS 9/1089/4, Records of the Special Operations Executive: Personnel Files: Noor Inayat Khan, National Archives, Kew.

22 Bailey (2008), p. 40.

23 7369, interview with Yvonne Cormeau (oral history), Imperial War Museum, London.

24 Squadron Leader Beryl E. Escott, *The Heroines of SOE: F Section: Britain's Secret Women in France* (Stroud: The History Press, 2010), p. 117.

25 Lieutenant Tongue, 15 February 1943, noted in E. M. Sloan, *When Songbirds Returned to Paris.* (Seattle: Booktrope Editions, 2016), p. 176.

26 L. Cpl Gordon, Group B, in E. M. Sloan (2016).

27 Lieutenant Tongue, 15 February 1943, in E. M. Sloan (2016).

28 Escott (2010), p. 123.

29 HS 9/339/2, Records of the Special Operations Executive: Personnel Files: Anne-Marie Walters, National Archives, Kew.

30 Escott (2010), p. 154.

31 Ibid., p. 155.

32 Michael Field, 'Pippa's astonishing story recognised', https://www.stuff.co.nz/national/63516307/pippas-astonishing-story-recognised (accessed 21 December 2022).

33 Ibid.

34 Escott (2010), p. 197.

35 HS 9/356, Records of the Special Operations Executive: Personnel Files: Pearl Witherington, National Archives, Kew.

36 'War heroine honoured 63 years on', http://news.bbc.co.uk/1/hi/uk/4898302.stm (accessed 21 December 2022).

37 32394, interview with Donald Arthur Farrington (oral history), Imperial War Museum, London.

38 'War heroine "not classed leader"', http://news.bbc.co.uk/1/hi/uk/7323747.stm (accessed 21 December 2022).

39 'War heroine honoured 63 years on', http://news.bbc.co.uk/1/hi/uk/4898302.stm (accessed 21 December 2022).

40 Documents.12636, private papers of Squadron Officer V. M. Atkins, eleven boxes containing documents, photographs and objects, Imperial War Museum, London.

41 Escott (2010), pp. 9–10.

42 Documents.12636, private papers of Squadron Officer V. M. Atkins, eleven boxes containing documents, photographs and objects, Imperial War Museum, London.

43 Lieutenant Colonel Tara Opielowski, US Air Force, Security Forces, interview with author, 2017.

44 First Lieutenant Harriet Randolph, US Air Force, interview with author, 2017.

45 Master Sergeant Sanya Bell, US Air Force, interview with author, 2017.

46 Major Meredith Doran, US Air Force, intelligence analyst, interview with author, 2017.

KEEP CALM AND CARRY ON

1 KV 4/227, Report on the work of MS (recruitment and operation of agents) during the Second World War, National Archives, Kew.

2 Peake (1993), p. 19. Air Commandant Dame Felicity Peake was the deputy WAAF administration staff officer at Bomber Command in 1943 and was promoted consistently until she eventually became the founding director of the Women's Royal Air Force in 1949.

3 Bingham, ed. (1999), p. 76.

4   11885, interview with Jean Hilda Mills (oral history), Imperial War Museum Archive, London.

5   Escott (1989), p. 186. Escott states that Bouchier later put his 'conversion' on record.

6   Hall (1985), p. 18.

7   Peake (1993), p. 33.

8   Sasson (2015), pp. 26–7.

9   Ibid., p. 31.

10 Squadron Leader Beryl E. Escott, *Our Wartime Days: The WAAF in World War II* (Stroud: The History Press, 2009), pp. 142–4.

11 13091, interview with Rosamond Grant Renton Barclay (oral history), Imperial War Museum Archive, London.

12 Collette Drifte, *Women in the Second World War* (Barnsley: Remember When, 2011), p. 64.

13 Peake (1993), p. 39.

14 Ibid.

15 AIR 28/384, Air Ministry and Ministry of Defence: Operations Record Books, Royal Air Force Stations, National Archives, Kew.

16 CEH14, notes pertaining to Mollie Thompson, Medmenham Collection Archive, RAF Wyton.

17 Luke (2003), pp. 7–8.

18 13091, interview with Rosamond Grant Renton Barclay (oral history), Imperial War Museum Archive, London.

19 Clayton (1980), p. 273.

20 Ibid., p. 48.

21 Younghusband (2009), p. 51.

22 Baughan (1996), p. 86.

23 Ibid.

24 Pushman (2006), p. 74.

25 Smith (2003), p. 76.

26 13927, interview with Edith Mary Kup (oral history), Imperial War Museum Archive, London.

27 Peake (1993), p. 42.

28 Younghusband (2009), p. 36.

29 Hall (1985), pp. 190–91.

30 Edith Kup, in Drifte (2011), p. 67.

31 Baughan (1996), p. 43.

32 Hall (1985), p. 33.

33 Ibid., p. 88.

34 Tape interview with Fay Gillon, in author's own possession.

35 Hall (1985), p. 32.

36 Ibid., pp. 32–3.

37 Ibid., pp. 33–4.

38 Drifte (2011), pp. 68–9.

39 Hall (1985), p. 32.

40 Ibid., pp. 186–91.

41 Ibid.

42 Ibid., p. 184.

43 Ibid.

44 Clayton (1980), p. 39.

45 Ibid.

46 Poem found in CEH24, notes pertaining to Mary Harrison, Medmenham Collection Archive, RAF Wyton; also cited in Halsall (2017).

47 24191, interview with Kathleen Mary Franck (oral history), Imperial War Museum Archive, London.

48 Clayton (1980), p. 274.
49 Halsall (2017), p. 149.
50 22232, interview with Mary Elizabeth Harrison (oral history), Imperial War Museum Archive, London.
51 Jones (2009), p. 303.
52 Stobbs (1989), pp. 42–3.
53 Arnold (2002), p. 130.
54 Younghusband (2009), p. 53.
55 Hall (1985), p. 46.
56 Jones (1983), p. 85.
57 AIR 2/8660, Women's Auxiliary Air Force: Personnel (Code B, 77/1): Substitution in signals trade, National Archives, Kew. Also: Escott (1989), p. 187.
58 Hall (1985), p. 25.
59 CEH53, notes pertaining to Jean Mary Youle, Medmenham Collection Archive, RAF Wyton.

CONCLUSION

1   Clayton (1980), p. 50.
2   AIR 40/2243, Air Ministry, Directorate of Intelligence and related bodies: Intelligence Reports and Papers, RAF Station West Kingsdown, National Archives, Kew.
3   AIR 24/646, Air Ministry and Ministry of Defence: Operations Record Books, HQ Fighter Command, National Archives, Kew.
4   Squadron Leader Beryl E. Escott, *The WAAF: A History of the Women's Auxiliary Air Force in the Second World War* (Risborough: Shire Publications Ltd, 2003), p. 38.
5   Ibid.
6   Dame Helen Gwynne-Vaughan, *The Junior Leader and Other Addresses* (London: Hutchinson & Co. Ltd, 1942), p. 8.
7   Escott (2003), p. 28.
8   Sasson (2015), p. 23.
9   Stella Rimington, *Open Secret: The Autobiography of the Former Director-General of MI5* (London: Arrow Books, 2002), pp. 90–91.
10 Ibid., pp. 122–4.
11 1276, interview with Betty Turner (oral history), International Bomber Command Centre Archive.

APPENDIX

1   Statistics from: Air Publication 3234 (the official history of the WAAF), held by Air Historical Branch, Appendix 4, pp. 134–8.

BIBLIOGRAPHY

PRIMARY SOURCES

The National Archives, Kew

ADM 223 – Admiralty: Naval Intelligence Division and Operational Intelligence Centre: Intelligence Reports and Papers

AIR 2 – Air Ministry and Ministry of Defence: Registered Files: policy, case, committee and miscellaneous papers and reports on a whole range of British air administration and related topics (including radar)

AIR 10 – Ministry of Defence and Predecessors: Air Publications and Reports

AIR 14 – Air Ministry: Bomber Command: Registered Files

AIR 16 – Air Ministry: Fighter Command: Registered Files

AIR 20 – Air Ministry and Ministry of Defence: Papers Accumulated by the Air Historical Branch

AIR 23 – Air Ministry and Ministry of Defence: Royal Air Force Overseas Commands: Reports and Correspondence (Y Service)

AIR 24 – Air Ministry and Ministry of Defence: Operations Records Books, Commands

AIR 28 – Air Ministry and Ministry of Defence: Operations Record Books, RAF Stations

AIR 34 – Air Ministry: Central Interpretation Unit, Predecessors and Related Bodies: Reports and Photographs

AIR 40 – Air Ministry, Directorate of Intelligence and Related Bodies: Intelligence Reports and Papers

AIR 51 – Mediterranean Allied Air Forces – Microfilmed Files (Y Service)

CAB 21 – Cabinet Office and Predecessors: Registered Files (1916 to 1965), Includes Files of the Joint Intelligence Sub-Committee

CAB 67 – War Cabinet Memoranda (WP(G) Series)

CAB 75 – War Cabinet, Home Policy Committee, later Legislation Committee, and Sub-Committees: Minutes and Papers

CAB 80 – War Cabinet and Cabinet: Chiefs of Staff Committee: Memoranda

CAB 81 – War Cabinet and Cabinet: Committees and Sub-Committees of the Chiefs of Staff Committee: Minutes and Papers

HS 9 – Records of the Special Operations Executive: Personnel Files

HW 14 – The Government Code and Cypher School: Directorate: Second World War Policy Papers

INF 1 – Ministry of Information: Files of Correspondence

INF 3 – Ministry of Information: Original Artwork

KV 1 – The Security Service: First World War Historical Reports and Other Papers

KV 4 – The Security Service: Policy Files, 1909–63

PREM 3 – Prime Minister's Office: Operational Correspondence and Papers, 1937–46

PREM 4 – Prime Minister's Office: Confidential Correspondence and Papers

WO 106 – War Office: Directorate of Military Operations and Military Intelligence, and Predecessors: Correspondence and Papers

WO 208 – War Office: Directorate of Military Operations and Intelligence, and Directorate of Military Intelligence; Ministry of Defence, Defence Intelligence Staff: Files

Imperial War Museum, London

Documents

Documents.12636, private papers of Squadron Officer V. M. Atkins, eleven boxes containing documents, photographs and objects, Imperial War Museum, London

Images

Art.IWM PST 0142, Fougasse's 'Careless Talk Costs Lives' poster, Imperial War Museum Archive, London

Art.IWM PST 13908, master copy of a variant with army personnel produced as part of a series of 'Careless Talk' posters, Imperial War Museum Archive, London

MUN 3854, annotated image of a Fieseler FI-103 V-1 flying bomb, Imperial War Museum Archive, London

Film

AMY 56, *Hush! Not a Word!*, Second World War 'Careless Talk' short film made to be shown to military personnel in 1943, Imperial War Museum Archive, London

AMY 59, *Missed Date*, Second World War 'Careless Talk' short film with a rhyming commentary made to be shown to RAF personnel in 1943, Imperial War Museum Archive, London

AMY 157, *RDF to Radar* film, Imperial War Museum Archive, London

Audio (Oral History)

7369, interview with Yvonne Cormeau

7463, interview with Petrea Winterbotham

9106, interview with Gwendoline Saunders

9551, interview with Vera Atkins

11885, interview with Jean Hilda Mills

13091, interview with Rosamond Grant Renton Barclay

13927, interview with Edith Mary Kup

16900, interview with Vera Ines Morley Elkan

22232, interview with Mary Elizabeth Harrison

23845, interview with Myra Collyer

24191, interview with Kathleen Mary Franck

28454, interview with Joan Fleetwood Varley

32394, interview with Donald Arthur Farrington

The Medmenham Collection

Collection of documents, photographs and objects pertaining to photographic intelligence carried out by the Royal Air Force at RAF Medmenham, held at RAF Wyton.

CEH11, notes pertaining to Pamela Howie

CEH14, notes pertaining to Mollie Thompson

CEH17, notes pertaining to Myra Collyer

CEH18, notes pertaining to Diana Cussons

CEH24, notes pertaining to Mary Harrison

CEH26, notes pertaining to Elspeth Macalister

CEH27, notes pertaining to Loyalty Howard

CEH34, notes pertaining to Millicent Laws

CEH4, notes pertaining to Constance Babington Smith

CEH50, notes pertaining to Jeanne Adams

CEH53, notes pertaining to Jean Mary Youle

CEH60, notes pertaining to Mollie Thompson

DFG4818, notes pertaining to Constance Babington Smith

DFG5003, *New York Times*, 6 October 1945

DFG9841, *The Times*, 5 June 2009

Kendall, Douglas, 'A War of Intelligence', unpublished account

Paper on the attributes of photographic interpreters, 1945, the Medmenham Collection Archive, RAF Wyton

Wood, Edward, letter circulated to all 'V' Section personnel at RAF Medmenham in 1945

The Military Intelligence Museum

Y Listening Service Archive Files

1682, Captain W. H. Wyllie, 'The History of Field SIGINT, 1939–45'

2259, Yvonne Jones, RAF Chicksands Priory, 1941–45

6107, report by Major Ellingsworth from Chicksands, 9 April 1941

7031, Margaret Porter, 'Memories of a WW2 WAAF Wireless Operator'

The BBC People's War Project

A1993098, Gwen Reading, 'Radar Operator in WW2', contributed 8 November 2003

A2121148, Joyce Anne Deane née Morley, 'War Memories: Plotting the Battle of Britain', contributed 9 December 2003

A2377460, Carol West, 'My Years at Bletchley Park – Station X', contributed 3 March 2004

A2423143, Dalma Flanders, 'Intelligence WAAFs in Y Service', contributed 14 March 2004

A2429561, Kathleen Godfrey, 'A WAAF at Bletchley', contributed 16 March 2004

The Bawdsey Radar Trust

Oral History Transcripts, 'Shout and Whisper' Oral History Project

Curtis, Joyce, radar operator

Davies, Olivia, radar operator

Pearson, Hilda, radar operator

Williams, Jean, radar instructor

Documents

Pearson, Hilda, radar operator, 1943, written memories

Other Archives

1276, interview with Betty Turner (oral history), International Bomber Command Centre Archive

1964, interview with Joan M. Wilson (oral history), International Bomber Command Centre Archive

Air Publication 3234 (the official history of the WAAF), held by Air Historical Branch

Baltimore News-Post, 18 May 1913, and *Daily Telegraph and Morning Post*, London, 18 May 1943. Copies of both obtained from the Lincolnshire Aviation Heritage Centre

Hansard, HC Deb, 20 August 1940, vol. 364, cc 1167 (Winston Churchill's 'Never in the field of human conflict was so much owed by so many to so few' speech)

Hansard, HC Deb, 18 June 1940, vol. 362, cc 51–64 (Winston Churchill's 'Finest Hour' speech)

Schmid, Joseph 'Beppo', head of Luftwaffe intelligence, report submitted 22 November 1939

Recorded Interviews

Tape interview with Fay Gillon, in author's own possession

Video interviews with WAAF personnel who served in Fighter Command, Association of Royal Air Force Fighter Control Officers, Barbara Davies, Sherry Lygo Hackett and Patricia Clark

Interviews Conducted by Author

Bell, Master Sergeant Sanya, US Air Force, interview with author, 2017

Doran, Major Meredith, US Air Force, intelligence analyst, interview with author, 2017

Knight, Mary, 'Second World War Memories', oral evidence recorded by the author, who is Mary's granddaughter, January 2016

Opielowski, Lieutenant Colonel Tara, US Air Force, Security Forces, interview with author, 2017

Randolph, First Lieutenant Harriet, US Air Force, interview with author, 2017

Memoirs and Written Second World War Personal Accounts

Arnold, Gwen, *Radar Days* (Oxford: Isis Publishing Ltd, 2002)

Arthur, Max, *Dambusters: A Landmark Oral History* (London: Virgin Books, 2008)

Ashbee, Felicity, *For the Duration* (Syracuse: Syracuse University Press, 2012)

Babington Smith, Constance, *Evidence in Camera* (London: David & Charles, 1957)

Bailey, Roderick, *Forgotten Voices of the Secret War* (London: Ebury Press, 2008)

Baughan, Joan, *The Inimitable Joan: The War Years* (Upton-upon-Severn: Square One Publications, 1996)

Bingham, Daphne, ed., *Bluebirds Fly Past: Memories of the WAAF West Sussex Group* (Bognor Regis: Woodfield Publishing, 1999)

Briggs, Asa, *Secret Days: Codebreaking in Bletchley Park: A Memoir of Hut Six and the Enigma Machine* (Barnsley: Frontline Books, 2011)

Buckmaster, Maurice, *Specially Employed: The Story of British Aid to French Patriots of the Resistance* (London: Batchworth Press, 1952)

Butler, Peggy L., *Searching in the Dark: The Story of a Radar Operator from 1942–1946* (Chichester: HPC Publishing, 1994)

Churchill, Winston, *The Second World War*, 6 vols (London: Cassell & Co. Ltd, 1948–54)

Clayton, Aileen, *The Enemy Is Listening* (London: Hutchinson & Co. Ltd, 1980)

Davison, Muriel, *A Wren's Tale* (Reigate: Mark Davison, 2011)

Gane Pushman, Muriel, *We All Wore Blue: Experiences in the WAAF* (Stroud: Tempus, 2006)

Gwynne-Vaughan, Dame Helen, *The Junior Leader and Other Addresses* (London: Hutchinson & Co. Ltd, 1942)

Hall, Grace 'Archie', *We, Also, Were There: A Collection of Recollections of Wartime Women of Bomber Command* (Braunton: Merlin Books Ltd, 1985)

Hinsley, F. H., *British Intelligence in the Second World War*, 6 vols (London: HMSO, 1979–90)

Jones, R. V., *Most Secret War* (London: Penguin Books, 2009)

Jones, W. E., *Bomber Intelligence: 103, 150, 166, 170 Squadrons – Operations and Techniques, '42–'45* (Leicester: Midland Counties Publications, 1983)

Lacey, Pat, *One O'Them Girls in Blue* (Oxford: ISIS, 2010)

Lorrimer, Claire, *You Never Know* (London: Hodder & Stoughton, 2016)

Luke, Doreen, *My Road to Bletchley Park* (Kidderminster: M&M Baldwin, 2003)

Millard, Joyce, *Mayday Calling Mayday: A Story of Rescue* (Felixstowe: Bluebelle Books, 1995)

Peake, Dame Felicity, *Pure Chance* (Shrewsbury: Airlife Publishing Ltd, 1993)

Peters, Yvonne, *'Have You Got Your Irons?' It's a WAAF's Life* (Northwich: Greenridges Press, 2004)

Pickering, Sylvia, *More Tales of a Bomber Command WAAF* (Bognor Regis: Woodfield Publishing, 2003)

— —, *Tales of a Bomber Command WAAF* (Bognor Regis: Woodfield Publishing, 2002)

Powys-Lybbe, Ursula, *The Eye of Intelligence* (London: William Kimber, 1983)

Rimington, Stella, *Open Secret: The Autobiography of the Former Director-General of MI5* (London: Arrow Books, 2002)

Rosier, Air Chief Marshal Sir Frederick, *Be Bold* (London: Grub Street, 2011)

Sasson, Molly J., *More Cloak Than Dagger: One Woman's Career in Secret Intelligence* (Ballarat: Connor Court Publishing, 2015)

Sawyer, Tom, *Only Owls and Bloody Fools Fly at Night* (Manchester: Crécy Publishing Ltd, 2000)

Settle, Mary Lee, *All the Brave Promises* (London: Heinemann, 1966)

Smith, Eileen, *Why Did We Join? A Former WAAF Remembers Service Life in World War II* (Bognor Regis: Woodfield Publishing, 2003)

Stobbs, Anne, *One-Oh-Eight Miller* (Marsworth: Bucks Literary Services, 1989)

Watkins, Gwen, *Cracking the Luftwaffe Codes: The Secrets of Bletchley Park* (Barnsley: Frontline Books, 2013)

Winterbotham, F. W., *The Ultra Secret* (New York: Harper & Row Publishers, 1974)

Younghusband, Eileen, *Not an Ordinary Life* (Cardiff: Cardiff Centre for Lifelong Learning, 2009)

— —, *One Woman's War* (Cardiff Bay: Candy Jar Books, 2013)

SECONDARY SOURCES

Books

Andrew, Christopher, *The Defence of the Realm: The Authorized History of MI5* (London: Penguin Books, 2010)

Basu, Shrabani, *Spy Princess: The Life of Noor Inayat Khan* (Stroud: The History Press, 2008)

Beesly, Patrick, *Room 40: British Naval Intelligence, 1914–18* (London: Hamish Hamilton Ltd, 1982)

Beevor, Antony, *The Second World War* (London: Weidenfeld & Nicolson, 2012)

Bishop, Patrick, *Air Force Blue: The RAF in World War Two* (London: William Collins, 2017)

— —, *Battle of Britain* (London: Quercus, 2010)

— —, *Fighter Boys: Saving Britain 1940* (London: HarperCollins, 2003)

Black, Adam and Charles Black, *The WAAF in Action* (London: Adam & Charles Black, 1944)

Braybon, Gail and Penny Summerfield, *Out of the Cage: Women's Experiences in Two World Wars* (London: Pandora Press, 1987)

Butcher, Catherine, *Edith Cavell: Faith Before the Firing Squad* (Oxford: Monarch Books, 2015)

Central Statistical Office, *Annual Abstract of Statistics 1938–50* (London: HMSO, 1951), vol. 88

Chorlton, Martyn, *Bomber Command: The Thousand Bomber Raids* (Newbury: Countryside Books, 2017)

Conyers Nesbit, Roy, *Eyes of the RAF: A History of Photo-Reconnaissance* (Stroud: Sutton Publishing, 1996)

van Creveld, Martin, *Men, Women and War* (London: Cassell & Co., 2001)

De Schaepdrijver, Sophie, *Gabrielle Petit: The Death and Life of a Female Spy in the First World War* (London: Bloomsbury Academic, 2015)

Donnelly, Larry, *The Other Few: The Contribution Made by Bomber and Coastal Aircrew to the Winning of the Battle of Britain* (Walton-on-Thames: Red Kite, 2004)

Downing, Taylor, *Spies in the Sky: The Secret Battle for Aerial Intelligence During World War II* (London: Abacus, 2012)

Drifte, Collette, *Women in the Second World War* (Barnsley: Remember When, 2011)

Dunlop, Tessa, *The Bletchley Girls* (London: Hodder & Stoughton, 2015)

Escott, Squadron Leader Beryl E., *The Heroines of SOE: F Section: Britain's Secret Women in France* (Stroud: The History Press, 2010)

— —, *Mission Improbable: A Salute to Air Women of the SOE in Wartime France* (Wellingborough: Patrick Stephens Ltd, 1991)

— —, *Our Wartime Days: The WAAF in World War II* (Stroud: The History Press, 2009)

— —, *The WAAF: A History of the Women's Auxiliary Air Force in the Second World War* (Risborough: Shire Publications Ltd, 2003)

— —, *Women in Air Force Blue: The Story of Women in the Royal Air Force from 1918 to the Present Day* (Wellingborough: Patrick Stephens Ltd, 1989)

Foot, M. R. D., *SOE in France: An Account of the Work of the British Special Operations Executive in France, 1940–1944* (London: HMSO, 1966)

— —, *SOE: The Special Operations Executive 1940–1946* (London: Pimlico, 1999)

Fountain, Nigel, ed., *Voices from the Twentieth Century: Women at War* (London: Michael O'Mara, 2002)

Frayn Turner, John, *The WAAF at War* (Barnsley: Pen & Sword Aviation, 2011)

Halsall, Christine, *Women of Intelligence: Winning the Second World War with Air Photos* (Stroud: The History Press, 2017)

Handel, Michael I., ed., *Intelligence and Military Operations* (London: Frank Cass & Company Ltd, 1990)

Hastings, Max, *Bomber Command* (London: Pan Books, 2010)

Helm, Sarah, *A Life in Secrets: The Story of Vera Atkins and the Lost Agents of SOE* (London: Abacus, 2005)

Hill, Marion, *Bletchley Park People: Churchill's Geese That Never Cackled* (Stroud: The History Press, 2004)

Holland, James, *The Battle of Britain* (London: Transworld Publishers, 2011)

Hunt, Felicity, ed., *Lessons for Life: The Schooling of Girls and Women, 1850–1950* (Oxford: Blackwell, 1987)

Jeffery, Keith, *MI6: The History of the Secret Intelligence Service 1909–1949* (London: Bloomsbury, 2010)

Jenkins, Roy, *Churchill* (London: Macmillan, 2001)

Keegan, John, *The Second World War* (London: Pimlico, 1997)

Kenyon, David, *Bletchley Park and D-Day: The Untold Story of How the Battle for Normandy Was Won* (New Haven: Yale University Press, 2019)

Knowles, Daniel, *Tirpitz: The Life and Death of Germany's Last Great Battleship* (Stroud: Fonthill Media, 2018)

Leaf, Edward, *Above All Unseen: The Royal Air Force's Photographic Reconnaissance Units 1939–1945* (Sparkford: Patrick Stephens Ltd, 1997)

Lee, John, '"Station X": The Women at Bletchley Park', in Celia Lee and Paul Edward Strong, eds, *Women in War: From Home Front to Front Line* (Barnsley: Pen & Sword, 2012)

McKay, Sinclair, *The Secret Life of Bletchley Park: The WWII Code-breaking Centre and the Men and Women Who Worked There* (London: Aurum Press Ltd, 2011)

— —, *The Secret Life of Fighter Command: The Men and Women Who Beat the Luftwaffe* (London: Aurum Press Ltd, 2015)

— —, *The Secret Listeners: How the Y Service Intercepted German Codes for Bletchley Park* (London: Aurum Press Ltd, 2012)

Ministry of Defence, *A Brief History of the Royal Air Force* (London: HMSO, 2004)

Morris, Richard, *Guy Gibson* (London: Viking, 1994)

Nesbit, Roy C., *The Battle of Britain* (Stroud: Pitkin Publishing, 2010)

Ogley, Bob, *Doodlebug and Rockets: The Battle of the Flying Bombs* (Westerham: Froglets Publications, 1992)

Proctor, Tammy, *Female Intelligence: Women and Espionage in the First World War* (New York: New York University Press, 2003)

Richards, Denis, *Royal Air Force, 1939–1945*, 3 vols (London: HMSO, 1974)

Shipman, Pat, *Femme Fatale: Love, Lies and the Unknown Life of Mata Hari* (London: Weidenfeld & Nicolson, 2007)

Smith, Michael, *The Secrets of Station X: How the Bletchley Park Codebreakers Helped Win the War* (London: Biteback Publishing, 2011)

Souhami, Diana, *Edith Cavell* (London: Quercus, 2010)

Stubbington, Wing Commander John, *Kept in the Dark: The Denial to Bomber Command of Vital Ultra and Other Intelligence Information During World War II* (Barnsley: Pen & Sword Aviation, 2010)

Summerfield, Penny, *Reconstructing Women's Wartime Lives: Discourse and Subjectivity in Oral Histories of the Second World War* (Manchester: Manchester University Press, 1998)

— —, *Women Workers in the Second World War: Production and Patriarchy in Conflict* (Oxon: Routledge, 2014)

Taylor, Leonard, *Airwomen's Work* (London: Sir Isaac Pitman & Sons Ltd, 1943)

Terraine, John, *The Right of the Line: The Royal Air Force in the European War, 1939–1945* (London: Hodder and Stoughton, 1985)

Thomas, Gordon and Greg Lewis, *Shadow Warriors of World War II: The Daring Women of the OSS and SOE* (Chicago: Chicago Review Press Incorporated, 2017)

Thomas, Gordon, *Inside British Intelligence: 100 Years of MI5 and MI6* (London: JR Books Ltd, 2010)

Turing, Dermot, *Alan Turing: The Life of a Genius* (Stroud: Pitkin Publishing, 2017)

Twigge, Stephen, Edward Hampshire and Graham Macklin, *British Intelligence: Secrets, Spies and Sources* (Kew: The National Archives, 2008)

Vargo, Marc E., *Women of the Resistance: Eight Who Defied the Third Reich* (North Carolina: McFarland & Company, Inc., 2012)

Webster, Charles and Noble Frankland *The Strategic Air Offensive against Germany* (London: HMSO, 1961)

Welch, David, *Persuading the People: British Propaganda in World War II* (London: The British Library, 2016)

Wheelwright, Julie, *The Fatal Lover: Mata Hari and the Myths of Women in Espionage* (London: Collins & Brown Limited, 1992)

White, Rosie, *Violent Femmes: Women as Spies in Popular Culture* (London: Routledge, 2007)

Williams, Allan, *Operation Crossbow: The Untold Story of the Search for Hitler's Secret Weapons* (London: Arrow Books, 2014)

Wood, Derek and Derek Dempster, *The Narrow Margin: The Battle of Britain and the Rise of Air Power 1930–1940* (Barnsley: Pen & Sword Aviation, 2010)

Articles and Papers

The Association of RAF Fighter Control Officers, 'Blazing a Trail for the Operational Employment of Women in the Royal Air Force', Briefing Paper (2012)

Bawdsey Radar Trust, 'A World First: The Story of Bawdsey Radar' (paper acquired from the Bawdsey Radar Trust)

Fox, Jo, 'Careless Talk: Tensions within British Domestic Propaganda during the Second World War', *Journal of British Studies*, vol. 51 (2012), pp. 936–66

The Institution of Electrical Engineers, ed., 'Seminar on the History of Radar Development to 1945' (London: The Institution of Electrical Engineers, 1985)

James, Mary, 'The Big Picture', *Royal Air Force Salute*, 2010

Thomas, Edward, 'The Achievements of Air Intelligence', paper given at the Air Intelligence Symposium by the Royal Air Force Historical Society and the RAF Staff College at Bracknell, copy held by the Royal Air Force Museum, Hendon

Willbond, T. C., 'The Battle of Britain – Another Perspective', Briefing Paper for the Association of RAF Fighter Control Officers (acquired from the Association of RAF Fighter Control Officers)

— —, 'Understanding the Dowding System', Briefing Paper for the Association of RAF Fighter Control Officers (acquired from the Association of RAF Fighter Control Officers)

Sound and Film

The Princess Spy, BBC Timewatch, 2006, prod. by John Hayes Fisher, interview with Sarah Helm

'Secrets and Spies: The Untold Story of Edith Cavell', BBC Radio Four, 16 September 2015

Websites

Air Transport Auxiliary, Museum and Archive at Maidenhead Heritage Centre, 'Women Join and Do a "Man's Job"', https://atamuseum.org/women-join-and-do-a-mans-job/ (accessed 28 April 2022)

Churchill's speech on the evening of D-Day, 6 June 1944, https://winstonchurchill.org/resources/speeches/1941-1945-war-leader/the-invasion-of-france/ (accessed 1 September 2022)

Hitler's War Directive No. 16, http://der-fuehrer.org/reden/english/wardirectives/16.html (accessed 16 April 2018)

Imperial War Museum, 'The Incredible Story of the Dambusters Raid', https://www.iwm.org.uk/history/the-incredible-story-of-the-dambusters-raid (accessed 28 April 2022)

International Bomber Command Centre, 'History of Bomber Command', https://internationalbcc.co.uk/history/the-history-of-bomber-command/ (accessed 28 April 2022)

Royal Air Force website, https://www.raf.mod.uk (accessed 18 April 2022)

Royal Air Force, 'Our History', https://www.raf.mod.uk/our-organisation/our-history/ (accessed 30 August 2022)

Secret Intelligence Service, 'Our History', https://www.sis.gov.uk/our-history.html (accessed 27 February 2018)

ACKNOWLEDGEMENTS

There are so many people to whom thanks are owed for their help in making this book possible. First and foremost, to my family, especially my husband and my parents, for their constant support and encouragement throughout this research. I am grateful for the way they have patiently endured my ramblings (the way all historians' families do). I am also very grateful for my great friends, Kristin Thue and Ashleigh Brett, for their encouragement and assistance in everything I do. This book began life as an academic thesis for my MPhil at Anglia Ruskin University, and I would like to thank the History Department there. From these wonderful people I have learned lessons for life, and I'm ever grateful for their help, instruction and encouragement. I especially thank my MPhil supervisors, Professor Lucy Bland and Dr Sean Lang, without whom this book simply would not exist.

During the course of my research, I have met many lovely people who have lent me their time, knowledge and skills. I'd like to thank the staff at the National Archives at Kew, the Imperial War Museum, the Military Intelligence Museum, the Lincolnshire Aviation Heritage Centre, the International Bomber Command Centre, the Bawdsey Radar Trust, the Association of Royal Air Force Fighter Control Officers, the Air Historical Branch, the Medmenham Association and Bletchley Park. I would particularly like to thank Tim Fryer and Mike

Mockford, volunteers at the Medmenham Association, who invited me to the Medmenham Collection Archive. Their knowledge and expertise, coupled with the records they granted me access to, were of great value to this research. Chris and Christine Halsall were also of great help, having personally interviewed many former WAAF photographic intelligence personnel. I embarked upon this research just a little too late to have this privilege myself, so it was wonderful to hear about it from those who did. Thanks are also owed to Joyce Hutton at the Military Intelligence Museum, Tim Willbond at the Association of RAF Fighter Control Officers and David Heath at the Bawdsey Radar Trust, for their provision of copies of sources, including expert papers and recorded interviews with former WAAFs. I am most grateful for these sources, which were essential to accomplishing my research aims. I am also very grateful to Heather Hughes and the staff at the International Bomber Command Centre, who have been working to catalogue and make electronically available in their brand-new online archive sources pertaining to the wartime personnel of Bomber Command. I also thank Charles Foster, nephew of the Dambusters pilot David Maltby, for helping with the research on Fay Gillon.

Huge thanks to my wonderful agent, Tom Cull, for believing in this book and making its publication a reality. Thank you also to Michael Smith for his expert help and guidance and to Ella Boardman and Olivia Beattie for making the editing and publication process so smooth and enjoyable.

Finally, my greatest and most emphatic thanks go to all of the people whose stories and voices are heard in this book. To the men and women of the wartime Royal Air Force and the Women's Auxiliary Air Force, and the women of the US Air Force 48th Fighter Wing who so graciously granted me interviews – for your service, courage and sacrifice – thank you.

INDEX